woodstock

Woodstock Music and Art Fair	Woodstock Music and Art Fair	Woodstock Music and Art Fair
FRIDAY	**SATURDAY**	**SUNDAY**
August 15, 1969	August 16, 1969	August 17, 1969
10 A. M.	10 A. M.	10 A. M.
$6.00	**$6.00**	**$6.00**
Good For One Admission Only	Good For One Admission Only	Good For One Admission Only
22270 NO REFUNDS	22270 NO REFUNDS	22270 NO REFUNDS

"Woodstock was beads and colors and flowers and sunshine and beautiful people."

JOHN SEBASTIAN

woodstock
Three days that rocked the world

Edited by Mike Evans and Paul Kingsbury

In association with

The
Museum
at Bethel Woods
CENTER FOR THE ARTS

STERLING

New York / London
www.sterlingpublishing.com

STERLING and the distinctive Sterling logo are registered trademarks of Sterling Publishing Co., Inc.

A CIP catalogue record for this book is available from the British Library.

10 9 8 7 6 5 4 3 2 1

Published by Sterling Publishing Co., Inc.
387 Park Avenue South, New York, NY 10016
Distributed in Canada by Sterling Publishing
c/o Canadian Manda Group, 165 Dufferin Street
Toronto, Ontario, Canada M6K 3H6
Distributed in the United Kingdom by GMC Distribution Services
Castle Place, 166 High Street, Lewes, East Sussex, England BN7 1XU
Distributed in Australia by Capricorn Link (Australia) Pty. Ltd.
P.O. Box 704, Windsor, NSW 2756, Australia

Sterling ISBN 978-1-4027-6623-7 (hardcover)
Sterling ISBN 978-1-4027-8034-9 (paperback)

Design and layout © 2009 Palazzo Editions Ltd
Text © 2009 Mike Evans and Palazzo Editions Ltd
Foreword © 2009 Martin Scorsese
Photographs © see picture credits page 285

Created and produced by
PALAZZO EDITIONS LTD
2 Wood Street
Bath, BA1 2JQ
www.palazzoeditions.com

Publishing director: Colin Webb
Art director: David Costa
Assistant art director: Terry Jeavons
Picture researcher: Dave Brolan
Managing editor: Sonya Newland

Printed in China

For information about custom editions, special sales, premium and
corporate purchases, please contact Sterling Special Sales
Department at 800-805-5489 or specialsales@sterlingpublishing.com.

CONTENTS

FOREWORD

My perspective on Woodstock is…limited.

How limited? Well, for most of that long weekend in August, 1969, I was confined to a platform about nine feet wide, just to the right of the stage, just below a bank of amplifiers, fiercely concentrating on the musicians and their performances. I was to be one of the film's editors and my job was to keep an eye out for images we would need when we started to put the film together. We had seven cameramen working every performance and, to the degree that I could communicate with them (surprisingly well, all hardships considered), I was trying to direct their attention to activity they could not perceive since their eyes were glued to their viewfinders. There were, from time to time, more pressing issues—like trying to stay upright in that tiny space jammed with people. All of us were dependent on one another for our well-being. If someone had shoved me out of his way, I could have been knocked off that platform. But that never happened—not to any of us. There was no way to get food or go to the bathroom. Probably the best hamburger I ever had in my life was courtesy of Arthur Baron, the documentary filmmaker, who somehow got a bag of them up to us during the Friday night concert.

I almost never saw the audience, so concentrated was I on the action on stage. It was simply a restive—potentially volatile—presence behind us. Every once in awhile I would catch a glimpse of Michael Wadleigh, the director, wielding his camera, head phones askew, trying to stay in touch with the other cameramen by radio microphone. Mostly we were getting what we could get, yet, it seems to me, we were curiously (maybe youthfully) confident that we would have something good to take back to New York and the editing rooms.

Which is where this adventure began. Wadleigh and I had met at the NYU film school and he had shot the 16 mm black and white footage for my first feature, *Who's that Knocking at My Door?* In the late sixties a group of us were sharing editing rooms on West 86th St. in Manhattan. I was working on my film, Jim McBride was next door, editing *David Holzman's Diary*, while Wadleigh and Thelma Schoonmaker—later to become my editor—were working on various documentary projects. We were all, naturally, passionate about film making, but Wadleigh and I were equally passionate about rock music. I thought then, and I still think, that it formed the score for many of our lives; we moved through the days to its swaggering rhythms. And Wadleigh and I were already feeling nostalgic about the pioneer rockers of the 1950s—Fats Domino, Little Richard, Jerry Lee Lewis, Chuck Berry—whose work was no longer being played very much. We got the idea of staging a concert featuring them and their music, which we would film. Then we began hearing rumors about the Woodstock concert. It soon became clear that it was going to include what was probably the greatest gathering of popular musicians ever assembled. Wadleigh decided to go upstate to see if it might be a model for what we wanted to do. We began getting calls from him, saying that we should make our film about this set of concerts instead.

Aside from our shared passion for the music, none of us—Jim McBride excepted—was what you would call a hipster, though Wadleigh had grown a significant beard before he attended Woodstock. When I first met him I thought, he looked like one of The Four Freshmen—a trim, short-haired very respectable looking young man from the Midwest, wearing button-down shirts. I had yet to acquire my first pair of jeans; I guess you could call my clothing style graduate school plain. And I was definitely not a country person. Afflicted with asthma, I was allergic to just about everything nature had to offer. Yet, there we all were—hungry, exhausted, struggling with the fact that the first priority among Woodstock's promoters was not the convenience or well-being of the filmmakers.

They had more pressing problems to contend with. I don't know how many people they expected to turn up that weekend—but not a half-million of them. And they were overwhelmed at every level—food, sanitation, medical staff. At least some of the lighting towers threatened to collapse and the grounds were turning into a sea of mud. It's no mystery why such a multitude made their way to Woodstock; it was the promise of hearing so many great musicians in one place, in a short span of time. To some it may be a mystery why, from beginning to end, Woodstock remained a peaceful gathering. I mean, anything could have gone wrong at any second. Sometimes I'd glance back and wonder, "What if something goes crazy? What if one of the drugs doesn't work, or works too well, and they decide to charge the stage." Today people sentimentalize the Woodstock spirit, but I do think it contained the never-fused elements of something more threatening.

I think it helped—it certainly helped me—that as early as the Friday night concert the idea that we were involved with something more than a rock concert, that we might be involved in a truly historic event, began to occur to some of us. By Saturday night, to borrow a cliché, "the whole world was watching"; Woodstock was all over television and the rest of the press. I think it's possible that a lot of people in the audience wanted to enforce a contrast between this peaceful assembly and the riotous events a year earlier at the Democratic convention in Chicago.

But we, the filmmakers, were not home free. Yes, Freddie Weintraub, the New York music entrepreneur—he owned The Bitter End—and was very well connected in the music world, had got in touch with John Calley, part of the new management team Steve Ross had installed at Warner Bros., and John had agreed to cover the costs of the documentary's camera rentals and film stock—a sum he later remembered as about $15,000 or as he put it, "sort of lunch in Las Vegas." He also remembered thinking that, if we struck out, he could recoup that modest sum just by selling what we shot as stock footage to documentarians in the future. But funding to complete the film was not guaranteed. I remember seeing Bob Maurice, our producer, with a phone to his ear, telling people—as the music blared behind him—that this was shaping up as an historic event and that they would be fools not to get in on it. I also remember Thelma, stuck at the lighting console—alternately yelling at and cajoling Chip Monck, who was a legendary concert lighting designer, to pour more light on the stage, so we could capture viewable images of the performers. He was the pioneer genius of rock concert lighting—and he didn't want to spoil his carefully calculated effects just to oblige a bunch of youthful filmmakers.

So *Woodstock*, the movie, was, on a lot of levels, a huge, closely run gamble. Shoots like this one nearly always are, but that was especially so in those days, when rock concerts were not the accepted genre that they now are. From the beginning there had been talk—especially from Wadleigh as I recall—of using a lot of split-screen imagery in the film. There was a lot of simultaneity about Woodstock—a sense of many things going on at once—that lent itself to this approach. A large open space above a pool hall also near West 86th had been rented so the raw Woodstock footage could be projected on the wall. The material from six or more cameras could be projected simultaneously on that wall. There was just something viscerally exciting about all that film running through the projectors all at once. That it became the stylistic hallmark of *Woodstock*; more important, by giving equal time to performance and crowd, it enabled Wadleigh to re-create the entire experience for the movie audience. He could not have done that with a purely linear movie.

There was enough usable material for a seven hour film, which is why in its various home video incarnations *Woodstock* has shape-shifted quite a bit over the years, without ever betraying its essence. But something more curious has happened over those forty years. I think that without the film Woodstock, the concert, would not be more than a footnote to the social and cultural history of the 1960s—represented by a still photo in a picture book, a line or two in the history books. What the movie did, and continues to do, is to distill the Woodstock experience and, more important, keep it vibrant and alive. The footnote has become a touchstone, a way for my generation to remind ourselves of who we were then and to measure the road we have traveled since. It has also been, more significantly, a way for newer generations to get in touch with the chaotic spirit of the 1960s. Or, rather, a part of that spirit—the happier part.

As for me, for various reasons, I left the film before it was finished. But it had an enormous impact on me. I went on to do other concert films, of course. But the experience marked me in other, more important, ways. I remember bitching and moaning about the hardships of the shoot (though I don't think I was alone in that). But as the years have gone by, I have come to think of Woodstock—the concert and the film—as a transcendent moment in my life—something that intimately connected me with my generation in many ways I still can't fully describe or analyze. I'm sure there's some evidence of Woodstock in my films—especially musically. I'm sure there are traces of the experience in some of the ways I think about my life and the world we all share. I suspect that's true of almost everyone who was present at Woodstock.

I hope this book, like the film, allows many more to see what we saw, taste what we tasted, as they re-encounter the "happening" that turned into one of the major cultural and historical events of its time.

MARTIN SCORSESE, MARCH 2009

Below: The Woodstock moviemakers (l to r) director Michael Wadleigh and editors Martin Scorsese and Thelma Schoonmaker.

Throughout the story of popular music there has been a handful of key events—Elvis's recording debut, the arrival of The Beatles in America, Dylan going electric—that are recognized as seminal moments, both cultural markers and catalysts in rock's tumultuous development. And this has never been more the case than with the Woodstock festival. It is acknowledged as the defining moment of the rock-driven counterculture of the late 1960s, when half a million fans descended on a small farm in upstate New York for what was promised to be "3 days of peace & music."

It wasn't the first large-scale gathering of its kind. Open-air music festivals had increasingly become features of the "flower-power" era of the late 1960s, since the template was established at the Monterey Pop Festival in the summer of 1967. Huge audiences, approaching 100,000 or more, had attended two festivals in Miami in 1968 and a similar marathon in Atlanta, Georgia, in July 1969, just a few weeks before Woodstock. All featured the key performers in cutting-edge rock and pop, attracted a predominantly young, white, middle-class audience, and were also demonstrative of a youth-led counterculture that challenged the lifestyle and values of mainstream American society.

It was a society increasingly fragmented over changing attitudes to civil rights, sexual liberation, drug use, and—most significantly for the younger generation—the escalating war in Vietnam. Opposition to that conflict was a great unifier for the throngs who made Max Yasgur's farm in Bethel their destination in mid-August 1969. Yet many were no doubt drawn together just as much by the music, the opportunity for free expression, and the allure of an instant youth community. Word soon spread that this would be the greatest gathering yet of the "alternative society"—the "Woodstock Nation" as it was dubbed in retrospect.

But it was due to the changing circumstances of the festival itself that Woodstock was unique. Even before the first artist performed, the logjam of vehicles along all routes leading to the site had made it almost impossible for any of the acts to arrive on time, precipitating a domino-effect of delays that saw the Friday-to-Sunday event ending on Monday morning. Those who did get there on the first day were greeted by an audience area filled with campers who had arrived days before, with fencing and ticket booths still being erected. Chaos threatened as the promoters hastily decided to abandon commercial considerations in favor of the advertised "peace." They declared it a free festival—and the very nature of the Woodstock Music and Art Fair began transforming before their eyes.

By the second day, heavy rainstorms had reduced the fields to a mudbath, and it was impossible for the audience (and to a lesser degree, the performers) to make their exit easily out of the area, and more were still on their way. With the huge numbers involved—more than three times the 150,000 anticipated were either at, or trying to get to, the festival—all provisions of food and drink, sanitary arrangements, and medical aid were rendered completely inadequate. As the authorities declared it a disaster area and the eyes of the nation (and the rest of the world) focused on a potential catastrophe, the "spirit of Woodstock" suddenly became apparent. A human drama unfolded in which a tangible feeling of mutual support and communion transcended all the problems.

The music—a mix of rock 'n' roll, folk, and even classical Indian—freedom of personal expression, a relaxed attitude regarding sex and drugs, and anger at the Vietnam conflict united the gathered tribe. Eyewitness accounts, from fans and musicians, local residents, and law officers, all speak of the fellowship between total strangers, the atmosphere of sharing, the lack of violence or aggravation, the sheer communality of the occasion—enacted against a backdrop of live music from some of the greatest performers of the era. In most cases the singers and musicians rose to the challenge, despite the far-from-perfect conditions. There were some landmark moments, including Richie Havens's rousing "Freedom" in the festival opener, a then-unknown Melanie alone on the nighttime stage as thousands of lighters glowed in the darkness, Country Joe's antiwar "Fixin'-to-Die Rag," the eleven-minute epic "I'm Going Home" from Ten Years After, and Jimi Hendrix's show-stopping version of "The Star-Spangled Banner."

The musical testament of Woodstock was preserved for posterity when it was decided at the outset to film and record most of the performances. The commercial success of the releases of both album and movie in 1970 extended the impact and reputation of the festival around the world. Since then, the happenings over that August weekend in Bethel have assumed almost mythical status. Innumerable accounts and sociological analyses have appeared over the years, usually focusing on a particular aspect of the event, or an individual's part in it.

With the aid of exclusive interviews, newspaper reports, and the invaluable archives of The Museum at Bethel Woods, this celebration, timed for the fortieth anniversary, presents a complete chronicle in words and pictures of the "3 days of peace & music" that came to define the music and culture of the late 1960s, the influence of which still reverberates today.

MIKE EVANS

TIMELINE To WOODSTOCK

1954 **March 1** First deliverable H-bomb tested by US on Bikini Atoll *(1)* **May 17** US Supreme Court outlaws racial segregation in schools **July 5** Elvis Presley cuts debut disc, "That's All Right" **July 17–18** First Newport Jazz Festival **November 11** First rock 'n' roll record in charts, Bill Haley's "Shake, Rattle, and Roll," reaches No. 7 spot

1955 **July 9** First rock 'n' roll record to top US chart: Bill Haley's "Rock Around the Clock" **July 17** Disneyland opens in Anaheim, California **September 30** James Dean dies in car crash *(2)* **October 27** *Rebel Without a Cause* released **November 22** USSR conducts its first H-bomb test **December 1** After Rosa Parks refuses to give up bus seat, Martin Luther King, Jr. leads 382-day bus boycott in Montgomery, Alabama

1956 **March 3** Elvis Presley's first pop No. 1 hit, "Heartbreak Hotel," debuts on the *Billboard* Top 100 pop chart **October** Allen Ginsberg's *Howl* published **November 26** Release of Brigitte Bardot's then-shocking film *And God Created Woman (3)* *Also: Elvis Presley is biggest-seller in record-industry history (4)*

1957 **September 5** Jack Kerouac's *On the Road* published **September 24** President Eisenhower enforces school racial integration in Little Rock, Arkansas **September 26** Teen-gang musical *West Side Story* opens on Broadway **October 4** USSR launches first artificial satellite, *Sputnik I (5)*

1958 **March 24** Elvis drafted into US Army *(6)* **April 2** The term "Beatnik" coined by San Francisco journalist **October 10** 10,000 people march in Washington, D.C., in the first Civil Rights youth march for integrated schools

1959 **January 1** Fidel Castro assumes power after revolution in Cuba **January** Military conflict begins between North and South Vietnam **February 3** Buddy Holly killed in plane crash **July 11–12** First Newport Folk Festival **July** William Burroughs' *The Naked Lunch* published in Paris

1960 **June 23** Birth-control pill approved for sale in US **October** Aretha Franklin's first commercial recordings **November 8** John F. Kennedy becomes youngest elected US president *(7)* **December** Vietnamese National Liberation Front (NLF) formed

1961 **February 21** The Beatles' first appearance at the Cavern Club, Liverpool, UK **March 1** Peace Corps established in US "to promote world peace and friendship" **April 5** Bob Dylan's first paid gig in New York City **April 12** USSR's Yuri Gagarin is first man in space *(8)* **April 15** CIA-trained Cuban émigrés fail to take Cuba in the abortive Bay of Pigs invasion **August 13** East Germany begins building Berlin Wall, escalating Cold War *(9)* **December 11** The Marvelettes' "Please Mr. Postman" is Motown's first US pop No. 1

1962 **June 15** Students for a Democratic Society (SDS) issue the Port Huron Statement, setting an influential agenda for student activism in America **July 12** Rolling Stones' debut gig, at London's Marquee club **July 16** Beach Boys sign with Capitol Records **August 5** Marilyn Monroe dies of barbiturates overdose **September** *Silent Spring*, Rachel Carson's environmental herald, is published **October** Cuban Missile Crisis *(10)*

1963 **February 19** Early feminist work *The Feminine Mystique* by Betty Friedan published **August 28** Civil Rights march on Washington: Joan Baez and Bob Dylan perform at Lincoln Memorial alongside Martin Luther King, Jr. *(11)* **October 10** Atomic Test Ban Treaty comes into force **November 22** John F. Kennedy assassinated in Dallas *(12)*

1964 **January 25** "I Want to Hold Your Hand" starts The Beatles' assault on US charts *(13)* **February 25** Boxer Cassius Clay (later Muhammad Ali) becomes World Heavyweight Champion **June 14** Ken Kesey's Merry Pranksters begin "acid test" road trip across US **July 2** Civil Rights Act of 1964 outlaws segregation in schools, employment, and public places

1965 **February 21** Malcolm X assassinated **March 7** "Bloody Sunday" as Voting Rights marchers attacked and beaten by police in Alabama **March 8** First US combat troops join 23,000 advisors in Vietnam **July** Bob Dylan moves to Byrdcliffe, Woodstock **July 25** Bob Dylan "goes electric" to mixed reaction at Newport Folk Festival **August 11** Riots erupt in Los Angeles black ghetto of Watts *(14)* **November 5** The Who release "My Generation" Ken Kesey's first "acid test" parties in California, with music by the Grateful Dead

1966 **March 4** John Lennon's "We're more popular than Jesus" comment appears in London newspaper *(15)* **April 11** Debut of Buffalo Springfield, including Stephen Stills and Neil Young **June 28–30** Feminist group National Organization for Women (NOW) formed **August 29** The Beatles play their last live concert at Candlestick Park, San Francisco **October 16** Grace Slick plays her first date with Jefferson Airplane **December 16** Jimi Hendrix Experience's debut single "Hey Joe" released

1967 **January 14** San Francisco "Human Be-In" heralds the Summer of Love **April 15** 400,000 antiwar protesters march from Central Park to the UN building in New York **June 1** The Beatles' *Sgt. Pepper's Lonely Hearts Club Band* LP released **June 16–18** Monterey Pop Festival **October 3** Death of folk-music legend Woody Guthrie **October 16** Joan Baez arrested with 123 others during nationwide anti-draft protests *(16)* **October 17** *Hair,* the "American Tribal Love-Rock Musical," opens in New York **October 21** 200,000 antiwar protesters march on the Pentagon **November 9** First edition of *Rolling Stone* magazine published

1968 **February 16–20** The Beatles leave for Rishikesh, India, for meditation with the Maharishi Mahesh Yogi **March 16** My Lai massacre in Vietnam **March** Joni Mitchell releases debut album, *Songs to a Seagull* **April 4** Martin Luther King, Jr. assassinated in Memphis **May 18–19** First Miami Pop Festival **June 6** Robert Kennedy assassinated *(17)* **July 1** USA, USSR, UK, and 59 other countries sign Nuclear Non-Proliferation Treaty **November 5** Richard Nixon elected US president **December 28–30** Second Miami Pop Festival **August 26–29** Antiwar protests at Democratic Convention, Chicago

1969 **March 18** US begins bombing North Vietnamese positions in Cambodia **March 25–31** John Lennon and Yoko Ono stage first "bed-in" at Amsterdam Hilton **June 26** *Easy Rider* released **July 4–5** Atlanta Pop Festival **July 20** US astronauts Neil Armstrong and Buzz Aldrin are first men on the moon *(18)* **August 1–3** Atlantic City Pop Festival **August 9** Actress Sharon Tate and four others murdered in Roman Polanski's home by the Manson Family

The Times
They Are a-Changin'

"**The 1960s were an amazing time, an eventful time of protest and rebellion.** An entire generation had permission to drink alcohol and die in a war at eighteen, but it had no voting voice until the age of twenty-one. Upheaval was inevitable. Talk made music, and music made talk. Action was in the civil rights marches, marches against the bomb, and marches against an escalating war in Vietnam. It was a march out of time, too—out of the restricted and rigid morality of the 1950s. The Beats had already cracked the façade and we, the next generation, broke through it." SUZE ROTOLO, NYC ARTIST

The Woodstock festival is considered the apogee of the youth-driven "counterculture" that flourished in the United States and other Western countries from the mid-1960s to the early 1970s. A reaction to the conservative attitudes of post-World War II society, and stimulated by opposition to the war in Vietnam, the counterculture espoused antimilitarism, racial equality, women's rights, artistic freedom, and sexual liberation. Although as a movement it embodied various social, political, and artistic groupings, it was most popularly represented by young people adopting the hippie lifestyle, which also encouraged "back to nature" communal living, an interest in exotic (often Eastern) spiritual teachings, and the widespread use of mind-altering drugs. And central to the counterculture was the new popular music of the 1960s, which "tribal" gatherings like Woodstock celebrated in all its variety.

This cultural revolution was the result of unprecedented social and political changes that had taken place across the Western world in general, and America in particular, in the decade following the end of World War II. Throughout the 1950s the US had enjoyed substantial economic growth, stability, and material wealth as had never been experienced before. In mainstream, white America, by 1955 some fifty percent of all families had at least one car, a TV set, a refrigerator—consumables not even considered luxuries, that came with the postwar economic boom. For the first time, such prosperity filtered down to young adults, "teenagers" (as they were first termed in the early 1950s). In recognizing this new consumer group with money to spend, entrepreneurs soon exploited the opportunity with targeted clothes, movies, and, most significantly, popular music. The new rhythms of rock 'n' roll, the teenage angst as portrayed in movies like *The Wild One* and *Rebel Without a Cause* were eagerly absorbed by the new young consumer. But such expressions of exuberance and affluence were tempered by a deep conservatism, an inward-looking society overshadowed by Cold War brinkmanship and the ever-present threat of nuclear annihilation.

At the start of the 1960s the scene was set for some radical social and political changes. First, in 1962, came the Cuban Missile Crisis, and for a time the whole world seemed to be counting down to atomic war. The following year, the assassination of President John F. Kennedy deeply traumatized the American public. Suddenly, young Americans began to question the political status quo that their parents had taken for granted. But the single factor that galvanized the concern of US youth like no other was their country's involvement in the Vietnam War. As the conflict escalated, and more and more young men were drafted to fight in Southeast Asia, the war became the main focus of protest throughout the 1960s.

Established standards and morals of society were also being challenged. Liberal attitudes toward race, sexual behavior (the contraceptive pill was introduced in 1960 and within two years over a million women were using it), artistic freedom, women's liberation (Betty Friedan's seminal book, *The Feminine Mystique*, was published in 1963), and drug-taking all took hold within a new, youth-driven culture that was finding itself increasingly out of sync with established conventions.

During the latter half of the decade, American society became increasingly polarized. The Civil Rights Movement had inspired people of all races, but following the assassination of Martin Luther King, Jr. in 1968, emotions had erupted into riots in the ghettos. Millions of young people (at least 50,000 of whom escaped to Canada), faced with the prospect of being drafted, opted instead to follow the mantra of Timothy Leary and "turn on, tune in, drop out." Student activists and other militants took to the streets to confront authority head-on—most famously at the 1968 Democratic Convention in Chicago, when hundreds of demonstrators were tear-gassed, beaten, and arrested by Chicago policemen, US Army troops, and National Guardsmen. The country was divided—not along the traditional lines of race or class, but by generation, attitude, and culture. The new counterculture suggested a new model for an alternative society, which many felt would be synthesized and expressed most completely at the "3 days of peace & music" that was to be the Woodstock festival.

Above: By 1955 a TV set was owned by fifty percent of all American families. Opposite (clockwise from top): US soldiers in Vietnam, 1969; Civil Rights March on Washington, 1963; anti-birth control protest, 1968; peace march, Oakland California, 1965.

"I HAVE A DREAM"

Rosa Parks's refusal to give up her bus seat for a white passenger in Montgomery, Alabama, in 1955, thereby instigating the Montgomery Bus Boycott, galvanized the Civil Rights Movement. Alongside the antiwar campaign, it was the other great cause identified by many young musicians and songwriters.

Initially most of this musical support came from the folk scene, which had a left-wing tradition inspired by artists like Pete Seeger and Woody Guthrie that went back to the Depression years before World War II. One prominent activist from the earliest days of the Civil Rights campaign was the African-American folk singer Harry Belafonte (who also enjoyed huge chart success in the 1950s). He led the first youth march for integrated schools in October 1958, in which more than 10,000 people, black and white, demonstrated in Washington, D.C.

Some of the earliest film footage of the young Bob Dylan performing "Only a Pawn in Their Game," was shot during a trip to Mississippi in 1963 in support of the nonviolent actions there. And when in 1963 Martin Luther King, Jr. stood before a quarter of a million supporters on the steps of the Lincoln Memorial in Washington and announced "I have a dream," his speech was preceded by a short set from Dylan and Joan Baez, which included "When the Ship Comes In" and "Only a Pawn in Their Game."

But despite the subsequent Civil Rights Act of 1964, which outlawed racial discrimination in all American states, the assassination of Dr. King in Memphis in 1968 sparked an angry response among poor African-Americans across the country. It led to riots in the poverty-stricken inner areas of over 100 cities, including Baltimore, Chicago, New York, and Washington, D.C., where damage wreaked in black ghettos was particularly severe.

The 1960s also saw the rise of militant groups like the Black Muslims and the Black Panther Party. Officially called the Nation of Islam, the Black Muslims were founded in 1930 in Detroit, and called for a separate state for black Americans. Their support grew during the first half of the 1960s, mainly through the charismatic appeal of their most famous spokesman, Malcolm X, but when he was assassinated just months after leaving the organization in 1965, their numbers gradually dwindled.

Founded by Huey P. Newton and Bobby Seale in 1966, the Black Panther Party was a Marxist-Maoist organization that initially called for "black power" to defend

African-American neighborhoods against what they saw as state-inspired police brutality. They gradually became more inclusive, however, condemning black nationalism as "black racism," and in doing so became accepted as one of the many quasi-political subgroups associated with the counterculture.

By the end of the decade it had become clear that African-American aspirations were not going to be served by legislation alone, though it did put an immediate end to the institutionalized discrimination rife in the southern states. Nor would those aspirations, for what was still largely an economic underclass, be resolved by the simple "peace and love" ethos of the counterculture. It was going to take a great amount of political will to effect necessary change over the coming years —from the injection of public funds into the deprived communities, to the recruitment of black men for city police forces patrolling those same ghettos— beyond the mere rhetoric of campaign slogans and protest songs.

But the power of music certainly had its place. From James Brown's 1968 soul-stirring with "Say It Loud—I'm Black and I'm Proud," there were African-American singers and songwriters producing increasingly politicized lyrics. They included performers like Nina Simone with "Young, Gifted, and Black," Marvin Gaye—whose early 1970s hits "What's Going On," "Mercy Mercy Me," and "Inner City Blues" addressed issues of poverty, discrimination, and political corruption—and Gil Scott-Heron, most famous for his 1970 debut single, "The Revolution Will Not Be Televised." It was a trend potently demonstrated at Woodstock when Richie Havens, the first act on stage, closed his set with "Freedom," a largely improvised and instantly acknowledged reference to the very real struggle continuing in that "other" America of the still racially defined inner cities.

"Good evening, ladies and gentlemen.
I understand there are a good many southerners in the room tonight. I know the South very well. I spent twenty years there one night. Last time I was down South I walked into this restaurant and this white waitress came up to me and said, 'We don't serve colored people here.' I said, 'That's all right. I don't eat colored people. Bring me a whole fried chicken.'"

DICK GREGORY, COMEDIAN AND SOCIAL ACTIVIST

Right: Tommie Smith and John Carlos giving a "black power" salute at the 1968 Mexico City Olympics. Opposite above: Bus protester Rosa Parks, Montgomery, Alabama, 1956. Opposite below: The historic March on Washington, August 28, 1963.

THE SPECTER OF VIETNAM

"And it's one, two, three, what are we fighting for? Don't ask me, I don't give a damn, next stop is Vietnam..."

COUNTRY JOE MCDONALD

Throughout the 1960s, America's increasing involvement in the war in Vietnam haunted the nation's youth. President Eisenhower had first sent in military advisers in 1956. Under President Kennedy, the number of US military personnel grew dramatically, and by the mid-1960s it seemed nearly every American family had a relative or knew someone serving in Vietnam.

As conscription (popularly known as "the draft") of males between the ages of nineteen and twenty-five was gradually escalated to meet the demands of the conflict, most young men lived with the very real prospect of being sent to fight a war on the other side of the world. At the time, the American government thought that if any Asian nation fell to Communism, others would inevitably topple as well, a line of thinking known as the "domino theory." That was the principal reason for the commitment to the war in Vietnam. Nevertheless, few young people fully understood the reason for the war, which was growing more unpopular by the day. A poll in 1965 indicated that sixty-one percent of the American population thought American involvement in the war was not wrong. By 1971 the tide had turned: the same percentage—sixty-one percent—thought the war *was* wrong.

Vietnam was the first war to be fully exposed on television. Horrifying images of the carnage were broadcast on the evening news to the homes of the majority of Americans almost as soon as they happened. With the advances in color photography, magazines such as *Time, Life,* and *Newsweek* were dominated by disturbing photo reportage, and the reputations of broadcasters and journalists such as Dan Rather and David Halberstam were made reporting from the battlefields.

These images resonated around the globe, but for young people in Europe and other parts of the world outside America, the vibrant youth culture of the Swinging Sixties seemed poles apart from the horrors of the Vietnam War. In the US they were inextricably linked. The average age of a GI in Vietnam was just nineteen, and the specter of war was as much a reality for the nation's youth as the music, fashion, and liberated attitudes that characterized their generation. Despite the dissent, this was a generation that genuinely loved its country. It was no aberration that patriotism as demonstrated by the display of the Stars and Stripes—albeit often with a peace symbol superimposed—was frequently seen at countercultural gatherings.

The antiwar movement, spurred by media coverage and supported by millions of young Americans, was associated from the start with the music of folk-protest singers led by Bob Dylan and Joan Baez, and later songs like Country Joe McDonald's "I-Feel-Like-I'm-Fixin'-to-Die Rag." And many Vietnam draftees took these songs with them, armed with guitars as well as rifles—indeed the conflict was often dubbed the "rock 'n' roll war."

Above: Draft card-burning at an antiwar demonstration at the Pentagon, October 1967.
Left: A soldier paraphrases the "Make Love Not War" slogan widely adopted by the counterculture.

COUNTING THE COST

US Troop Numbers

Total US troops in Vietnam: 2,594,000
Draftees: 648,500 (25%)
12% of draftees were
college graduates

Peak Troop Strength

April 1969: 543,482
Draftees at end 1968: 38%

Average age of GI in Vietnam:

19

13% of troops were African American,
but 28% of combat units
were African American

US Dead, Wounded, and POWs

Total US dead: 58,193
Draftees killed: 17,725 (over 30%)

Wounded in action: 303,704
Severely disabled: 75,000
Lost limbs: 5,283
Multiple amputations: 1,081

Prisoners of war: 766
Died in captivity: 114

Civilian Deaths
Estimated between 500,000 and
one million for North and
South Vietnam (1960–75)

"Now we have a problem
in making
our power credible,
and Vietnam is the place."

JOHN F. KENNEDY, 1961

"Woodstock was against the background of what had happened in the years before … you had had so many terrible, terrible years here. In 1968 Martin Luther King was assassinated, and Robert Kennedy was assassinated; we went from a terrible president, LBJ, who was really detested by that time, to Nixon, who was so much worse. We knew we were being lied to, and people had gone on so many marches, protests and everything. And Woodstock was basically an antiwar event more than anything else. I'm sure people came along for the ride for other reasons, but mainly it was a way of showing that a lot of people did not want the war to go on. People had sort of run out of ideas about how to make a statement."

ISABEL STEIN, WOODSTOCK ATTENDEE

1954 At Geneva Conference, Vietnam is split into North and South at the 17th Parallel • French colonial troops leave North Vietnam • **1956** French colonial government and troops leave South Vietnam • US military advisors begin training South Vietnamese troops • **1957** Weapons and men from Communist North Vietnam begin infiltrating the South • **1959** The first US servicemen die in Vietnam • **1960** Number of US military advisers rises to more than 600 • **1962** Number of US military advisors in South Vietnam rises to 11,000 • US military employs poisonous defoliant Agent Orange to expose trails used by rebel Vietcong forces • **1963** Vietcong defeats South Vietnamese Army in Battle of Ap Bac • President Kennedy assassinated in Dallas; Lyndon B. Johnson assumes presidency • **1964** Gulf of Tonkin incident, in which North Vietnamese boats allegedly fire torpedoes at American destroyer • Congress approves Gulf of Tonkin Resolution, authorizing President Johnson to "take all necessary measures to repel any armed attack against forces of the United States and to prevent further aggression" • **1965** Over 180,000 US combat troops sent to Vietnam • Bombing raids on North Vietnam commence; referred to as Operation Rolling Thunder, the air raids continue for three years • 9th Marine Expeditionary Brigade arrives in Vietnam • Students at American universities start mass protests against US policy in Vietnam • **1966** B-52s bomb North Vietnam • American protests against the war continue as students are joined by veterans of World Wars I and II • **1967** Antiwar protests continue; Martin Luther King, Jr. and others call for draft evasion • US troop strength increases to 389,000 men • US Secretary of Defense Robert McNamara admits that US bombing raids failed to meet objectives • **1968** Tet Offensive: Vietcong attacks 36 South Vietnamese cities and towns; the fierce fighting convinces the American public that the war will not end quickly • My Lai village massacre of 450–500 people by a company of US soldiers • Peace talks take place in Paris between North Vietnamese and Americans; they are unsuccessful • Faced with increasing unpopularity because of the war, President Johnson announces he will not run for re-election • Richard Nixon elected US president • **1969** More than 540,000 US troops in Vietnam • President Nixon announces planned withdrawal of 25,000 US combat troops • President Nixon authorizes covert bombing of Cambodia to destroy supply routes • News coverage of My Lai massacre shocks America, leading to numerous antiwar demonstrations

"In America, which was totally patriotic, these young people loved their country and yet the country was telling them to do something which they couldn't agree to, to go and fight a war they couldn't see any reason for, and if they didn't they would be jailed ... so they burnt their [draft] cards and all that kind of stuff. And all those people at Woodstock had some kind of connection with that. I think the patriotic thing was really hard for people, with the burning of the flag and such. It was a very poignant moment."

MIKE HERON, THE INCREDIBLE STRING BAND

Left: Flag-burning at Washington antiwar rally, 1969, and protest button badges. Opposite: The peace symbol worn on the frontline in Vietnam.

21

.... and peace

The peace symbol, a familiar icon at antiwar demonstrations and counterculture events in the late 1960s, actually had its origins in England over a decade before the Woodstock festival.

☮ It was created by designer Gerard Holtom for the Direct Action Committee, a UK peace group pledged to civil disobedience in protest against nuclear arms.

☮ The symbol was based on the semaphore flag signals for the letters "N" (holding two flags down in an inverted V-shape) and "D" (one flag pointing straight up, one pointing straight down), initials for "Nuclear Disarmament."

☮ It first appeared in public at a three-day march from London to the atomic weapons research establishment in Aldermaston, organized by the DAC over the Easter weekend of 1958.

☮ Soon after the march, it was adopted as the official symbol of the Campaign for Nuclear Disarmament, which had a huge following—especially among the young—in the UK during the late 1950s and early 1960s.

☮ It was first seen in the American media when a pacifist protester, Albert Bigelow, sailed a small boat displaying a CND banner into a US nuclear test zone in the Pacific Ocean in 1958.

☮ The iconic symbol was imported into the US by University of Chicago student Philip Altbach. He was visiting Britain in 1960 on behalf of the US Student Peace Union, and returned to Chicago with a bag of CND peace buttons, after which the SPU also adopted it as their badge.

☮ Over the next few years the "chickentrack" buttons appeared among students and other peace protesters across the US, and by the end of the decade it had become an instantly recognizable symbol of the antiwar movement, and the counterculture generally.

Below: The peace symbol at Woodstock 1969.
Opposite: And at the 25th anniversary festival in 1994.

CHICAGO 1968

The Students for a Democratic Society (SDS), formed in 1960, was a central force in the "New Left" movement that would galvanize American society. It had evolved out of the Student League for Industrial Democracy that had existed at the start of the century, and held its first meeting in Ann Arbor, Michigan. At its first convention, in 1962, the manifesto known as the Port Huron Statement was adopted. Largely written by activist Tom Hayden, it criticized American politicians for failing to achieve international peace or to address effectively various social ills including racism, poverty, and exploitation. And in occasionally naïve language it urged the younger generation to take part in civil disobedience and "participatory democracy," sowing the seeds for a culture clash based not on race or class, but generation.

Initially the SDS focused on supporting the Civil Rights Movement and improving conditions in the urban ghettos, but by the mid-1960s—in the face of growing "separatist" militancy on the part of groups like the Black Panthers—it was mainly concerned with opposition to the Vietnam War. In April 1965, the SDS organized a national march on Washington as a visible war protest. With its slogan "Make Love, Not War" the SDS was an integral factor in the emergence of the counterculture. The first teach-in to protest the war was at the University of Michigan, which led to hundreds more held all over the country, and to demonstrations like the 1969 draft-card burning in New York's Central Park (which drew half a million protesters—as many as attended Woodstock a few months later).

But the most notorious confrontation between radical students and the authorities came at the 1968 Democratic Convention in Chicago, when Mayor Richard Daley's police attacked 5,000 unarmed antiwar protesters—a coalition

of the SDS, the National Mobilization Committee to End the War in Vietnam, the "Yippies" (Youth International Party), and other groups—in what observers later called a "police riot." After Chicago the lines were drawn, and America (even middle-class, white America) seemed divided as never before. The SDS itself dissolved at its last convention in 1969, but subsequently there would be an even more tragic encounter between student demonstrators and the powers-that-be in May 1970, when Ohio National Guardsmen shot and killed four antiwar protesters on the campus of Kent State University.

Above and below: Police, troops, and demonstrators at the 1968 Democratic Convention, Chicago. Opposite: SDS leader Rennie Davis lies injured and bloodied by police at the Chicago protest rally.

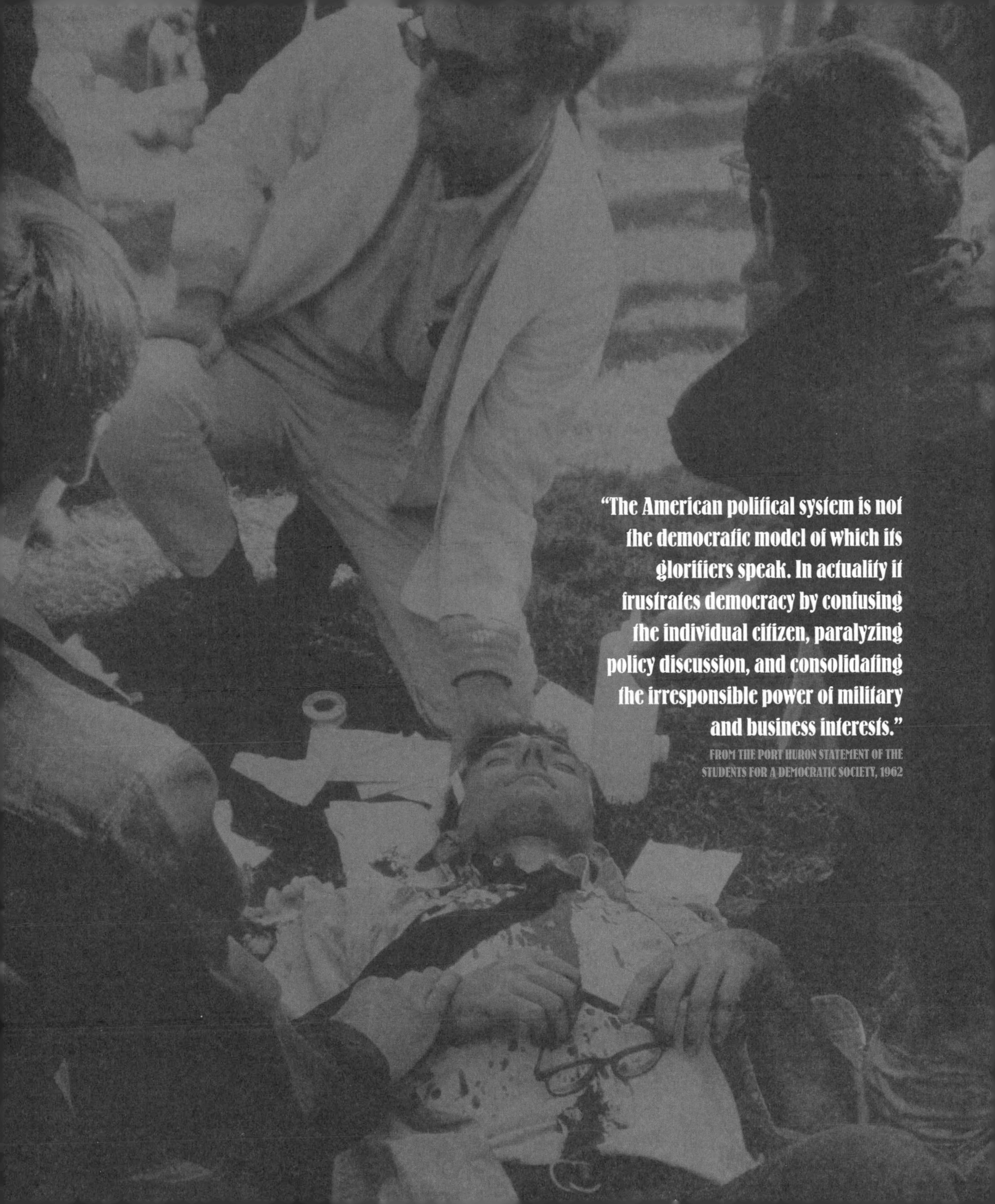

"The American political system is not the democratic model of which its glorifiers speak. In actuality it frustrates democracy by confusing the individual citizen, paralyzing policy discussion, and consolidating the irresponsible power of military and business interests."

FROM THE PORT HURON STATEMENT OF THE STUDENTS FOR A DEMOCRATIC SOCIETY, 1962

All You Need Is Love

By the start of the decade pop and rock had evolved from the wild, overtly sexy rock 'n' roll of Little Richard, Jerry Lee Lewis, and pre-Army Elvis to become like just another stream of the established record business. The prevailing idols were typified by clean-cut crooners such as Paul Anka, Fabian, Bobby Vinton, Brian Hyland, and Bobby Vee (although Bob Dylan had started off playing in Vee's backing group, The Shadows). But their time in the spotlight was to be short-lived.

In 1964 the American music scene was revolutionized when, from across the Atlantic, The Beatles stormed the US charts. The Fab Four heralded an invigorating invasion of numerous British artists who brought their own brand of rock and rhythm & blues back to the land where it had originated.

Meanwhile, one of the prime sources for The Beatles' early repertoire, contemporary Black American R&B—exemplified in barnstormers like The Isley Brothers' "Twist and Shout"—was undergoing its own metamorphosis. While the studio pop of Smokey Robinson, The Supremes, and others was making Motown in Detroit the most successful African-American label in history, a tougher version of soul music—pioneered by labels such as Atlantic in New York and Stax in Memphis—was reflecting the struggle being played out in society at large. Titles like Aretha Franklin's "Respect" and James Brown's "Say It Loud—I'm Black and I'm Proud" (making *Billboard* No. 1 and No. 10 respectively in 1967 and 1968) represented the new black consciousness that characterized the latter half of the decade.

At the same time protest-folk music, enjoying its own success with mainstream audiences, was evolving into folk rock, influenced by the impact of The Beatles on Bob Dylan and others. The parallel R&B boom epitomized by The Rolling Stones—while reviving the careers of Muddy Waters, John Lee Hooker, and other blues legends—similarly inspired the burgeoning wave of (mainly white) US electric-rock groups.

In 1967, as The Beatles released their *Sgt. Pepper* album and the anthemic single "All You Need Is Love," the so-called Summer of Love arrived under the influence of hallucinogenic drugs, particularly lysergic acid diethylamide (LSD). Timothy Leary, psychology professor at Harvard, was the most prominent LSD researcher, and was described by Richard Nixon as the most dangerous man in America. Psychedelic rock soon emerged, pioneered by West Coast bands like the Grateful Dead and Jefferson Airplane, and largely based in the epicenter of the "flower power" revolution in the Haight-Ashbury district of San Francisco.

On a broader front, the good vibes coming out of California were evident in mainstream pop, in hit singles by the likes of The Mamas & the Papas ("California Dreamin'"), The Byrds ("Eight Miles High"), The Beach Boys ("Good Vibrations"), and Scott McKenzie, who had a worldwide smash with the anthemic "San Francisco (Be Sure to Wear Flowers in Your Hair)." The hippie-led counterculture had arrived, and music—even more so than the omnipresent marijuana—was both its main driving force and its common denominator.

In the variety of performers taking the stage, Woodstock reflected 1960s music in all its diversity, from the politico-protest of Tim Hardin and Joan Baez to the blues of Janis Joplin and Paul Butterfield, from Richie Havens's "Freedom" to the proto-heavy rock of Mountain, British mod-rock from The Who, the modern soul of Sly Stone, the boogie R&B of Canned Heat, the good-time music of Country Joe, the poetic Americana of The Band, and the outer reaches of psychedelia represented by the Airplane, the Dead, and Jimi Hendrix.

Right: Joan Baez and Bob Dylan (top), Scott McKenzie (center), and James Brown while playing for US troops in Vietnam in June 1968. Opposite: The Beatles performing "All You Need Is Love" on a worldwide TV broadcast, 1967.

"Rock 'n' roll is the new form of communication for our generation."

PAUL KANTNER, JEFFERSON AIRPLANE

> "There was jazz music, with its roots in the poor, black inner-city locations, and money—Newport, Rhode Island, vacation paradise for the class whose idea of work was telephoning their stockbroker for the latest Dow Jones news."
>
> BILL MACALLISTER, "JAZZ ON A SUMMER'S DAY"

THE NEWPORT JAZZ FESTIVAL

The concept of an open-air music festival was not new by the time Woodstock was planned. As well as its immediate antecedents, the Monterey Pop Festival (1967) and the Miami Pop Festivals (1968), Woodstock's forerunners and influences can be traced as far back as 1954 and the first Newport Jazz Festival.

Staged annually in the upscale Rhode Island resort, the festival was originally held at the Bellevue Avenue estate of millionaire Louis Lorillard, whose jazz-loving socialite wife Elaine had persuaded impresario George Wein to promote it with financial help from her husband. With audiences mainly in a college student-to-adult (rather than teenage) demographic, it was a comparatively staid affair, reflecting its genteel surroundings. The crowd was seated in neat rows of folding chairs and politely applauded each band and the individual soloists. Captured potently in *Jazz on a Summer's Day,* Bert Stern's award-winning documentary film of the 1958 festival, it was up on the stage rather than in the crowd that the sparks most often flew.

The most famous Newport musical moment occurred in the 1956 appearance by Duke Ellington's Orchestra. During an up-tempo blues number entitled "Diminuendo and Crescendo in Blue," tenor sax player Paul Gonsalves performed an amazing twenty-seven-chorus R&B-style solo. The crowd was whipped into a frenzy hitherto seen only at rock 'n' roll concerts. Prompted by a single blonde girl who started dancing on her seat during Gonsalves' seventh chorus, similar outbursts erupted around the audience, and before the end of the marathon solo the whole crowd was on its feet, hundreds dancing in the aisles and crammed down at the front of the stage—a heaving mass of gyrating humanity. The good folk of Newport had never seen anything like it.

However, far more disturbing for the locals (and festival organizers) were the events on the Saturday evening of the 1960 festival. Initially sparked by 300 ticketless fans who stormed the gates, a full-scale riot ensued, involving 10,000 drunken college kids hurling bottles and smashing windows. Police retaliated with tear gas and hundreds of arrests. Inside the grounds Ray Charles was turning up the temperature with his barnstorming "What'd I Say," oblivious to the ruckus outside. The pretty Victorian streets of Newport were in a state of near-martial law, as three companies of the National Guard were called in to restore order.

Apart from a blues concert the following afternoon, the rest of the festival was canceled. Despite fears that this would be the end, the Newport Jazz Festival resumed in 1961 and continued annually until 1972, when it moved to New York City. It became a two-site festival from 1981, when it ran in both Newport and NYC. Now known as the JVC Jazz Festival, it is the longest-running event of its kind.

Right: Duke Ellington's tenor sax virtuoso Paul Gonsalves during his legendary twenty-seven-chorus solo at the 1956 Newport Jazz Festival.

THE NEWPORT FOLK FESTIVAL

Following the successful jazz festival, in 1959 George Wein—along with folk performers Theodore Bikel, Pete Seeger, and Oscar Brand—launched the Newport Folk Festival. It tapped into the folk-music revival which, alongside jazz, had been discovered and promoted by college students. Inspired in the early 1950s by the music of Woody Guthrie and Pete Seeger, and centered around the bars and coffeehouses of New York's Greenwich Village, the folk boom had spread nationwide by the end of the decade, and had encouraged a new generation of singers and musicians to begin their careers.

George Wein's partner in the venture was Albert Grossman, who later started managing his own stable of new folk talent, including Peter, Paul & Mary, Odetta, Phil Ochs, and Bob Dylan—the most talked-about *enfant terrible* on the Village scene in the early 1960s. The Newport Folk Festival became a natural launch pad for these artists and others like Joan Baez, who first appeared at the 1959 festival as an unannounced guest of Bob Gibson, a leader of the revival and Grossman's earliest signing. Dylan made his Newport debut in 1963, alongside his friend and sometime collaborator Baez, in what is generally regarded as his first national-profile performance. For the next two years the pair reigned as unofficial king and queen of the new protest-driven folk movement.

The festival was also associated with the blues revival of the early 1960s, during which Delta bluesmen like John Lee Hooker and Mississippi Fred McDowell were "rediscovered." This in turn had a direct impact on the burgeoning underground rock movement (both in the US and, more significantly, the UK) that revolutionized pop music.

The most significant catalyst in the eventual synthesis of folk, rock, and blues also occurred at the Newport Folk Festival when, on July 25, 1965, Bob Dylan famously "went electric." His groundbreaking album *Bringing It All Back Home,* which was half-acoustic and half-electric, had just been released so it should have come as no surprise when, after a Newport "workshop" appearance the previous day in which he played a couple of acoustic numbers, he opted for an electric backing for his Sunday evening headliner. Using members of the Paul Butterfield Blues Band (who were also appearing at the festival), minus Butterfield himself, he roared through frantic—and for the folk crowd, deafening—versions of "Maggie's Farm," "Like a Rolling Stone," and "It Takes a Lot to Laugh, It Takes a Train to Cry," amid catcalls from the audience (though many were merely calling for the band to play quieter so they could hear Dylan). But old-guard

folkies like Pete Seeger—who tried to disconnect the power—were appalled. Having abandoned the stage, Dylan was persuaded to return for two acoustic songs, "Mr. Tambourine Man" followed by "It's All Over Now, Baby Blue," which were received ecstatically.

But the die was cast. Dylan would not appear at the Newport Festival for the next thirty-seven years. He had severed ties with the folk-music establishment, folk rock was born, and popular music would never be the same again. The emerging counterculture, which reached its apogee at Woodstock four years later, had found its prime mover and shaker—although it was a role Dylan would himself refute at every opportunity.

> "We had the precedent with [Duke] Ellington of being a place where things can happen. When we started the folk festival the first year, some people had that expectation. Folk was becoming the big thing, and Newport was the place to be." GEORGE WEIN

Above: Dylan "goes electric" at Newport '65. Top: Dylan at the 1963 Folk Festival, flanked on his immediate right by Joan Baez, then Peter, Paul & Mary, and on his left by The Freedom Singers, Pete Seeger, and Theodore Bikel.

MONTEREY

The Monterey International Pop Music Festival (to give it its official title) was the first cultural manifestation of the "alternative society" that reached its zenith two years later in Max Yasgur's field at Bethel, New York.

Organized by record producer Lou Adler, Michelle and John Phillips of The Mamas & the Papas, booking agents Ben Shapiro and Alan Pariser, and ex-Beatles publicist Derek Taylor, it was staged at the Monterey County Fairgrounds in California on June 16–18, 1967—and was regarded as the apex of the "Summer of Love." The hippie counterculture had its epicenter in the San Francisco district of Haight-Ashbury, and the Monterey event just down the coast was a large-scale celebration of the music-led, flower-power philosophy that was spreading around the world.

Monterey set the scene for the US debuts of The Who, Jimi Hendrix (who was booked on the insistence of board member Paul McCartney), and—in a non-classical context at least—Indian sitar virtuoso Ravi Shankar. All subsequently appeared at the Woodstock festival, as did the more established performers Country Joe & the Fish, the Grateful Dead, and Jefferson Airplane. Filmmaker D. A. Pennebaker, who had made *Don't Look Back,* the groundbreaking Bob Dylan documentary, in 1967, captured the festival in *Monterey Pop,* which established the precedent of seeing the cinematic possibilities of such events and influenced the subsequent Woodstock movie.

One of the highlights of the festival, and likewise the movie, was when Jimi Hendrix astounded the audience by pouring lighter fuel on his guitar and setting it on fire—a piece of now-classic rock 'n' roll theater directly inspired by The Who's Pete Townshend and his guitar-smashing "auto-destructive art." The incendiary set by Memphis soul singer Otis Redding was equally memorable, his rendition of the slow ballad "I've Been Loving You Too Long" considered by many to be the finest single performance of the festival.

The presence of black artists like Hendrix, Redding, Lou Rawls, Booker T, and Hugh Masakela alongside their white counterparts, as well as a number of racially integrated bands, would have been unimaginable just a few years earlier. It demonstrated how far the Civil Rights Movement had come since the beginning of the decade, and how racial intolerance was rejected by the young, predominantly white, audience.

Although Monterey was preceded a couple of weeks earlier by the Fantasy Fair and Magic Mountain Music Festival in Marin County, California, it was nonetheless the first widely promoted rock festival in the world. With attendance figures of roughly 50,000 for each of the three days, it set a template for subsequent large-scale music festivals, of which Woodstock would become the most famous and celebrated example.

> ## "We had the social consciousness and free spirit of San Francisco combined with Los Angeles' broader musical tastes and business sense, and it worked."
>
> **LOU ADLER, RECORD PRODUCER**

Right: Jimi Hendrix sets his guitar alight at Monterey. Far right: Other Monterey stars included Ravi Shankar (top), and—here in the audience—Michelle Phillips and Cass Elliott of The Mamas & the Papas.

MIAMI AND ATLANTA

Monterey had set the scene for a number of open-air pop festivals that took place ahead of Woodstock, although few of them registered as anything special. The first Miami Pop Festival was significant, though, largely due to the fact that it was promoted by the twenty-three-year-old Michael Lang—later the prime instigator of Woodstock. The festival took place at the Gulfstream Racetrack just north of Miami on May 18 and 19, 1968, and attracted a crowd of over 40,000. The lineup included Steppenwolf, The Mothers of Invention, Blue Cheer, Crazy World of Arthur Brown, Chuck Berry, Pacific Gas & Electric, and Three Dog Night.

In retrospect, the biggest act to appear was the Jimi Hendrix Experience. Although the group had appeared to enthusiastic audiences at Monterey and had subsequently made the US album charts, they were not considered headline material for the all-star bill at the time of Miami. Three stages operated at the event, with two bands playing at any given time. As the Experience were getting ready to play on one stage, Frank Zappa & the Mothers of Invention were finishing their set on another, and Hendrix attracted only a few hundred of the dedicated or just plain curious.

So successful was the May event that another Miami festival was staged at the same venue between December 28 and 30, though this time Michael Lang wasn't directly involved. This featured an equally spectacular lineup, with high-profile names of the day including Fleetwood Mac, Buffy Sainte-Marie, Chuck Berry, Flatt & Scruggs, Steppenwolf, Richie Havens, Sweetwater, Terry Reid, The McCoys, Pacific Gas & Electric, Marvin Gaye, Joni Mitchell, The Box Tops, Iron Butterfly, Jr. Walker & the All Stars, Joe Tex, the Grateful Dead, The Turtles, and Ian & Sylvia. An estimated 99,000 attended over the three days.

Held over July 5 and 6, 1969, a festival in Atlanta, Georgia, attracted more than 110,000 fans. Held at the Atlanta International Raceway, it was organized by Alex Cooley, who staged the Texas International Pop Festival just two weeks after Woodstock. In the searing heat—with temperatures at nearly 100 degrees Fahrenheit, the local fire department used their hoses to create sprinklers for the crowd to cool off—an all-star lineup included Janis Joplin, Johnny Winter, Blood, Sweat & Tears, Canned Heat, Joe Cocker, Creedence Clearwater Revival, Sweetwater (all of whom would play Woodstock), plus Al Kooper, Chicago, Pacific Gas & Electric, and Led Zeppelin—the new British superstars-to-be.

"I guess the seed for Woodstock was sown during the Miami Pop Festival."

MICHAEL LANG, WOODSTOCK ORGANIZER

Opposite: Richie Havens at the second Miami Pop Festival. This page: The December '68 event also included singer/guitarist José Feliciano (above left) and soul legend Marvin Gaye (below).

SOUNDOUTS

Since the early twentieth century the small town of Woodstock in upstate New York had been host to a thriving colony of artists, writers, and musicians. In 1957 a body calling itself the Woodstock Festival Committee published the first edition of an annual booklet, *The Woodstock Festival,* publicizing the arts scene there. As well as advertising local shops and businesses, it carried calendar listings of galleries, art classes, plays, poetry readings, and musical events. And every year local artists submitted drawings of a dove, one to be chosen for the front cover of the next edition.

By the mid-1960s this bohemian community was beginning to reflect the emerging youth counterculture, attracting among others various well-known musicians—including the emerging superstar Bob Dylan. He was already familiar with Woodstock through his manager, Albert Grossman, who had a huge house and grounds in nearby Bearsville. In 1965 Dylan purchased an eleven-room mansion called Hi Lo Ha in the district of Byrdcliffe, where an Arts and Crafts Movement colony had flourished since the 1900s. Other musicians, including Tim Hardin, Richie Havens, and The Band, moved to the Woodstock area soon after Dylan. Performers such as Joan Baez, Peter Yarrow (of Peter, Paul & Mary), Janis Joplin, and Jimi Hendrix were regular visitors, just hanging out or recording at the Bearsville Studio, which Grossman had opened on his sprawling estate.

The key figure as far as the local scene was concerned, however, was a woman in her fifties named Pansy Drake Copeland. Pan, as she was known, opened Anne's Delicatessen on Tinker Street, and this day-and-night hangout quickly became a nerve center for the burgeoning music fraternity. On the same street Pan's son, Franklin Drake, ran the Espresso Café (where Dylan rented a tiny one-room apartment for a short time), which featured live music by local singers and groups.

It was Pan Copeland's farm—across the town line in Saugerties, just off the Glasco Turnpike—that provided the setting for the genuine forerunner of the 1969 festival: a series of open-air jam sessions staged between 1966 and 1968 and initially dubbed Soundouts. Held in Zena High Woods and organized by local health-food store owner Jocko Mofit, the Soundouts (later called the Woodstock Sound Festival) featured an amazing list of up-and-coming musicians and bands, including Tim Hardin, The Flying Burrito Brothers, Larry Coryell, Don McLean, James Taylor, The Mothers of Invention, members of Jefferson Airplane, and early psychedelic pioneers The Blues Magoos. There was even a light show.

The Soundouts attracted hundreds of people from outside the Woodstock area, who paid a few dollars for a weekend and camped out, cooking their own meals or sharing food with others. Facilities included parking, water, and firewood, plus simple sanitary arrangements and a single food concession—both constructed from refurbished chicken coops. For the musicians, the get-togethers were a rare opportunity to jam in an informal situation, away from their professional life on the road. Filmmaker David McDonald, whose documentary *Woodstock: Can't Get There From Here* traced the origins of the 1969 festival back to the Soundouts, recalled: "Everybody was up there at one time or another. It was like rock 'n' roll summer camp."

"The big turning point was when the rifle shop turned into a psychedelic shop. By '68, it had just mushroomed and you started seeing some really famous people walking around town."
GEORGE QUINN, WOODSTOCK RESIDENT

Right: Bob Dylan on his Triumph Tiger 100 in the streets of Woodstock (where he would have his fateful motorcycle accident in 1966) in July 1964, with singer John Sebastian riding behind.

34

THE VENTURE

Not long after staging the Miami Pop Festival in May 1968, promoter Michael Lang moved to Woodstock, attracted by the thriving musical community there. At the time he was managing a group called The Train, and while in New York City hustling to get them a recording contract, he met twenty-six-year-old songwriter and producer Artie Kornfeld, who had become the youngest vice-president of Capitol Records five years previously. The two men—both natives of the Bensonhurst district of Brooklyn—hit it off immediately, and quickly became close friends. They came up with the idea of setting up a recording studio in Woodstock (which in fact never progressed beyond the planning stage). To help fund it, they conceived an idea for a series of concerts—or, better still, a fully fledged festival—hopefully recruiting some of the better-known talent in the area. But for the festival idea to take off, they would also need some capital.

Meanwhile, an advertisement had appeared in the small ads section of the *Wall Street Journal*. It ran:

YOUNG MAN with unlimited capital looking for legitimate investing opportunities and business propositions. Box B-331, The Wall Street Journal

A similar ad ran in the *New York Times*. These had been inserted by two would-be venture capitalists, Joel Rosenman and John Roberts, who were hoping to write a television series about two young guys "with more money than brains," as Rosenman later recalled. "And the only thing we didn't have was plots—we couldn't think what kind of nutty business ventures these two nutty men would get into. In desperation we took an ad out in the *Wall Street Journal,* claiming to be a young man with (quote) 'unlimited capital' looking for business propositions." They ran the ads as a hook to meet people with unusual business ideas, which Roberts and Rosenman could then presumably turn into television scripts.

Like a self-fulfilling prophecy, a genuine venture evolved from one of the many replies to the phoney ad—a recording-studio project in New York called Media Sound. Michael Lang's lawyer, Miles Lourie, knew of Roberts and Rosenman and their fledgling studio, and fixed a meeting at which Lang and Kornfeld proposed a Woodstock studio and initial concert to fund the project.

But along the way the four plunged into the notion of a Woodstock festival. Not long after, the young straight-suited money men had thrown in their lot with the two hippie-looking characters, with an initial investment of $500,000, forming a four-man partnership called Woodstock Ventures.

Of the two entrepreneurs, twenty-three-year-old Roberts was the main source of the investment capital, having an inheritance from his wealthy family business (the Pycopay dental/pharmaceutical company), the first payment of which he had received at the age of twenty-one.

Before he decided to take his chances in financial speculation with Roberts, Joel Rosenman's background was in law—an invaluable asset for the new enterprise. Of the four, Artie Kornfeld had the most experience and contacts in the music business, while Michael Lang—who had run a hippie "head shop" in Florida before producing the Miami Pop Festival—was the visionary, and the one who most clearly understood the counterculture with which the festival would identify.

Right: The inspiration behind the whole Woodstock project, Michael Lang, in his office at the festival. Opposite above: Entrepreneurs Joel Rosenman (left) and John Roberts in the 1970s. Opposite below: Joel Rosenman at the time of the Woodstock festival.

"I laid this out to my father why I was doing this, and he said, 'You've rented a field a hundred miles from New York City, and you're going to expect 50,000 people to come up there to listen to rock music, and you're going to put your own money into this venture.' And I said, 'Yeah, Dad, I am. I really think it's a great idea. There's a whole new thing going on in the world—hey man, this is the Sixties.' And he said something like, 'I just knew it.... I just knew it. I just knew the minute you got your hands on your inheritance, you would do something like this.'"

JOHN ROBERTS, WOODSTOCK ORGANIZER

"John and Joel were in charge of ticketing, and accounting and contract vetting. Joel was a lawyer. He never actually practiced law, but Joel was a lawyer, so he was good at reviewing boilerplate for us on the contracts we issued. But basically their responsibility was of the financial sort, keeping track of the money and the ticketing operation. They put up all of the initial capital—well actually it was John Roberts' money. He put up $200,000 as the cash money we needed for the festival, and he put up $275,000 to build the studio.... This for them was a financial deal. It was an investment. Certainly for John. But they're good guys, and obviously they would judge the project by how well it went, and how well people did, how safe it was, and how good a time everybody had.

They were not counterculture people, but they were good guys, so they had that perspective as well, but it was basically a financial deal for them." MICHAEL LANG

THE TEAM

The next stage for Woodstock Ventures was to recruit a team to put the plan into action. After securing some offices in Manhattan, Lang's first move was to bring in Stanley Goldstein, who had worked with him on the Miami Pop Festival, to act as a headhunter, lining up various technical experts. Another teammate from the Miami show was Mel Lawrence, who would act as director of the site operations, dealing with the layout, landscaping, and coordination of everything that had to be built. And the design and construction of the stage itself, and the management of the stage and between-acts set-ups, was the responsibility of production stage manager Steve Cohen.

Described by Michael Lang as "a genius," Chris Langhart had taught theater design at New York University, and helped put together the nearby Fillmore East rock venue. He was appointed technical director for Woodstock, overseeing the stage design, electrical arrangements, and even the plumbing. For lighting Lang hired Chip Monck, who had done the Monterey Festival in 1967, and was considered the best lighting man in the business. Monck in turn recommended John Morris to look after artist relations—his official job description was "production coordinator" —a role he had fulfilled at Fillmore East, where he virtually ran the operation.

As the team grew, so more people were recommended—everybody knew someone who would suit a certain job. What Lang defined as the core group soon included Joyce Mitchell, the administrator of the New York office, an old Miami friend Peter Goodrich in charge of concessions, and Jim Mitchell who became the purchasing agent. Lang hired Ticia Bernuth as his personal assistant, and together they found Wes Pomeroy (former head of the president's Crime Commission, and assistant to the US attorney general) to take control of security.

And, crucially, Stan Goldstein brought in the state-of-the-art sound engineer Bill Hanley, who had also worked at the Miami event.

Left: Michael Lang (rear) and lighting man Chip Monck (right) during a planning meeting.
Right: Displaying his "credentials," director of operations for Woodstock Ventures, Mel Lawrence.
Below: Michael Margetts (left), the British filmmaker originally hired to cover the building of the White Lake site, and Michael Lang's assistant Ticia Bernuth.

WOODSTOCK AND WALLKILL

The site originally planned for the festival, owned by Alexander Tapooz In Woodstock itself, was rejected after objections from local residents. Then, in March 1969, Lang and Kornfeld found a landowner in nearby Saugerties who was willing to lease his property for the event. However, when Roberts and Rosenman subsequently met with his attorney, it became apparent the landowner was having second thoughts—possibly because he was unsure about the financial security of the whole Woodstock Ventures setup. The next site to be considered was identified by Roberts and Rosenman, an undeveloped 600-acre patch called the Mills Industrial Park in the town of Wallkill, about thirty-five miles south of Woodstock. Its owner, Howard Mills, readily agreed to lease the property to Woodstock Ventures for $10,000, but once again protests from local citizens made the prospect untenable.

> "The fact that we'd gotten thrown out of Wallkill had thrown our plans into the wastebasket. We tried to explain to what by then was 50,000 to 60,000 people who'd already bought tickets, that there was still going to be a festival, and why we had moved it from one community to another, which was that we weren't welcome, and we didn't want to throw three days of peace and music where we weren't welcome."
>
> JOHN ROBERTS, WOODSTOCK ORGANIZER

Right: The original poster for the proposed event at Wallkill. Created by rock industry designer David Byrd, it celebrated the "Age of Aquarius" popular in hippie lore at the time, with its announcement of an "Aquarian Exposition" and a picture of the Zodiac water carrier, Aquarius.

WOODSTOCK MUSIC & ART FAIR PRESENTS

AN AQUARIAN EXPOSITION

WALLKILL, NEW YORK
AUGUST 15·16·17

40

PEACEFUL ROCK FETE PLANNED UPSTATE

BY LOUIS CALTA

The promoters of a rock music festival planned for mid-August in Wallkill N.Y., met here yesterday to plan security measures. They hope to prevent disorders such as those that marred similar activities in California last weekend. The promoters anticipate a crowd that could reach 150,000.

The Wallkill event is named the Woodstock Music and Art Fair, although it will take place about 20 miles away from Woodstock. The original site proved not large enough and not easily accessible, according to the promoters.

The promoters, Michael Lang and Artie Kornfeld, met with security personnel at the Village Gate, a Greenwich Village nightclub. They said they hoped the California incidents would not "set a precedent for other festivals this summer."

The rock program will take place Aug. 15, 16 and 17 and will present 17 major acts including Janis Joplin, the Jefferson Airplane, Blood, Sweat and Tears and the Grateful Dead.

Wesley A. Pomeroy will be in charge of security. Mr. Pomeroy, who was Attorney General Ramsey Clark's special assistant for law enforcement, was named by President Johnson to be one of two associate administrators of the Justice Department's anticrime agency.

"I'm not worried about the security particularly," he said, adding, "if people have enough to do, there won't be any trouble."

Last weekend's disturbance occurred at the Newport (Calif.) Music Festival after young people who could not gain admittance attempted to force their way in.

Mr. Lang said 600 acres would be available for the festival-goers to use for camping and for activities other than music listening. The main performance area will consists of 150 acres. He said that the crowd was expected to range from 50,000 to 150,000.

"We don't anticipate that we'll have to turn anyone away," Mr. Lang said. Three hundred policemen will be recruited for the festival. None will be in uniform and none will carry weapons, Mr. Pomeroy explained. State and Federal officers also will be present.

NEW YORK TIMES, JUNE 27, 1969

"I'm sitting in the basement of my house where my office was, and I had just placed an ad in the New York paper 'property for rent.' This was property that I was going to develop and I wasn't using it at the moment.

And two young men walked into my office, well dressed, stating that they had seen my ad and wanting to rent my property for a small musical fair or something, consisting of probably 5,000 people. My accountant was sitting there next to me, and before it was over I had agreed to rent them the property for $10,000 for the season. And when they left [I thought] 'Where in the hell are they going to find 5,000 damn fools to sit in a field.' So that's where it started.

I was not really aware of the drug culture and what the world was evolving into, and I had no knowledge of it, until I started to get threatening phone calls into the middle of the night, and my wife did, to get rid of these people. And I was really quite unaware of what the reason was, and then of course it became a political issue, as people started to complain they wanted it out of there.... I had a contract with them for a property, I had no way to get rid of them. And then the town put the injunction on it, and in fact our lives were even threatened at some points, and I considered moving my family up to Lake Placid for the summer. The state police advised me against it, because they could only watch me in one place.

I had legal advice trying to find a way out of this contract, then came the injunctions from the town council. And at the time I knew Governor Rockefeller very well because of the economic development group I was in. I got a phone call from him one morning saying, 'Howard, I don't know what is going on down there, but get rid of it.' That was a short conversation from him, and then the story went that they'd moved to Bethel.

I was with the Woodstock promoters a bit, on the property they had made trails, they had carved statues in trees, made carvings on rocks and paintings. And they had a very short time to get out and move to Bethel, when they finally were given permission to come up there. All those things were moved, it was impossible what they did—those kids, they moved trees, they moved plants, huge boulders, all the things they had worked on all summer, had been moved from the Wallkill site to Bethel. It was really quite some maneuver to watch them do that."

HOWARD MILLS, WALLKILL SITE OWNER

WHITE LAKE

How did Woodstock Ventures ever find the sleepy hamlet of White Lake just east of Bethel and Yasgur's farm? A fellow named Elliot Tiber had something to do with that.

As of 1969, the thirty-four-year-old interior designer from Brooklyn had spent more than a decade of his spring and summer weekends helping his Jewish immigrant parents run the El Monaco, their dilapidated and failing Catskills motel. He was looking for an escape hatch.

Tiber got involved in the arts and theater community of the Bethel/White Lake area. Eventually, he became president of the Bethel Chamber of Commerce ("which was ridiculous," joked Tiber, "because there was no commerce!"). As such he had a regular permit to hold outdoor music and arts festivals in the town limits. The "festivals" he held prior to 1969 were so small they barely rose above the level of backyard barbecues. "I had done music and theater festivals for ten years without any success," said Tiber. "Very few people came." All that was about to change.

In the middle of July 1969, Tiber read in the local White Lake newspaper that the town of Wallkill had rejected the Woodstock festival. Instantly, he had a eureka moment: he could invite the festival to White Lake, and the festival could not be expelled because he already held a legal permit. (The permit, Tiber explained, "allowed me, as the president of Bethel Chamber of Commerce and the property owner of the El Monaco, to hold a music and arts festival. Period. It was that loose.") Even better, the festival could bring much-needed business to his parents' beleaguered motel.

In short order, he invited Michael Lang and company to White Lake, showed them the permit, and made a deal with Lang for Woodstock Ventures to use the El Monaco Motel as a base of operations—and performers' accommodation—for the festival. It proved a lucrative deal for Tiber and his parents.

Initially, Tiber thought that the festival could be held on the motel's grounds, but the property proved to be ill suited—too small and too swampy. According to Tiber, he then led Lang to the affable local dairy vendor, Max Yasgur, introduced Lang, and vouched for him to his local banker, Charlie Prince, who helped ensure the Woodstock Ventures accounts flowed freely. Michael Lang, however, has said a local real-estate agent was involved in finding the Yasgur farm.

After the festival, flush with El Monaco money paid by Woodstock Ventures, Tiber left the El Monaco behind and moved to Belgium, where he became a successful writer for television, movies, and theater.

Surprisingly, up until 2008, Tiber's story had barely figured in any published accounts of the festival. But with the publication in 2007 of his well-received memoir *Taking Woodstock,* and the Ang Lee-directed film comedy based on that book, Elliot Tiber's story has become part of Woodstock lore.

> "Elliot Tiber called my office and spoke to my assistant, Ticia. He said he had a site and a permit and he wanted us to come up. So we went up to see him at the El Monaco Motel. The site was a swamp behind his motel. As we were already there we toured the area with a local realtor and that's how we met Max Yasgur."
>
> MICHAEL LANG

Left: The dried-up swimming pool at Elliot Tiber's near-derelict El Monaco Motel.
Inset: An ad published to announce the festival's move from Wallkill to Bethel, designed by Arnold Skolnick who also created the classic "dove" poster for the Music and Art Fair.

THE FARM

Having made contact with dairy farmer Max Yasgur, Woodstock Ventures' Michael Lang and John Roberts, along with their attorney Richard Gross, visited him. Looking at possible sites on his extensive property in White Lake, Bethel, thirty miles west of Wallkill and forty-five miles from Woodstock, they agreed to rent what they assumed would be enough land for the festival, for $50,000. But even after the site was near completion, there were objections. A last-minute court hearing withdrew an injunction against it taking place, called for by a small group of objecting property owners whose land adjoined the Yasgur farm.

POP ROCK FESTIVAL FINDS NEW HOME

BY RICHARD F. SHEPARD

An ambitious pop rock festival is going west 30 miles in the hope of finding a warmer reception than the one received in Orange County's Wallkill, where the climate of opposition led to the search for another site in the state.

The new home of the festival, the Woodstock Art and Music Fair, is to be Bethel, 10 miles west of Monticello, in Sullivan County. The dates remain Aug. 15 through 17.

Among the performers expected to lure as many as 200,000 people over the three days are Joan Baez, Janis Joplin, Ravi Shankar, the Jefferson Airplane and Blood, Sweat and Tears. A group of people in the Bethel area approached Woodstock Ventures, the sponsor of the event, seeking to bring the fair there.

With 60,000 tickets already sold, Woodstock Ventures was busy yesterday publicizing the change of address and informing buyers whose names were known because they had bought tickets by mail.

The quest for a new location began a week ago when the town of Wallkill, which is near Middletown, rejected the fair's application to stage its event on private property there. Many people in Wallkill were reluctant to welcome a festival that they believed threatened to over-tax the town's ability to deal with security, sanitation, and traffic.

A citizens' group in Wallkill has applied for an injunction to keep the fair out, but no decision has yet been handed down by the court. Woodstock Ventures said last week that it did not recognize the town's authority to approve or disapprove the fair and that it would go ahead as scheduled in Wallkill. However, at the same time, it began looking for a place in the area that would be more receptive.

The sponsor also said that it would file suit against "town agencies and individuals" in Wallkill. Joel Rosenman, first vice president and director of Woodstock [Ventures], said yesterday that the damage suit had not yet been filed but that he anticipated that it would be for "millions of dollars" to cover the costs of the move.

Woodstock Ventures and the fair itself derive their names from the Town of Woodstock, N.Y., where the sponsor makes its headquarters. The village is 45 miles from Bethel.

The first estimate of the cost of producing the festival was $750,000. Of this, $450,000 was said to have been committed in the form of contracts with the guest artists.

Mr. Rosenman said that all equipment and temporary facilities that can be moved will be moved from the 200-acre Wallkill site to the 500-acre farm in Bethel that has been leased for the festival.

He did not say what the status of the Wallkill lease was as a result of the change.

The Woodstock group made its presentation to the Bethel Town Board, Zoning Board of Appeals, and Planning Board on Monday night. Mr. Rosenman said that while "there was concern expressed" by residents, "this was taken care of by our presentation."

Fred Obermeyer, town clerk of Bethel, which has a population only of 2,366 as against Wallkill's 10,000, said that the event was "not fully cleared yet," but that it would take a day or so until Woodstock had presented all of its material.

He said that the town wanted to see the $3-million insurance policy that Woodstock said it had taken out as a precaution against developments that might lead to town expenditures.

Woodstock Ventures has stressed the measures it is taking to insure in policing and in handling, health, and traffic problems. It is seeking 300 off-duty New York City policemen to staff the festival.

The fair, to be held on the property of Max B. Yasgur, a prominent dairy farmer, does have some detractors in Bethel. The opposition has not coalesced into a formal group, but a 2½-by-4-foot sign has appeared in the town. It reads:

"Stop Max's Hippie Music Festival. No 150,000 hippies here. Buy no milk."

In Wallkill, the feeling against the festival culminated in the formation of the Wallkill Concerned Citizens Committee, which had hundreds of residents sign petitions asking the local government to ban the festival. Spokesmen for the committee emphasized that they were not against music or festivals, but that they were worried about an event that threatened to bring 60,000 or more people a day into an area that they said was ill-equipped to receive them.

NEW YORK TIMES, JULY 23, 1969

"At the beginning they were only gonna use one small field.

They originally had told him [Max] that they wanted a field where they could accommodate between 10,000 to 15,000 people. When he got here and we drove out, he started to show them that he had a number of big, large fields that could readily accommodate that many people. Then for the first time they really told him that they were expecting to sell 50,000 tickets, and they felt that they would have at least another 50,000 people trying to come without paying.

And he said, 'Wait a minute. You're—you're now at 100,000 people.' He said, 'That's a lotta people.'

And he said, 'I will really have to think whether or not I really want to be involved in something that large.'" RICHARD GROSS, WOODSTOCK VENTURES' ATTORNEY

MAX YASGUR

"Michael Lang and Johnny Roberts came to the house, and they were looking to rent a field for three days. No one anticipated it would be what it was. And it was a simple, straight deal: 'Can you rent us a field for three days?'...

The summer of '69 was a very wet summer. We couldn't get hay in the barn. When you have that many cattle, and you've gotta put up enough hay to get 'em through the winter, and you can't make it yourself, the prospect of having to buy that amount of hay was daunting to say the least. Johnny Roberts and Mike Lang came—I think it was a Sunday afternoon— and said they'd like to rent a field for three days.

Sometimes dubbed the "Angel of Woodstock," and even the "Patron Saint of Woodstock," Max Yasgur was an unlikely candidate for either accolade. Born in 1919 and raised on a farm, he had studied at New York University before he went back to farming in the 1940s—first at the family home in Maplewood, New York, before moving to Bethel to expand his business. By the time he came into contact with the Woodstock Ventures entrepreneurs, the Yasgur Dairy Farm had flourished to the extent that it was the biggest milk producer in Sullivan County.

After agreeing to rent some of his land to the festival organizers, Max had second thoughts, as the potential numbers involved seemed to rise day by day. But although basically a conservative, no-nonsense man of the land, when various neighbors began to object to the plans—and urged a boycott of his milk in the process—he dug his heels in on the side of the festival and its youthful audience, becoming a countercultural hero as a result.

Above: Michael Lang with Max Yasgur backstage during the festival.
Right: Lang, with Chip Monck assisting, uses a tractor to pull his Porsche out of a ditch.
Overleaf: The view across Max Yasgur's farmland as building begins.

This field would be appropriate because it has a bowl-shaped topography. And that's all it was, 'for a few days.' Then things changed, and they changed fairly dramatically, because some of the neighbors had a very negative reaction to what were then called hippies, coming to western Sullivan County. And that bothered Dad.

I can remember him saying to one of them, 'Look, the reason you don't want them here is because you don't like what they look like. And I don't particularly like what they look like either. But that's not the point. They may be protesting the war, but thousands of American soldiers have died so they can do exactly what they're doing. That's what the essence of the country is all about.' And, from that point on, he became a champion.

He believed that they had a right to express themselves. He believed that they were the next generation who were going to have the opportunity to take their turn at bat, and make the country a better place. He certainly didn't have anything in common with them. He was a forty-nine-year-old hardworking man. Lived all his life on a farm, which meant very long days. He had a family. He had no comprehension at the time this thing started about their culture, certainly not about their music, but those things didn't make any difference to him.... He genuinely believed that people had a right to express themselves, he believed that people had a right to be left in peace." SAM YASGUR, MAX YASGUR'S SON

"It's perfect, perfect, perfect." MEL LAWRENCE, AFTER HIS FIRST SIGHT OF YASGUR'S FARM

Rona Elliot had worked as a backstage PR person at the second Miami Pop Festival at the end of 1968, and via Mel Lawrence, her then-boyfriend and Woodstock Ventures operations director, was hired for a similar role by Michael Lang. The major thrust of her job before the actual event took place was to smooth the way, in terms of public relations, with the local Sullivan County populace—especially after the festival had been expelled from its first site at Wallkill.

Above: Rona Elliot. Opposite (clockwise from left): Michael Lang, Mel Lawrence's assistant Penny Stallings, and Mel Lawrence at the wheel.

"I was in Algeria, and I got a telegram from Mel Lawrence, saying, COME HOME, FESTIVAL IN UPSTATE NEW YORK. I had been planning on staying in Algeria for the Pan African Cultural Festival, which at that point was being run by Tim Leary and [Black Panther leader] Eldridge Cleaver. It was a lunatic decision to make, but I just had a feeling, and I went back from Algeria to Paris, Paris to JFK. Mel picked me up and off we went to upstate New York. This was May of 1969, and we were at the first site [Wallkill]. So that's how I got there....

I told Mel I was gonna go pitch Michael on a job, on what I knew how to do, which was local PR. I knew a lot about radio stations. If you're thinking there were jobs [with Woodstock Ventures], there weren't, not for some people at least. So I went and I had a meeting with Michael, as far as I can recall. I said, 'I'll go out and talk to the local radio stations, the local TV stations, I'll call the newspapers, I'll go give speeches to the Kiwanis Club, the Elks Club, meet with local merchants and tell them why this is good for the community.' Which, if you think about it, is hilarious....

By the time we got to the second site, it was fine. I went to work every day, I did my job. I reached out to people, I gave speeches, but they didn't know what was about to hit them. And what we were really trying to do, and what I was in particular trying to do, was to assuage them and calm them, that whatever level of people were going to be coming through their community, they were going to end up with a good monetary reward. We were friendly. We weren't trying to upset them....

I remember we attended in full force ... a square dance! And there I am, with a flower in my hair in my headband, at a square dance with a lot of the other staff members, and the local people in White Lake. It's hilarious! I mean, it's unbelievable! It was insane. And it was nice, and I couldn't have been nicer. I remember speaking to the Kiwanis Club or the Elks Club and getting a certificate, and standing up in a leather skirt and leather boots, and I'm sure they thought I was from outer space.

There was a company that Michael hired, Wartoke ... that were doing bigtime PR out of New York. But what I did, I believe, was to just really stay in touch with people."

RONA ELLIOT, FESTIVAL PUBLICIST

"It was the first event ever to be promoted nationally. There had never been a national music event before that. We were on every college and underground radio station in the country. Artie had a lot of connections in radio. We hired publicists called Wartoke who were already reaching out to the counterculture representing artists like Jimi Hendrix. They had a pretty good network of people in the underground press. We did some press conferences with the underground and college press, and held debates to discuss what the festival should be. So we really reached out." MICHAEL LANG

THE POSTER

With the move from Wallkill to Bethel, a new poster appeared—which now had to be turned out very quickly. John Morris, who had run Bill Graham's Fillmore East venue in New York City, had been hired as the festival's production coordinator, booking the acts and generally overseeing the running of things. Through Morris, Woodstock Ventures had already acquired the services of Arnold Skolnick, a New York–based graphic designer, to come up with a new poster image for the Music and Art Fair. Even before the change of venue, Michael Lang hadn't been happy with the original Art Nouveau style of the Wallkill poster, created by rock industry designer David Byrd, and suggested they use a dove on a guitar to represent "3 days of peace & music." (Coincidentally, the annual Woodstock festival booklet, publicizing the art scene in the town, had featured a dove on its cover since its inception in 1957). Based on drawings he'd made of catbirds earlier that summer, Skolnick came up with the "dove" image that would become an icon.

"It starts off I have a friend who is an architect, and he was hired to design a hotel in St. Thomas called the Lime Tree. It was a hotel for rock music, and they hired a guy called John Morris to book the acts. This is probably a year before the Woodstock festival.... Anyway, he [Morris] finally quits, and these guys who are starting this little festival in Woodstock hire him to book the acts. So he called me in on a Thursday and asked me if I could come up with a poster by Monday morning.

They wanted a poster, and they wanted ads, and they wanted a brochure.
So I called up a friend of mine who was a writer, his name was Ira Arnold.
I called Ira and said 'Look we're gonna need a brochure....'
They said they wanted it to be a festival for three days,
they wanted it to be very peaceful, with a lot of music."

"I was living on 9th Street and 5th Avenue, they were on 6th Avenue, and I was going back and forth all the time, designing the advertising campaign. It was a funny meeting we had; we had a certain amount of money to spend, so how do we reach all the kids in the country? We tried to figure out where were all the kids, and where were they going to be going as it was summer. And we hit various areas in the country ... the New York, Boston, Philadelphia area, the Chicago area, San Francisco/Los Angeles, Texas.... I came up there one day, there were two girls sitting there half nude, counting dollar bills in a room—everybody was stoned. The whole thing was like a surrealist movie. And I kept saying, 'You guys, it's gonna be much bigger than....' The money was coming in to buy tickets, and it started to snowball, and they didn't know how to deal with this, it got out of hand—already, before the festival opened."

"I sat around all weekend to try and figure out how to do this thing. That summer I'd been staying in a place at the end of Long Island, Shelter Island ... and there were these catbirds—I'd been out there drawing and sketching this bird about the place—and that Monday morning I sat down, and I took a razor blade, and I cut all these shapes out. I cut out all the pieces, and I put it on blue, because blue is for peace, and I sat there all morning from seven, eight, nine, ten—it comes to eleven o'clock, and something was wrong.

I had my own set of rules about design—you only have to say something once, you don't have to say it twice, and the bird already said "peace." So I ran to the store and bought this red paper. I put all the pieces out on the red paper, and it just said it, that was it.

I pasted it up, and I went running to these guys and they said, 'Great, yeah...' and that was it." ARNOLD SKOLNICK

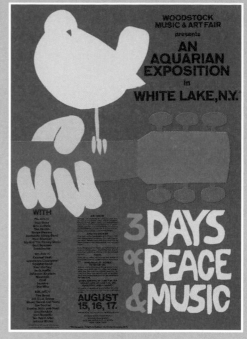

Overleaf (l to r): Festival founders Artie Kornfeld and Michael Lang with production coordinator John Morris.

THE HANLEY SOUND

Now a legend among sound engineers, Bill Hanley was undoubtedly the best-qualified man in America to organize the audio setup at Woodstock.

Born in 1937 in Massachusetts, his first sound job was at his high-school record hop at the age of thirteen, and through his teens he developed his skill (and reputation) to the extent that promoter George Wein hired him to mix the sound at the 1957 Newport Jazz Festival. From there on he—and his company, Hanley Sound—was the premier name when it came to large outdoor events, with most of the rival outfits specializing in indoor, theater presentations. He did indoor venues as well, of course—he cut his teeth in the rock world with early theater gigs by Velvet Underground and Jefferson Airplane—but found his particular niche in stadium shows featuring the biggest names in the business, including The Rolling Stones and The Beatles: he looked after the sound for the entire eastern leg of The Beatles' final US tour in 1966, including Shea Stadium. And such was his reputation that he was engaged to do the sound for prestigious nonmusical events, such as President Johnson's 1965 inauguration in front of the Capitol in Washington, D.C.

The first Hanley heard about the upcoming Woodstock festival was when he got a call from Woodstock Ventures' "fixer," Stan Goldstein. Goldstein's job included finding and hiring various technical personnel, and he had used Hanley previously for the Miami Pop Festival early in 1968, also run by Michael Lang. At Miami, Hanley just mixed the sound, but this time he was hired to design, build, and coordinate the whole setup, before the stage and performance area were actually built.

Hanley was initially contracted for the aborted festival at Wallkill, which was canceled the day he got there to view the site. Shortly afterward, he was whisked over to Bethel in a rented limousine to look at another possible site, and to meet with Max Yasgur, the local farmer who owned the land.

Hanley built special speaker columns on the hills facing what would be the stage area, and had sixteen loudspeaker arrays in a square platform going up to the hill on seventy-foot towers. They set it up for 150,000 to 200,000 people, never expecting half a million to show up.

On Hanley's specification, audio company Altec Lansing built speaker cabinets that weighed half a ton each, were six feet high, almost four feet deep and three feet wide. Each of the woofers (for lower-frequency sound) carried four fifteen-inch Lansing D140 speakers, while the higher-frequency tweeters consisted of four two-Cell and two ten-Cell Altec Horns. Behind the stage were three transformers providing 2,000 amps of power. For many years the system pioneered at Bethel was collectively known as "the Woodstock Bins."

"We arrived thirty days beforehand. In fact, it was either the next day or that afternoon we went there, when [Lang] received word that they were canceled [at Wallkill]. Max and I and Michael went out looking at his field. We got to the first field and I said, 'Good. Let's go here.'... I picked it out myself. We never went to any of the other fields that Max had. We were going to go around to all of them, and I took one look at it, and decided that that was good...."

"I designed and laid out those big, long fences on either side to keep the crowd funneled in. And I had to make the walls twelve feet tall so that people— from my experience with other festivals—people would be able to walk out and have some kind of freedom to get in and out. That's why the fences were so high at the sides. That was the crowd-control idea behind it. And it was ten foot in front, so that if you kept pushing to the stage, then you'd get so close you couldn't see anymore. The stage was higher [than ten foot] I believe. And then the wall in front of it—that had the cameras and stuff in between the stage— they had the wall so that they could film it all close up. And then the crowd came, and then if you pushed yourself in from the crowd, then you'd push yourself out of your sightline. The rest of the fences in the funnel—if you look at the shots from the plane, you'll see that there's these great big green areas. That was my idea to keep everybody in the range of the sound system. I designed that and placed the stage, then designed the sound system around that."

BILL HANLEY, SOUND ENGINEER

Opposite: The vast superstructure that took shape around the festival stage, with the artists' main access being the wooden bridge to the right.
Above: In addition to the thousands of feet of electric wiring on the site itself, mains power (there was insufficient on the Yasgur farm) had to be supplied from Bethel via eight miles of cable.
Overleaf: Top right: Michael Lang and Chip Monck on site. Bottom, center, and right: Stage manager Steve Cohen supervising the build. Bottom left: Lang, with assistant Ticia Bernuth (in hat) in background. Center: Monck and Cohen (in middle).

"The staff that I put together was really what made Woodstock work. A lot of people thought it was overstaffed or top-heavy, but that's the reason we managed to get through in one piece, because these people were just the best at what they did, and they gave everything they had.... That initial group, that core group, was a really miraculous group of people."

MICHAEL LANG

"We got within a mile of the venue, and there was just traffic everywhere. This was six o'clock in the morning, Friday morning, I remember walking that last mile up to the site and seeing, basically, the sun come up over the hill and looking at the site and there's this stage that's in a total disarray. They're not even finished yet. There's this structure going on the top, there's this series of wooden pieces that are holding together this … protection for the artists, and it's just a mess and I'm thinking to myself, 'Good God, we're gonna be….' It was seven or eight in the morning, a few hours later we're supposed to be on….

Above: One of the huge lighting towers under construction.
Opposite: The ill-fated "revolving stage" apparatus.

... There was a device that was built with the intention of making the movement of one band to the next easy. And it was essentially a round stage that had been built with wheels, and divided in half. The first band is on the first half, they would finish, and you would turn the podium, it would go around, and you would have the next band already set up. After the first band played, they tried to turn, all the wheels fell off and it just sat there like that through the entire show.

So that gives you an indication of what it was like. Communication between the stage and the [sound-mixing] truck stopped after the first hours. I remember going down to see what was going on with the PA system. This was just before the first artist, before Richie Havens went on. There's about twenty minutes to go. Just let me run out and have a quick look. And there was this little shed, maybe twenty rows out from the stage that had been built to protect the PA, the front of house PA, and Bill Hanley was running this.

I poked my head in to have a look, and all I saw was this guy bent over the console, this console was propped up on a wooden stick and there was smoke pouring from it and I said, 'Yes, I think I'm going to leave now, I'm going back to the truck, where I know what I'm doing.' It was chaotic, but an enormous amount of fun."

EDDIE KRAMER, RECORDING ENGINEER

Woodstock FESTIVAL

Bethel, N.Y.

LOAD HERE

YESTERDAY, WHILE LAST-MINUTE PREPARATIONS WERE BEING MADE IN BETHEL, THOUSANDS OF YOUNG PEOPLE CONGREGATED IN THE PORT AUTHORITY BUS TERMINAL ON 41ST STREET AND EIGHTH AVENUE, WAITING FOR THE SPECIAL SHORT LINE BUSES, WHICH LEFT EVERY 15 MINUTES FROM 7:30 A.M. TO 10:15 P.M. EACH ONE HELD 45 PASSENGERS.

"I've never seen anything like this," said Charles Newell, terminal manager for the Short Lines Bus Company, which rented 20 extra buses to carry the young people to Bethel. "The line will have 15 buses waiting at 7:30 this morning to take the first load north. Sometimes over the Fourth of July or Labor Day, we have a big crowd, but never so many thousands going to one place."

Carrying sleeping bags and tents, canned food, and guitars, dressed in beads, leather, bandanas, and long gowns, the young people spoke of sleeping out under the stars and possible riots.

Vicki Kamp, 18 years old, of Philadelphia, was one of the many who had to overcome parental opposition in order to attend. "They were so upset," she said. "I've never done much traveling and they were so afraid of riots and police trouble and drugs. We had to sit down and talk it all out."

In the crowd around her were two teenagers from Westbury, L.I., Neal Sobel and Robert Spevack. Their parents had refused to let them go unless they could pay for the $12.45 round-trip bus fair and $7-a-day ticket themselves.

"We didn't know what to do," Neal said. "Finally we went to Roosevelt Raceway, hoping we might win some money." They did—$45 on the daily double....

"My parents knew there'd be drugs there, that it'll be a bit wild. They didn't want me to come," said one 16-year-old, standing with the group of teenagers from Westbury. "I know there'll be drugs everywhere and I wonder what it will all be like. I've never been away from home before. I wonder what will happen to all of us."

NEW YORK TIMES, AUGUST 15, 1969

Right: A fan heading for Bethel, his Ford Mustang covered in antiwar graffiti.
Opposite: Fans gathering at the 41st Street Port Authority terminal in New York City, waiting to board Short Line buses to Bethel.

"My friend and I drove in from Rochester. When we got there, we were amazed at the people. We parked miles away and walked.

We weren't planners, however, and brought very little food with us.

We thought there would be concession stands and restaurants in town!

We stayed til 3 a.m. the first night and headed back to our car to sleep." CECELIA, WOODSTOCK ATTENDEE

200,000 THRONGING TO ROCK FESTIVAL JAM ROADS UPSTATE

BY BARNARD L. COLLIER

BETHEL, N.Y., Aug 15

A crowd estimated at more than 200,000 poured into this Catskill Mountain hamlet today for a three-day rock and folk music festival, creating massive traffic jams and a potentially serious security problem.

The police reported that an increasing number of cars were being abandoned by motorists on the shoulders of highways as drivers decided to walk to Bethel. Estimates of the total number of people both at the festival and in the surrounding area were as high as 400,000.

Wes Pomeroy, director of security for the Woodstock Music and Art Fair, who issued the 200,000 figure, warned late this afternoon that Bethel should be avoided.

"Great Big Parking Lot"

"Anybody who tries to come here is crazy," he said. "Sullivan County is a great big parking lot."

At about midnight, the festival promoters announced that, with their full cooperation, the state police and local authorities would start turning back all cars heading for the fairgrounds. This would primarily affect vehicles attempting to reach Route 17B from the Quickway (Route 17). A state police officer said, "We're just going to reroute everybody, Sullivan County is filled up."

Lines of cars were still stretching up to 20 miles from the fair at midnight. The Automobile Club of New York warned that traffic in the Catskills was "at a virtual standstill," and predicted that "conditions are not likely to improve until after the Woodstock Fair folds its tents sometime early next Monday morning."

Traffic on the five key roads that lead and feed into Bethel—Routes 17, 17B, 42, 55 and 97—was bumper to bumper up to four and one-half hours today. An auto club spokesman called the situation "an absolute madhouse." At some points all four lanes of traffic were heading in the same direction. Trapped on Route 17B—the road that lead to Monticello 11 miles northwest to Bethel—was a group scheduled to open the festival, the Sweetwater, a six-man group. The musicians and their instruments were finally air-lifted by helicopter to the bandstand.

NEW YORK TIMES, AUGUST 16, 1969

Above and right: The total gridlock on all routes leading to the Bethel site ensured that, by road at least, the festival was effectively cut off from the rest of the world.

"Parked cars jammed roadways in all directions for up to 20 miles, and thousands of festival-goers, weary after long walks to get here, had to spend the night sleeping on the rain-soaked ground. They awoke to find food and water shortages."

Barnard L. Collier, *New York Times*, August 17, 1969

day one

"Three million people to me,
or even half a million people,
constitute just a nice,
big, large spirit."

RICHIE HAVENS

richie havens

Friday, August 15, 5:07 p.m.
Richie Havens: guitar, vocals
Paul "Deano" Williams: guitar
Danielle Ben Zebulon: percussion, conga drum

Richie Havens, with his eclectic, soul-tinged take on the folk-rock genre (characterized by highly original cover versions) was already a veteran of music festivals, having appeared at the Newport Folk Festival in 1966, Monterey in 1967, and the Miami Festival in 1968. By the time he got to Woodstock he had released three highly acclaimed albums—*Mixed Bag, Electric Havens,* and *Something Else Again*—and he was beginning to receive some serious national exposure.

The traffic jams that had been building up on all the access routes were already making it difficult for both fans and performers to reach the Bethel site, but by Friday afternoon Havens and his backing band (with the exception of his bass player) had arrived, so he agreed to go on first. Playing the opening set established his presence as a key performer at Woodstock, which was later movingly recorded in the movie.

It was originally planned for Havens to do just four songs, but he was happy to "kill time" for the organizers—who were still waiting for subsequent acts to arrive—and among the extra material he performed were three covers of Beatles songs. Other performers would also perform Lennon-McCartney numbers at Woodstock, a reflection of the fact that the Liverpool quartet were still the biggest thing in rock music, their influence ever-present through the sheer familiarity of their already classic songbook. Richie Havens closed his set with the largely improvised and highly spontaneous "Freedom." Based on the old folk spiritual "Motherless Child," it was one of the true anthems to come out of the three days of peace and music.

While most attendees agree on who played at Woodstock, the exact order of the artists (and sometimes even on which day they performed) remains uncertain. There is also uncertainty still about the exact set lists performed by each artist. In spite of the event having been so well-chronicled in film and audio, individual memories, recordings, books and other public works contain significant discrepancies. The editors have carried out their own intensive review and have also relied upon their own interviews and the most recent information provided for the CD reissues of Woodstock tracks with set lists identified by Andy Zaks and published in Michael Lang's memoir.

Set List: From the Prison / Get Together / From the Prison, I'm a Stranger Here, High Flying Bird, I Can't Make It Anymore, With a Little Help from My Friends, Handsome Johnny, Strawberry Fields Forever, Freedom (Motherless Child)

> ## "I thought to myself, 'Oh God, they're going to kill me. I'm not going out there first.'"
> ### RICHIE HAVENS

"I was supposed to do maybe forty minutes, thirty-five, forty minutes ... and when I walked off the first time they said, 'Richie, you gotta do four more songs.' So I said 'OK.' I went back, and I did four more songs. I walked off again, and they said, 'Richie, three more....'

So I went out on the stage and [in the movie] you see me kind of stalling because that's exactly what I was doing. That long intro to what is 'Freedom' the song, was me trying to figure out what to sing. I sang every song I knew.... And I think the word 'Freedom' came out of my mouth, because I saw it in front of me. I saw the freedom we were looking for. And every person was sharing it, and so, that word came out. And 'Motherless Child' I hadn't sung in nineteen years. And it's amazing. I was singing with a family, a choir, and that's when I learned that song and sang it. And that same family had sang another song, which was part of a different song, which part of came out in the 'Freedom' song as well. It's the one about mother, father, sister, brother— that section. That came from another hymn. And I'm going, 'Where is this coming from?' And I got up and walked in the back, and they said, 'Thank you.' And I was, 'Wow, that's pretty far out.' For me, the oddest thing was, I had to go see the movie to see what I did. I actually did. I remember 'Freedom,' and I remember 'Motherless Child,' but I didn't remember how it was structured. Just the song existed. And I went to the movies and I saw it.

It was the first time I saw myself on the screen, anywhere."

RICHIE HAVENS

"I don't think we'd ever heard of Richie Havens, but when he came on stage and started singing 'Freedom,' you know it just stopped you in your tracks. Because we were all very focused in that time on the Vietnam War, and you know it was our brothers and our friends who were fighting in the war or were scheming on ways to get out of the war, out of going to the war.
And so when he came and started singing 'Freedom,' it really did just sort of grab you, and it became from that moment on ... it became a really spiritual experience about peace."

DIANA THOMPSON, WOODSTOCK ATTENDEE

"I am overwhelmed with joy to see the entire youth of America gathered here in the name of the fine art of music.

In fact, through the music, we can work wonders. Music is a celestial sound and it is the sound that controls the whole universe, not atomic vibrations. Sound energy, sound power, is much, much greater than any other power in this world."

sri swami Satchidananda

Friday, August 15, approx. 7:10 p.m.

During the latter half of the 1960s there was a growing interest among young people, and in the counterculture generally, in Hindu-related religious and philosophical movements, and yoga-inspired meditation disciplines. A number of groups representing these various ideas were present at Woodstock—among them the guru Sri Swami Satchidananda with an entourage of his followers.

After teaching his own brand of "integral yoga" in Sri Lanka through the late 1950s and early '60s, in 1966 Satchidananda visited New York City at the request of an American follower, the artist Peter Max. The guru eventually acquired US citizenship, and continued to spread successfully his teachings of yoga and enlightenment in his adopted country. Among his best-known disciples over the course of his life were the poet Allen Ginsberg, actor Laura Dern, and the singer-songwriter Carole King. The fifty-four-year-old, white-bearded swami and his party, who was not originally scheduled to appear, arrived at the festival site by helicopter on the Friday, his entourage having earlier approached the organizers suggesting Satchidananda could speak to the crowd.

The fifty-four-year-old, white-bearded swami and his party, who was not originally scheduled to appear, arrived at the festival site by helicopter on the Friday, his entourage having earlier approached the organizers suggesting Satchidananda could speak to the crowd. While the acts following Richie Havens were still arriving, the guru addressed the Woodstock audience with an invocation of peace and love, to mark the opening of the festival. And as he concluded his ten-minute appearance, with his white-garbed disciples lined across the stage either side of him, Satchidananda led the crowd in repeating the mantra "Hari Om" together.

"If these pictures or the films are going to be shown in India, they would certainly never believe that this is taken in America. For here, the East has come into the West. And with all my heart, I wish a great, great success in this music festival to pave the way for many more festivals in many other parts of this country. But the entire success is in your hands, not in the hands of a few organizers. Naturally, they have come forward to do some job. I have met them. I admire them. But still, in your hands, the success lies.

The entire world is going to watch this. The entire world is going to know what the American youth can do to the humanity.

So, every one of you should be responsible for the success of this festival."

SRI SWAMI SATCHIDANANDA

Friday, August 15, approx. 7:30 p.m.

Nancy Nevins: lead vocals

Albert Moore: flute, vocals

August Burns: cello

Alex Del Zoppo: keyboards, vocals

Fred Herrera: bass, vocals

Elpidio Cobian: conga drums, percussion

Alan Malarowitz: drums

Formed in 1967 by friends who jammed at various Los Angeles coffeehouses, Sweetwater were very much a band of the wide-open, "anything goes" 1960s. Their psychedelic mix of rock, classical, Latin, and jazz influences—with similarly eclectic instrumentation that included flute, cello, and conga drums played by a racially diverse white/black/Latino lineup—defied categorization. Yet they toured nationally, made a number of TV appearances, and performed at most of the major festivals of the day (Miami Pop Festival, Atlanta Pop Festival, Texas International Pop Festival), all without the benefit of a hit single or a bestselling album. When they appeared at Woodstock, they had just one album under their belts, issued on the Reprise label in 1968.

Sweetwater agreed to the booking with the stipulation that they would be the first act to perform at Woodstock. That's because keyboardist Alex Del Zoppo had enlisted in the Air Force reserves (to avoid active duty in Vietnam) and was scheduled to attend training the next day, Saturday, in Riverside, California. He feared that if he missed the training, he would be shipped immediately to Vietnam. As it turned out, because of the traffic jams, Sweetwater arrived late at Bethel and appeared third at Woodstock—after Richie Havens and Swami Satchidananda.

Though Del Zoppo left immediately after their set, the traffic congestion kept him from arriving at the Air Force base until late Sunday night. Fortunately, he was let off with a virtual slap on the wrist: the loss of two days' pay. The band, though, was unable to capitalize on their rising stock. In December 1969, lead singer Nancy Nevins was seriously injured in an automobile accident when she was hit by a drunken driver, resulting in a damaged vocal cord that was never the same again. Sweetwater carried on briefly without her and then disbanded early in the 1970s, but they have subsequently re-formed from time to time.

Set List: Motherless Child, Look Out, For Pete's Sake, Day Song, What's Wrong?, My Crystal Spider, Two Worlds, Why Oh Why, with closing medley: Hey Jude, Let the Sunshine In, and Oh Happy Day

"We hit the ground around five or six thinking we were going to have to run immediately onstage and play, and all of sudden somebody said, 'No, the Swami's going to go onstage before you.'" FRED HERRERA, SWEETWATER

Right: August Burns, Albert Moore, and Nancy Nevins.

"We were actually slated to go on in the afternoon on Friday, and we left the hotel around noon. We had plenty of time under any reasonable circumstances to go the twelve or fifteen miles to get there from the Holiday Inn in Liberty, New York, to the site. But nobody knew there would be quite so many people.... We figured Woodstock would be attended lightly, although there were some really great groups on there. But even so, there were great groups on a lot of festivals in those days. We didn't think it was going to be much of anything until we saw all the traffic. And then we thought: Well, maybe they just can't manage traffic very well up here. We didn't really get it until we flew over the scene in a helicopter, and we saw all the people. I couldn't even believe they were people. I thought they were flowers down there. You just saw colors from one end of the horizon to the other. I literally asked the pilot what the crop was, and he says, 'Those are people.' And then we realized: This is the big one."

ALEX DEL ZOPPO, SWEETWATER

FREEDOM!

By the time the festival got underway, it was apparent that the sheer numbers of people descending on the site (literally hundreds of thousands more than anticipated or planned for) were making it impossible to operate a conventional entry by ticket system. A failure in forward planning was partly to blame. While days in advance some of the rented land had been designated as well-signed parking lots, the lack of actual fencing and entry gates meant that thousands of early arrivals were already camping in the audience area before the festival began. And ticket booths were still being set up on the Friday as some fans, of the opinion that the event shouldn't have been organized for profit, started to storm the hastily erected perimeter fence.

Michael Lang and associates considered their options. They realized that if they tried to clear the performance area of the early (ticketless) attendees, 50,000 angry hippies could wreck the festival and the prospect of a film, and so a free festival was declared from the stage by production coordinator John Morris, with the added caveat "that doesn't mean anything goes." Nevertheless, agitated fans—and at least one protest group, the quasi-anarchist UAW/MF (Up Against the Wall, Motherfuckers)—continued to tear down sections of the fence.

"There were already people arriving three or four days before. The fences were not put up, because Max Yasgur wouldn't allow them to put up the fences [until too late]. Because if the fences were put up the cows wouldn't chew the cud, the cows wouldn't give the milk, and the cows wouldn't be productive. And therefore Max wouldn't let Michael put up the fences. So the situation was obviously out of anyone's normal control."

RONA ELLIOT, FESTIVAL PUBLICIST

"There were lots of social—or should I say antisocial—groups at the festival. The Up Against The Wall Motherfuckers came up from New York City. They were from the East Village in Manhattan, and their claim to fame was running through the streets smashing garbage cans. Their trip was just being anti-everything. One guy was running around backstage screaming, 'Tear down the gates, tear down the gates!' trying to incite people to some sort of action. He came up and started to argue with me. I said, 'Listen, there aren't any gates.' The guy didn't want to hear it; that didn't seem to matter to him. So one of our security guards removed him."

MICHAEL LANG

"Yeah, I got a standing ovation ... on their way to the bathrooms!" BERT SOMMER

bert Sommer

Friday, August 15, approx. 8:20 p.m.
Bert Sommer: guitar, vocal
Ira Stone: electric guitar, Hammond organ, harmonica
Charlie Bilello: bass

Singer-songwriter Bert Sommer was appearing, after a brief spell in the baroque-pop group Lefte Banke, as Woof in the "American tribal musical" *Hair* (his frizzy Afro-style hair famously featured on the posters for the Broadway show) when he was signed to a recording and management deal with Artie Kornfeld in 1968. He had released *The Road To Travel*, the first of two albums cut with Kornfeld as producer, just a few months earlier, and now faced the most challenging appearance of his career. He opened with a song from that first LP, "Jennifer," about the singer Jennifer Warnes, who had appeared with him in the LA production of *Hair*. But the highlight of his hour-long set was a version of Simon & Garfunkel's "America," which was about to appear on his second Kornfeld-produced album, *Inside Bert Sommer.* Moved by the combined resonance of Paul Simon's lyrics and Sommer's delivery, the audience rose to its feet as one, shouting for more.

Set List: Jennifer, The Road to Travel, I Wondered Where You'd Be, She's Gone, Things Are Going My Way, And When It's Over, Jeanette, America, A Note That Read, Smile

> "We went on stage and played a full ten-song set. The eighth song into the set, we did that cover of Simon & Garfunkel's 'America' and got the first standing ovation of the festival. Looking into Bert's eyes and hearing the roar of that huge audience ... WOW! We finished our set and were totally blown away. All of us were unaware at that time what this concert would later become!" IRA STONE, BERT SOMMER'S GUITARIST

Left: Bert Sommer (right) backstage at Woodstock, with guitarist Ira Stone.

Friday, August 15, approx. 9:00 p.m.

Tim Hardin: vocals, guitar

Richard Bock: cello

Ralph Towner: guitar, piano

Gilles Malkine: guitar

Glen Moore: bass

Steve "Muruga" Booker: drums

Once regarded as one of the great singer-songwriters of the era, Tim Hardin ended up as one of its casualties. Although he could be a charismatic performer (an appearance at the 1966 Newport Folk Festival was very well received), his appearances were often marred by late-showing or canceled dates, and were sometimes chaotic—a long-term heroin habit lying at the core of his problems. His prime success was as a result of other performers covering his songs. His biggest chart hit was Bobby Darin's version of "If I Were a Carpenter," which made the *Billboard* Top 10 in 1966. The song was also covered by, among others, The Four Tops and Johnny Cash & June Carter.

Attracted by its relaxed atmosphere and rural setting, plus its proximity to New York City, Hardin moved to Woodstock in the late 1960s. Throughout the 1970s Hardin made some critically acclaimed albums, such as *Bird on a Wire* (1970) and *Nine* (1973), and was even considered for the role of Woody Guthrie (eventually given to David Carradine) in the 1976 biopic *Bound for Glory*. He died of a heroin overdose in Los Angeles in December 1980.

Set List: Hang on to a Dream, Susan, If I Were a Carpenter, Reason to Believe, You Upset the Grace of Living When You Lie, Speak Like a Child, Snow White Lady, Blue on My Ceiling, Simple Song of Freedom, Misty Roses

Above: Hardin relaxing backstage. Right: Crossing the precarious-looking bridge that led artists to the stage area.

tim hardin

"I really wanted Tim Hardin to be at the festival. I figured Woodstock could be Tim's big break. I had told him about it months and months before and he got really excited about playing, but when he got to the site he got high and did a disappointing set. It was a shame."

MICHAEL LANG

ravi shankar

Friday, August 15, 10:00 p.m.
Ravi Shankar: sitar
Maya Kulkarni: tamboura
Ustad Alla Rakha: tabla

Ravi Shankar had been an acknowledged master of the sitar since the 1950s, and the most celebrated exponent of the instrument outside his native India. His name became familiar to an even broader public in the West, however, after he famously gave a few initial lessons on the instrument to George Harrison of The Beatles, who had been introduced to his work in 1965 by David Crosby of The Byrds. Harrison went on to champion Shankar whenever the opportunity arose, and was largely responsible for having him included at the Monterey Pop Festival in 1967.

It was a time when many young people in the West—particularly those identified with the counterculture—were turning to the music, philosophies, and religions of the Indian subcontinent for inspiration. The most publicized example of this was when The Beatles (along with other rock stars and celebrities) became interested in the teachings of Maharishi Mahesh Yogi, and in 1968 attended the guru's Transcendental Meditation training course in Rishikesh, India.

In the broad-based cultural atmosphere that characterized the late 1960s, therefore, it came as no surprise that Shankar was included on the bill at Woodstock, especially as he had made a huge impression at Monterey. Unfortunately he was the first victim of the rain that plagued the festival, his performance being cut short by a downpour after just thirty-five minutes.

Set List: Raga Puriya-Dhanashri/Gat In Sawarital, Tabla Solo in Jhaptal, Raga Manj Kmahaj, Alap Jor, Dhun In Kaharwa Tal, Medium & Fast Gat In Teental

Above and left: Ravi Shankar (right) with Alla Rakha on tabla.
Inset: Tamboura player Maya Kulkarni.

"My few experiences at the rock festivals continued until Woodstock, in August 1969. This was a terrifying experience. If Monterey was the beginning of a new movement or beautiful happening, I think Woodstock was almost the end. We had to go by helicopter from the motel where we stayed many miles away, and landed just behind the stage. I performed with Alla Rakha accompanying me on tabla, in front of an audience of half a million—an ocean of people. It was drizzling and very cold, but they were so happy in the mud; they were all stoned, of course, but they were enjoying it. It reminded me of the water buffaloes you see in India, submerged in the mud. Woodstock was like a big picnic party, and the music was incidental. I wish I hadn't performed there, but because of my commitment I had to. The thought of my instrument getting wet and spoilt was worrying me so much that it was not a very inspired performance, although I did my best. When I looked out there was no way of communicating to the crowd—it was such a vast audience."

RAVI SHANKAR

Left: Ravi Shankar chats backstage with Joan Baez; in the background, tamboura player Maya Kulkarni.

Friday, August 15, approx. 10:50 p.m.
Melanie Safka: vocals, guitar

After Ravi Shankar had to abandon his set at 10:35 p.m. in the face of the downpour, The Incredible String Band refused to follow on: although they could have played an acoustic set, their repertoire now turned on a basically electric instrumentation that would have been impossible in such conditions. So twenty-two-year-old Melanie Safka—a completely unknown folk singer-songwriter from Queens—took over, and totally captivated the crowd. In just two numbers she became one of the stars of the festival, and her appearance at Woodstock launched her career.

Before Melanie's set John Morris, the festival's production coordinator, had announced from the stage: "This is the largest crowd of people ever assembled for a concert in history, but it's so dark out there we can't see and you can't see each other. So when I say 'three,' I want every one of you to light a match." Melanie's later hit, "Lay Down (Candles in the Rain)" (1970), was directly inspired by the sight of the Woodstock crowd holding up candles and lighters *en masse* that night.

Set List: Close to It All, Momma Momma, Beautiful People, Animal Crackers, Mr. Tambourine Man, Tuning My Guitar, Birthday of the Sun

"I was in the same office building, with Buddha Records, as Artie Kornfeld and Michael Lang. I just walked into them and said, 'I hear you're doing like a concert, in the park, or up in Woodstock or somewhere—and I'd like to be there.' I was picturing like a picnic in a field, with families and picnic blankets.... I thought it sounded really nice ... arts and crafts and so on. I just asked could I do it, and they said, 'Yeah, yeah, come.'"

"I drove up with my Mom and we hit traffic, and we made a phone call and were told we had to go to a different place, to a hotel, and then we'd be taken to the site. At first with all this traffic, I thought it was an accident.... When we got to the hotel I wondered if the traffic was because of the gig, because there were media trucks all over the parking lot, you couldn't get in the door for bodyguards and so on. So me and my mother went through the door, and there's Janis Joplin in the lobby, and she was a big famous person and I'd never met a famous person ... I was just a singer and songwriter who sang in Greenwich Village, and here's Janis Joplin, surrounded by the media.

I got asked, 'What are you doing?' 'I'm Melanie, I'm singing 'Beautiful People.' I only had one record ... it was the only claim to fame I had at that moment. So if anybody asked me, I would break into a few lines of 'Beautiful People,' and then I would be OK. So they said, 'OK, the helicopter's right over there,' and I think, 'Helicopter? What'd you mean helicopter?' I'd never been in a helicopter. So my mother and I started walking towards this helicopter, and somebody says, 'Wait, who's she?' and I said, 'It's my mother' and they said, 'No, only bands and managers'—and I didn't even have the sense to say, 'She's my manager.' I just said, 'Goodbye, Mom,' and I felt awful about leaving her behind.

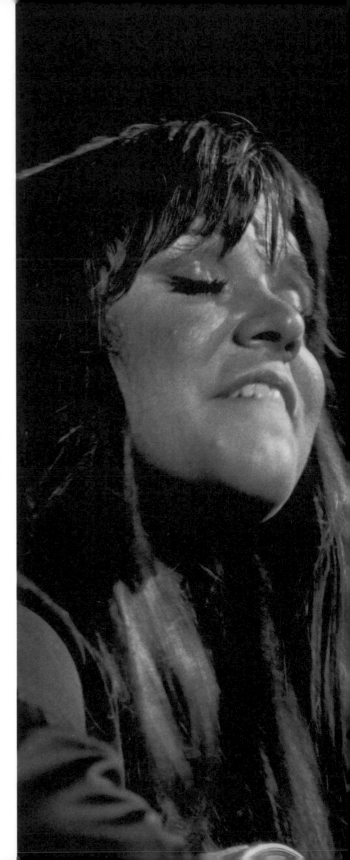

melanie

I got on the helicopter all by myself. So that's how I got there.

I'm in this helicopter and the terror is starting to mount. I'm in a helicopter to a concert.... So there we go, miles to the site, and as we're descending I didn't even know that those were people under me. 'What is that?' and the pilot says, 'It's the people, and that's the stage over there,' and I see this massive thing, and now I'm like, 'This is no picnic in the park.'

They led me to a little tent, and I have vague memories of a larger tent, where I could see the upper echelons of performers were. I had a smaller tent, that's where I stayed. Now I have, I still do, a bronchial cough when I get nervous.... And I started to cough, deep bronchial, it sounded like demons ... and I guess Joan Baez must have heard me from the bigger tent, or had been passing by, and she sent over one of her helpers. She had a flower ring around her head, and she came to my tent and said, 'Hello, Joan Baez heard you coughing, and thought you might like this,' and she'd sent over a pot of tea. And that was my first Woodstock moment."

"As I walked that plank, I left my body. That was my very first out of body experience. I actually left my body. Everything was quiet, and I saw myself sit down, I saw myself sing, it was all quiet, I was watching a girl sing. And at some point I came back, and when I came back, I was looking at a field that had started to alight with little flickering candles. And it was just the most amazing, spiritual experience. I felt this incredible flow of human connected power. This sort of warm, total caring, from a mass of humanity. That image will never leave me—it was just like fireflies dancing. And the whole field started lighting up." MELANIE

Above: The spectacle of hundreds of lights in the crowd as Melanie took the stage. She was to have many more "moments," becoming the "Woodstock icon," and performing at nearly every large outdoor festival for years to follow.

arlo guthrie

Friday, August 15, approx. 11:55 p.m.
Arlo Guthrie: vocals, guitar
John Pilla: guitar
Bob Arkin: bass
Paul Motian: drums

Son of Woody Guthrie, the legendary folk singer and political activist, Arlo Guthrie had become something of a hero himself among the hippie community following the huge success in 1967 of "Alice's Restaurant Massacre"—an eighteen and a half-minute antiwar and pro-counterculture message song. His reputation was further enhanced by the 1969 movie *Alice's Restaurant,* based on the song, and he was thus perfectly placed to follow newcomer Melanie in front of the Woodstock crowd. His short set consisted of "Coming into Los Angeles," his classic song referencing the paranoia of folk carrying illegal drugs, Bob Dylan's "Walkin' Down the Line," and the anthemic American hymn "Amazing Grace." The penultimate act that night, all that was left was for Arlo Guthrie to hand over the stage to Joan Baez—the leading female voice of the folk-song movement.

Set List: Coming Into Los Angeles, Wheel of Fortune, Walking Down the Line, Arlo speech: Exodus, Oh Mary, Don't You Weep, Every Hand in the Land, Amazing Grace

"It was a wonderful and breathtakingly exhilarating.... Scary ... to play for that many people.... I knew, at that time, that I would never, ever again perform before that many people.... Unfortunately, I didn't know I was supposed to play that day, so I was doing what everybody else was doing, so I had no business actually performing. So, you know, this was one of those moments you wished you could have done it again. But it is still one of the fonder memories of my entire life. I will never forget it and I wish I had more sense years ago.... If I knew I was going to play in one event, I mean, the biggest single event in the history of the music world, I probably would have done it under better circumstances had I had some foresight.

But, at eighteen, you don't have a lot of foresight...." ARLO GUTHRIE

Saturday, August 16, approx. 12:55 a.m.
Joan Baez: vocals, guitar
Richard Festinger: guitar
Jeffrey Shurtleff: vocals, guitar

In the heady anti-Vietnam war atmosphere that prevailed at Woodstock, Joan Baez was the perfect choice to close the first day's proceedings, although following the delays she appeared just as the second day started. She had been instrumental in getting political songs—particularly those of contemporary writers like Phil Ochs and Bob Dylan—popularized in the musical mainstream since the start of the folk boom in the early 1960s. It was on the second volume of *Joan Baez in Concert*, recorded live in 1963, that she first recorded Dylan material, with "Don't Think Twice It's Alright" and the antiwar song "With God on Our Side." And her first taste of success on the singles charts came with two political songs, "We Shall Overcome" (1963) and her cover of Phil Ochs' "There But for Fortune" (1965).

Baez heard about the stage that had been built outside the festival fence so that those who did not have tickets could be entertained by amateur bands and audience members performing "open mic" spots. She decided it would be appropriate and in the spirit of the festival to entertain those who could not get close to the main stage, even after the festival had been declared free and the fence was torn down. Consequently—and she was the only major star to do so—Baez played to a fringe audience for a full forty minutes before her manager found her and reminded her that she still had to play a set on the main stage.

After relating the story of how, on July 15, 1969, federal marshals came to take her husband, draft-resister David Harris, into custody, the visibly pregnant Baez opened her set with "Joe Hill"—a folk song dedicated to the labor organizer and activist who was executed for murder in 1915 after a controversial trial. Her set also included a duet with accompanist Jeffrey Shurtleff, and the traditional spiritual "Swing Low Sweet Chariot."

Closing with "We Shall Overcome," the unofficial anthem of the Civil Rights Movement and the broader US protest movement—and with large sections of the crowd joining in—Baez helped confirm the overtly political stance that characterized the counterculture generally, and the Woodstock gathering in particular.

Set List: Oh Happy Day, Last Thing on My Mind, Joe Hill, Sweet Sir Galahad, Hickory Wind, Drug Store Truck Drivin' Man, One Day at a Time, Why Was I Tempted to Roam, Let Me Wrap You in My Warm and Tender Love, Swing Low, Sweet Chariot, We Shall Overcome

joan baez

"Woodstock? Hell, I was already pushing my luck. I'd been on the music scene for ten years and still didn't take dope or use a backup band.

But Woodstock was also me, Joan Baez, the square, six months pregnant, the wife of a draft resister, endlessly proselytizing about the war. I had my place there. I was of the Sixties, and I was already a survivor." JOAN BAEZ

"We flew in over upstate New York. I pushed Mom in the helicopter after Janis Joplin, and we chopped our way above the patchwork farmlands and the hordes of roving backpackers.

Janis clutched her ever-present bottle of booze and everyone leaned out over the door, the wind blowing us into wild people, blue and black clouds ahead of us and all around. Was it just the bizarre weather, or did we all sense history in the making? They put me in the bridal suite of the Holiday Inn. People were crashed all over the floor in the lobby and I got the bridal suite. I must have given it away because I was in another room the next morning when I heard a great thundering racket and saw a helicopter landing in the parking lot just outside my window. I stuffed some toast in my mouth and flapped my arms at the pilot, who was grinning into my bedroom. He nodded he'd wait. I bundled off with some press and I cannot remember who else. The whole event had me so wired up I didn't mind flying around cumulo-nimbus thunderbusters in a tiny helicopter. Ours was the last flight into the golden city that day. And my mom didn't make it till the next day because of the mud. Scoop, the lunatic roadie, was driving and kept getting stuck deeper and deeper, and telling Mom that everything would be OK. Finally he just stopped and smoked a joint, and everything was OK, at least for him." JOAN BAEZ

Above, left, and opposite:
As conditions grew worse, so
the spirit of mutual self-help
seemed to grow among the
Woodstock crowds.

"Friday was folk night, and was finished with an inspirational 'We Shall Overcome' by Joan Baez. Appropriately, the song applied to the rain and mud as well as political protest."

VARIETY, AUGUST 20, 1969

"Everybody was very nice to each other. I mean it started to rain that night, and people who didn't even know each other, if they had a tent they were offering people to stay in their tent. People were sharing things. I brought some sandwiches and I shared them with the people around me. There were all kinds of different people, young people, old people, bikers—from that point of view I think it was very nice. Overnight people were having bad drug trips, and helicopters were coming in, medical teams were lifting people out, and they were running out of food, and there weren't enough toilets, and it rained a lot.

It was obvious to me it was a bit more than they had planned for." ISABEL STEIN, ATTENDEE

THE PLEASE FORCE

The Merry Pranksters had been a key element in the evolution of the counterculture. The group had first been celebrated by Tom Wolfe in his book *The Electric Kool-Aid Acid Test* (1968), based on the LSD-fueled road trip they made in 1964. The trip was organized by author Ken Kesey, and together they established "acid test" LSD parties at their base in San Francisco. Music at these events was provided by The Warlocks—an early incarnation of the Grateful Dead. Through one of the leading Pranksters, Hugh Romney—later known as Wavy Gravy—they also had links with the Back to the Land movement, which encouraged migration from the big cities to rural-based communes. It was Romney who, in 1965, founded one such commune in California, the Hog Farm, so-called because in exchange for occupying the land of a farmer who had suffered a stroke, members of the commune fed and looked after his forty-five hogs. The Hog Farm had relocated to New Mexico by the time it attracted the attention of Michael Lang and Woodstock Ventures. Lang sent Stan Goldstein (who was coordinating the campgrounds at Bethel) to invite the Hog Farmers to help set up support facilities for the festival. Two weeks before the event, eighty Hog Farmers were flown in on a private jet that had been rented at a reported cost of $16,000.

As well as running the kitchens and a "freak-out tent" where people were talked down from bad LSD trips, the Hog Farmers assisted with security on the site. Wavy Gravy called the laidback security team the Please Force, referring to their non-confrontational method of keeping order: "Please don't do that, please do this instead." On the rare occasions that a fight looked like breaking out, the solution was a cream pie in the face, slapstick style!

"In the mountains of New Mexico the Hog Farmers, a bunch of crazies, were celebrating the summer solstice, hundreds of us ... and up walks Stan Goldstein and he says, 'I want you guys to come to Woodstock and help us ... you know, with fixing up the paths, and the booths, and the medical tents and things like that.' And we said, 'Sure, sure, OK.' He kept calling, and kept calling, and pretty soon he said, 'I'm going to send a jet to get you,' and at that point we said, 'This guy's serious.'" LISA LAW, HOG FARMER

Above, left, and opposite:
Inspired by the Merry
Pranksters' original "acid-test"
bus, the "psychedelic" vehicles
of the Hog Farm and other
groups were often home to
a traveling family commune.

"Good morning! What we have in mind is breakfast in bed for four hundred thousand."

WAVY GRAVY, TO THE WOODSTOCK CROWD

Above: Wavy Gravy (with Chip Monck) addressing the crowd.
Overleaf: Wavy Gravy with Michael Lang.

"I thought, 'The last thing we need are these mouths to feed, and who is this commune anyway from New Mexico, we're gonna bring them up here on a jet plane, and have them here as our responsibility for the weekend ... don't we have enough problems...?' And Stanley [Goldstein] spent about ten minutes explaining it to me, and I instantly realized—thanks to the way he put it across—that this was a very smart idea. And it turned out to be much better than even he had imagined, because as much as anything they were responsible for maintaining the tone of this event." JOEL ROSENMAN

"When I personally got to Woodstock the Hog Farm had been there, the advance Hog Farmers with Kesey's bus *Further,* were already there, and they'd set up a little kitchen for the Hog Farmers themselves, and we had discussions about how we were going to feed these people that were coming. And we were out scrounging around for some aluminum pots and this and that ... and I looked at the whole scene and I said,

'We don't need to scrounge, let's go get the real equipment.'

So I decided I was going to go into New York, and took one of the Hog Farmers with me to show me around New York—because I'd only been there once—and where to go to buy this stuff.

I ended up buying 160,000 paper plates, forks, knives, and spoons, and about 160,000 paper cups.... And it's a good thing I did, because they all went, everything went." LISA LAW

Left: Tom Law, whose wife Lisa helped organize the Hog Farm kitchen. Opposite and above: The Hog Farm kitchen was soon able to rely on volunteer help from regular fans to meet the huge demand.

"Between the Hog Farm tent and the stage was a forest, and in the forest was where all the art was going on. Because it was 'music and art,' so the entire forest was filled with booths, and it looked beautiful.

There are a lot of festivals that go on today like that, with art.... I think those people probably sold out the first day, of everything they had. But it got pretty muddy in there too. But we built the trails for that.... And maps where to go to get things, giant wooden maps, hand painted. And there was a wonderful playground they built for kids, a beautiful playground made out of logs with swings and slides, a Jungle Gym." LISA LAW

"Another group came early and played around with ideas for kids. They helped create the very successful playground. They piled bales of hay, and everyone jumped from a tree structure on to the haystacks. A tripod was erected with a tremendous rock weighing several tons suspended from it by ropes. Just under that swaying rock was another rock on the ground, and little kids would lie down between them and squeal in mock terror." JEAN YOUNG, WOODSTOCK ATTENDEE

"Where we had parked our camper and pitched a little tent was, I think, about a ten-minute walk from the big field where the stage was, and that big sort of natural amphitheater place. And so to walk from the music site back to where we were, was like walking through a village. And there were, as I recall, little paths through the woods.... There were a couple of different ways to get there. Along these paths, people had set up little market stalls essentially and were selling lots of drugs. But they were also selling other stuff—beadwork, and I don't know what else—whatever people could think of to sell.

And there was a whole sort of commercial enterprise going on in the woods. And there were also people having sex in the woods, and tripping in the woods, and wandering lost in the woods, and running around naked in the woods. Everything was happening. Not just in the woods, but all around too.

But it did have this feeling of there being a kind of village center where the music was, and then going back to the more residential areas where people were camped out and getting fed and that sort of thing."

ERIC STANGE, WOODSTOCK ATTENDEE

Opposite: The sense of community in the woods even extended to the pathways being signposted like village streets.

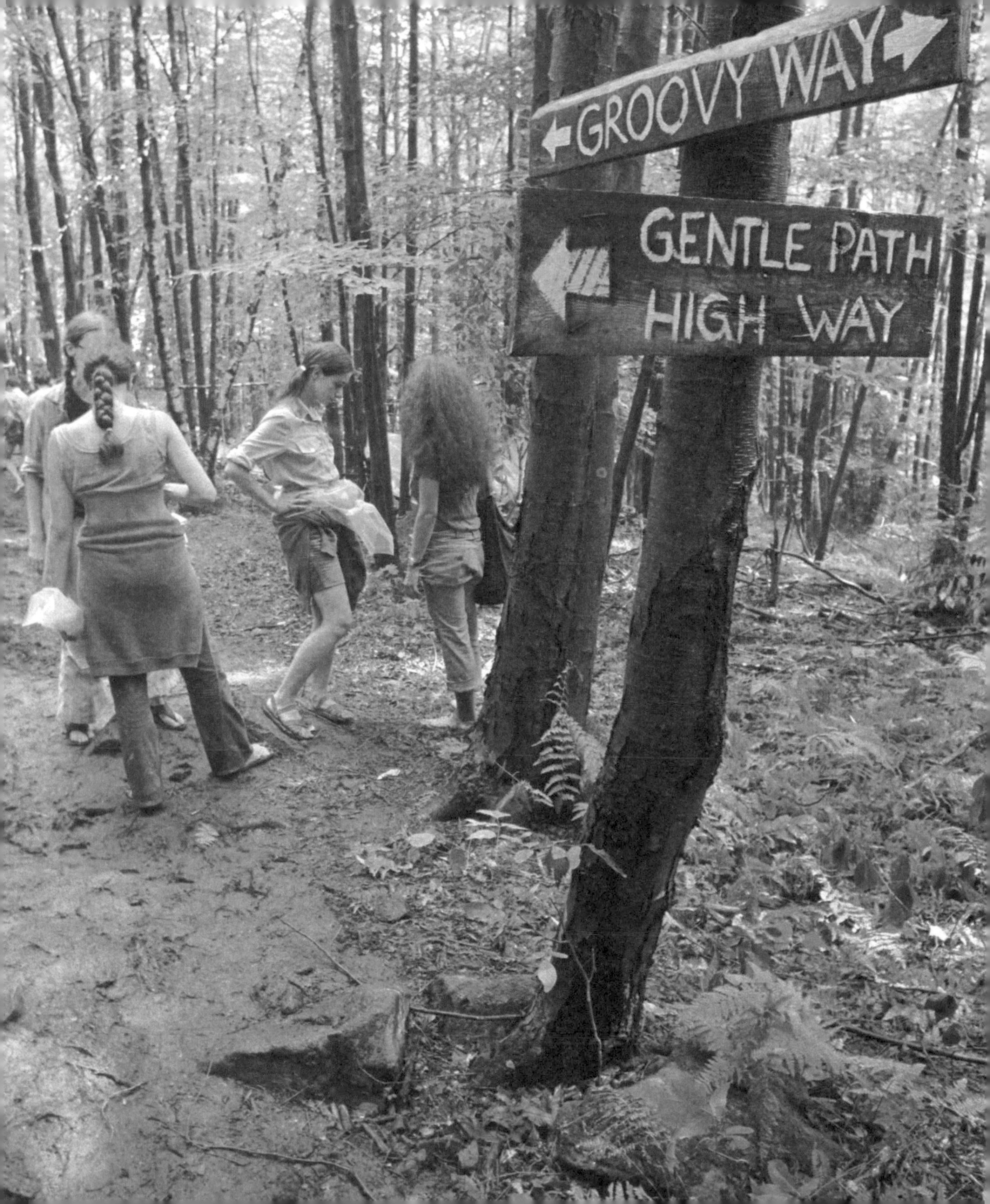
GROOVY WAY
GENTLE PATH
HIGH WAY

day two

"Rainless Saturday concerts bring euphoric peaks.
Participants groove to the tunes of Quill, Keef Hartley,
Santana, Mountain, Canned Heat, Creedence Clearwater Revival,
the Grateful Dead, Janis Joplin, Sly & the Family Stone, The Who,
and the Jefferson Airplane. Gladiator gods at the frontlines of
consciousness, these bands lead the masses past breakthrough
peaks. Rock's Freedom Beat by moonlight unites the tribes at the
apex of a decade. Woodstock's field of dreams awakens ancient
rites and Sabbat dance. The music is a fruit rooted in Blues,
ripening sweet in a half-million heads. It is the Saturnalia of the
Century, casting possession frenzy 'til dawn...."

MICHAEL J. FAIRCHILD, AUTHOR OF ROCK PROPHECY

Saturday, August 16, 1:20 p.m.

Dan Cole: vocals

Jon Cole: bass, vocals

Norman Rogers: guitar, vocals

Phil Thayer: keyboard, saxophone, flute

Roger North: drums

Quill, a five-piece from Boston, originally formed by singer-songwriter brothers Jon and Dan Cole, was signed to a management deal by Michael Lang, then booked by Woodstock Ventures for a series of public-relations gigs ahead of the festival. As well as spending the preceding week living at the setup camp at a nearby motel—providing entertainment for stage crew and other festival workers—the band was also hired to play goodwill concerts at nearby state prisons, mental institutions, and halfway houses, as a gesture by the Woodstock promoters to offset growing community concerns about the upcoming event. Quill had built a healthy following over the previous couple of years, with a stage show that included handing out percussion instruments for the audience to join in. They repeated the exercise at Woodstock, throwing maracas and such into the crowd, but although they were received enthusiastically the band never made it into the Woodstock movie. A technical hitch, which meant the audio and film were not synchronized properly and rendered the footage unusable, was only resolved after they had left the stage.

Set List: That's How I Eat, They Live the Life, Driftin',
Waitin' for You

Left: Vocalist Dan Cole, filmed by director Michael Wadleigh. Opposite: Dan Cole and (back to camera) guitarist Norman Rogers.

Saturday, August 16, approx. 2:20 p.m.
Country Joe McDonald: guitar, vocals

Although Country Joe and his band The Fish were not due to play Woodstock until Sunday evening, the opening running order on Saturday had been disrupted as a result of programmed acts having not yet arrived at the festival. Country Joe and John Sebastian (who was not even scheduled to appear) were prevailed upon to help out. Although his band had not yet arrived, Country Joe agreed to perform a solo acoustic set and was in a position to deputize for artists still struggling to reach the site one way or another.

Country Joe had become something of a counterculture hero in the mid-1960s, with his satirical antiwar anthem "I-Feel-Like-I'm-Fixin'-to-Die Rag." It was preceded here as usual by his trademark "Fish Cheer" ("Give me an 'F,' Give me a 'U,' Give me a 'C,' Give me a 'K.' What's that spell?"), which had the crowd in full call-and-response mode—although before the audience participation, the rest of his acoustic set had received a lukewarm response. A day later Joe appeared before the Woodstock thousands once more, this time in his "official" Sunday evening slot with the full Fish lineup.

Set List: Janis, Donovan's Reef, Heartaches by the Number, Ring of Fire, Tennessee Stud, Rockin' 'Round the World, Flying All the Way, I Seen a Rocket, Fish Cheer / I Feel Like I'm Fixin' to Die Rag

"So I walked back in front of the mic and yelled 'Give me an F!' and it exploded. And I remember thinking 'Wow, it's too late to stop now' and I got really bold and really energized. And it worked out really good. The reason that the audience responded that way was because the song was … produced on a little record but it became an underground classic, and in New York City there was a radio station that had played it every day. We had invented the 'Fuck' cheer at the Shaffer beer festival about a year before that in New York City. And about ninety percent of the people who were there were from the New York City area. And so they didn't know who I was, they didn't know what I was doing, until I yelled 'Give me an F' and then it was like Pavlov's dog, the whole audience stopped what they were doing and yelled 'F.' It was something." COUNTRY JOE MCDONALD

country joe mcdonald

Saturday, August 16, approx. 3:10 p.m.
John Sebastian: vocals, guitar

John Sebastian was a major artist at the time, his group The Lovin' Spoonful having made the *Billboard* Top 40 singles chart ten times between 1965 and 1968 before disbanding. He had lived in Woodstock off-and-on since the mid-1960s, and went along to the festival just as one of the crowd, with no intention of doing a set—he had not even taken a guitar.

Once backstage amongst friends and other performers he was quickly "volunteered" into playing by stage coordinator Chip Monck, who needed time for the stage to be cleared of rainwater. Monck turned to Sebastian as someone else, like Country Joe earlier, who could play an acoustic set and hold the audience while the sound system was readied for the next electric band to set up. Hastily borrowing a guitar from Tim Hardin, Sebastian strode out on stage to a huge cheer from the audience, which immediately recognized him.

Considered objectively, his set wasn't what it could have been, and he seemed to forget the words to some of his own songs. On his own admission he was tripping on LSD, but it could also have been the result of performing in front of a 500,000-strong crowd with no preparation, and trying to improvise new material while he was at it. Regardless, many agreed that the sheer spontaneity of his performance confirmed a tangible *frisson* that characterized Woodstock—an atmosphere that anything could happen over the coming days.

Set List: How Have You Been?, Rainbows All Over Your Blues, I Had a Dream, Darling Be Home Soon, Younger Generation

> "At Woodstock he [John Sebastian] unwittingly found some kind of place in the annals for creating the biggest impression in front of the largest audience without actually having been booked to appear."
>
> JERRY GILBERT, *ZIG ZAG* MAGAZINE

Above: John Sebastian backstage with the Harmony Sovereign guitar loaned from Tim Hardin. Opposite: Sebastian, unscheduled, alone in front of the Woodstock multitude.

"I wanted to be a spectator, but because all my friends were backstage, I ended up backstage ... and people began to go, 'Oh, great! When are you playing?' And I'm going, 'I'm not playin'. I don't even have a guitar.' Well, it just so happened that my old pal Timmy Hardin did have a guitar and was there. It was somewhere in the second day, somebody hadn't showed up yet, and it had started to rain. So I get summoned into the sort of war room, there in the center of the backstage area. And Chip Monck ... asked me, 'Look, it's raining. We're havin' trouble with the sound system. We're afraid to put an amplifier on the stage. We're figuring we could keep this audience's attention if we had a guy with one guitar who could hold 'em. You're elected.' So I go to Timmy and I say, 'Timmy, I need a guitar.' He lends me a Harmony Sovereign. This is the great workhorse guitar, for people buying instruments for under $60. And so with that instrument and a slight buzz, I went on in the rain and, as it happened, the rain had stopped by the time I finished." JOHN SEBASTIAN

Saturday, August 16, approx. 4:00 p.m.

Keef Hartley: drums

Miller Anderson: guitar, vocals

Jimmy Jewell: saxophone

Henry Lowther: trumpet, violin

Gary Thain: bass

Drummer Keef Hartley was assured at least a minor place in the rock history books when he replaced Ringo Starr in the Liverpool group Rory Storm and the Hurricanes in 1962, following Ringo's move to The Beatles. Then, after playing with John Mayall's Bluesbreakers—one of the seminal bands on the British blues scene—he formed his own jazz-oriented blues-rock outfit in 1969, and quickly became a regular feature on the UK club and festival circuit. Precise details of what the band played at Woodstock are hard to establish, as there appears to be no film or audio record of their performance: their manager apparently refused to have them filmed without a written contract. However, the most definitive listing certainly includes a medley of songs from their 1969 debut album *Halfbreed*.

Set List: Spanish Fly, She's Gone, Too Much Thinkin', Believe in You, (Halfbreed Medley), Sinnin' for You (intro), Leaving Trunk, Just to Cry, Sinnin' for You

Opposite: Keef Hartley. Above: Guitarist Miller Anderson.
Below: Henry Lowther, trumpet (left) and Jimmy Jewell, tenor saxophone.

the keef hartley band

FARMER WITH SOUL MAX YASGUR

BETHEL, N.Y., Aug. 17

Until a few days ago Max Yasgur was just another dairy farmer in Sullivan County. Now he gets phone calls threatening to burn him out. And even more calls praising him and asking how the callers can help. The reason for his unwonted prominence is that it was on 600 acres of his land that hundreds of thousands of youngsters gathered for Woodstock Music and Art Fair, their cars blocking roads and overflowing onto lawns.

But Mr. Yasgur, a dairy farmer since boyhood, has the stubbornness of most farmers. He also avoids the phone these days.

"I never expected this festival to be this big," he told an acquaintance the other day. "But if the generation gap is to be closed, we older people have to do more than we have done."

He Gives Away Food

A gaunt man of 49, with glasses, he looks even taller than his 5 feet 11 inches. He is trying to do his bit to bridge the generation gap by giving large amounts of dairy products to the youngsters at the festival, sometimes at cost and often free.

His red barn, fronting on Route 17B, with its long line of parked cars, displays a big sign reading, "Free Water."

He put up this sign when he heard that some residents were selling water to the youngsters at the festival. He slammed a work-hardened fist down on the table and demanded of some friends:

"How can anyone ask for money for water?"

The other day, as he was preparing to give away substantial quantities of butter and cheese, someone asked what the youngsters would put the butter on.

That evening a relative brought a car filled with loaves of bread to the farm.

Mr. Yasgur and his wife, Miriam, have two children, a daughter, Lois, and a son, Samuel, who is an assistant district attorney on the staff of District Attorney Frank S. Hogan of Manhattan.

The gently rolling Yasgur farm is the home of a herd of 650 cows, mostly Guernsey. Mr. Yasgur raises some of the corn used as feed for his dairy herd.

Friends Concerned on Health

As he paces nervously in the heavy work shoes he has worn almost all his life, his friends become increasingly concerned. He has a cardiac history and they fear another heart attack.

Mr. Yasgur has been getting very little sleep at night and refuses to ease up during the day, often flying over the music festival area in a helicopter.

A man in this county who has known Mr. Yasgur for many years, and who thinks the festival was a terrible mistake, said:

"I don't doubt that Max made a good business deal. But I think he was motivated at least as much by his principles as by the thought of making money." Sponsors of the fair said they had paid $50,000 to rent the farm.

And a successful businessman who has been dealing with the daily farmer for a long time declared:

"Max is not just a successful farmer. He is an individualist."

NEW YORK TIMES, AUGUST 18, 1969

"I'm a farmer ... I don't know how to speak to twenty people at one time, let alone a crowd like this. But I think you people have proven something to the world—not only to the town of Bethel, or Sullivan County or New York; you've proven something to the world. This is the largest group of people ever assembled in one place. We have had no idea that there would be this size group, and because of that you've had quite a few inconveniences as far as water, food, and so forth. Your producers have done a mammoth job to see that you're taken care of ... they'd enjoy a vote of thanks. But above that, the important thing that you've proven to the world is that a half a million kids— and I call you kids because I have children that are older than you are—a half million young people can get together and have three days of fun and music and have nothing but fun and music, and I God Bless You for it!" MAX YASGUR

"Dad had come over to deal with the promoters, at what was known as the administration building up on top of the hill. We were having some difficulties with getting access for our neighbors, who were pretty upset that they couldn't get milk out, they couldn't deal with their own cattle because of the crowds here, and because the roads were totally congested.

So he came over to meet with Johnny and Michael and the others, to talk with them about what could be done to free up the space a little bit. And some of the kids saw him, and they asked Max to come down to the stage. If you look at the video, he's very, very tired. He'd gone through a couple of really hellish days. We had taken an oxygen tank off the acetylene welder's set in the shop and brought it down to his office.

Dad had a bad heart, he was in real distress. He saw perhaps his life being ruined by this event. You know, the neighbors were angry, and rightly so, and he was really upset. So when he came down, he was not thinking about doing anything with the crowd. He was certainly bone weary. But he got on the stage, and he started off that famous little one-minute speech by saying, 'I'm just a farmer,' and then he told them that he was proud of them. And they responded.

They had heard the stories during the weekend about what he was doing for them, how he was providing free water and milk and everything else, and he was championing their cause as it were—and the crowd stood up and [there was] amazing applause, for a man that they shouldn't have been able to relate to." SAM YASGUR, MAX YASGUR'S SON

Saturday, August 16, approx. 5:15 p.m.

Carlos Santana: guitar
Gregg Rolie: vocals, keyboard
David Brown: bass
Jose "Chepito" Areas: timbales, congas, percussion
Mike Carabello: timbales, congas, percussion
Michael Shrieve: drums

A Mexican by birth, Carlos Santana moved to San Francisco in 1962 at the age of fifteen. There he quickly became embroiled in the local music scene, often sneaking into Bill Graham's Fillmore Auditorium to hear his favorite musicians, who included Muddy Waters and local heroes the Grateful Dead. His first group, known as the Santana Blues Band, hung out in the city's Aquatic Park where conga players would get together and jam, and soon their percussion-driven Latin rock came to the notice of promoter Graham, who signed them to a management deal.

Carlos Santana's own recording debut came in September 1968, when he guested on a live album by Mike Bloomfield and Al Kooper, *Live Adventures of Mike Bloomfield and Al Kooper,* recorded at the Fillmore. And it didn't take Bill Graham long to secure a contract for the band (which had by this time shortened its name to just Santana) with CBS Records, although their debut album—*Santana*—would take several months and various changes of personnel before it was finally completed. Meantime Graham convinced Michael Lang and his Woodstock partners to book the group, even though the album was yet to be released.

The band's set captivated the audience, its hypnotic rhythm and exotic texture touching a nerve on the humid day in the aftermath of the first rainstorms. Their performance was one of the sensations of the festival, and—along with the LP release later that month and the subsequent film—thrust them into the national, and international, spotlight.

Set List: Waiting, Evil Ways, You Just Don't Care, Savor, Jingo, Persuasion, Soul Sacrifice, Fried Neckbones and Some Home Fries

"We were going on without having an album out and a lot of people didn't know us from Adam. It was kind of scary going out in front of that much of a crowd. But I felt if Bill [Graham] believed we could do it, we could do it." CARLOS SANTANA

Above right: Michael Shrieve, Carlos Santana, and cameraman/director Michael Wadleigh.
Right: Michael Shrieve. Opposite: Bass player David Brown.

"We arrived by helicopter and, yes, organizationally it was a disaster area. Anybody who had food was sharing it. All the freeways were closed for almost fifty miles radius. It was like one of those Orson Welles movies where time just stood still. Cars parked all over the freeway, everything just abandoned. This is why, to this day, it shocks the straight world that such a thing could have happened. And no fights."

"We got in at about eleven o'clock in the morning and the first person that I saw was Jerry Garcia. We were both looking out over this live ocean of flesh, and he says, 'Man, just look at it.' And I say, 'Yeah, it's incredible.' He says, 'I don't think there'll ever be another one like this.' I say, 'I think you're right.' He says, 'They say there's 450,000.' I say, 'Wow.' He says, 'What time are you gonna play?' I say, 'Well, we're supposed to play around four o'clock this afternoon.' He says, 'Well, we're supposed to be playing right after you and we're not going on until two o'clock in the morning, so you probably won't go on until at least midnight.' So one thing led to another and I took some mescaline. I thought, 'If I take it now, by the time I come to play I'll be coming down and life is beautiful,' you know? Wrong! As soon as I took it, and I turned on, all I can remember is some face saying, 'You gotta go on right now. If you don't play right now you're not gonna play at all, period.'" CARLOS SANTANA

Below: Santana bass guitarist David Brown and (back to the camera) drummer Michael Shrieve.

"They landed on the moon on my birthday, July 20, and the next month we were at the meeting of the tribes. I was really peaking on mescaline before I went on. I remember praying, 'Lord, help me to stay in tune and in time.' The music made the people move like leaves in a field." CARLOS SANTANA

Saturday, August 16, approx. 6:30 p.m.

Mike Heron: multi-instrumentals

Robin Williamson: vocals, multi-instrumentals

Christina "Licorice" McKechnie: organ, vocals, multi-instrumentals

Rose Simpson: bass, vocals, multi-instrumentals

With their brand of psychedelic folk-rock perfectly in tune with the mystical, fairytale side of flower power, The Incredible String Band's 1967 debut album *5000 Spirits Or The Layers of the Onion* was hailed in the their native UK as the folk scene's equivalent to The Beatles' *Sgt. Pepper's Lonely Hearts Club Band*. They were making similar inroads in the US after an acclaimed appearance at the 1968 Newport Folk Festival, and the Woodstock booking would have been a useful opportunity to further their reputation by playing on the same bill as Joan Baez, Ravi Shankar, and others during an ongoing American tour.

But the experience didn't quite work out like that. They were due to follow Ravi Shankar on the Friday evening, but when his set was cut short due to rain, they were faced with a dilemma. There was no way they could play their electric repertoire in the wet conditions, so stage manager John Morris offered them an alternative spot the following day; their manager Joe Boyd wasn't sure—he was convinced they would make a better impression doing just an acoustic set after Shankar, that would precede Arlo Guthrie. Boyd was overruled by the band, who refused to consider an acoustic performance.

In the event, Boyd's instincts were probably right. Melanie, who jumped into the spot they had vacated, was an instant hit, while their set on the Saturday afternoon—among much heavier company like Santana and Canned Heat—hardly cut it with a crowd now hyped up on a night in the rain and mud, a day's worth of drugs, and loud, heady music to match.

Set List: Invocation (spoken word), The Letter, Gather 'Round, This Moment, Come with Me, When You Find Out Who You Are

the incredible string band

"The sylvan beauty of the hippie crowd the day before had changed beyond recognition; now it looked like a battle zone."

JOE BOYD, THE INCREDIBLE STRING BAND'S MANAGER

Opposite top: Robin Williamson. Opposite bottom: (l to r) Mike Heron, Robin Williamson, "Licorice" McKechnie, Rose Simpson. Below: Mike Heron.
Overleaf: Lunch backstage (l to r) Williamson, McKechnie, Heron, Simpson.

"Joe Boyd, he was managing us at that time, penciled in this American tour we were doing. I think we were doing Carnegie Hall either before or after, and he said, 'This thing has come up, this festival, and I think it might be worth doing it, this little festival in the country,' and so he slotted it in to the tour. It was completely amazing, we didn't realize it was such a huge thing.

So when we arrived there it was a complete roaring thunderstorm, and there was no cover really, so nobody electric wanted to go on … which is why all those people like Richie Havens and Melanie were bunged on because they didn't have electric stuff. The most unfortunate thing for us was we were going through a phase when we were incorporating the girls, Licky and Rose, into the band…. We got the girls doing lots of things with the band, and a lot of it was electric. So—and Joe has never forgiven us—we refused to go on, because we didn't really want to go on and do an acoustic set, it would have been unfair on the girls.

It was very high up, the stage, and wasn't fantastically secure. We'd never really been on a stage like that, and we were all a bit wary of heights. We'd come in on one of these helicopters with no sides, like a military thing, then after that we had to struggle up this rickety ladder to this very high stage, and the girls were in these little flimsy kind of English rose outfits, little frocks, so it was kind of against the elements. Joe always thought that was why we didn't make an impact, because by the time we did go on, on the Saturday afternoon, everyone had been living in the mud and eating beans for a day, and they were into things like Canned Heat and those kind of bands, they were more likely to relate to than delicate little English hippies. And they were on to maybe heavier drugs than they had been. They were not as light and spiritual as they were on the Friday.

So he did have a point, but I don't know what we could have done about that really. And for years and years Robin [Williamson] and I have been saying it was so terrible, but actually the footage is not bad at all. I mean, the bad thing about it is we didn't do our hits, we did songs we were doing at the time, we didn't really do the songs we were known by. That was the mistake we made really, and I think Joe's right, but I don't know how we could have gone on on the Friday—though obviously the people that did go on, Melanie and so on, they all went on and got some kind of following." MIKE HERON, THE INCREDIBLE STRING BAND

Saturday, August 16, approx. 8:00 p.m.

Alan "Blind Owl" Wilson: guitar, harmonica, vocals

Bob "The Bear" Hite: vocals, harmonica

Harvey "The Snake" Mandel: guitar

Larry "The Mole" Taylor: bass

Adolpho "Fito" de la Parra: drums

Los Angeles-based Canned Heat were a natural choice for the Woodstock event, with two Top 40 singles to their credit—"On the Road Again" and "Going Up the Country"—and a big live following for their blues-tinged boogie rock. But they very nearly didn't make it to the festival. Just two days before the opening, guitarist Henry Vestine left the band after a bust-up with bassist Larry Taylor, following which drummer Adolpho de la Parra quit, complaining they didn't have time to rehearse a new guitarist before the gig. Manager Skip Taylor would have none of it, however, and forced his way into the drummer's locked room to persuade him otherwise. Taylor managed to get the group into one of the helicopters ferrying acts between the site and their accommodation in local hotels, and Canned Heat arrived just in time for their performance. It was a good-natured set: in the movie a guy can be seen clambering on to the stage, but instead of trying to get him off, lead singer Bob Hite shares a cigarette with him.

Although they enjoyed another decade in the limelight, Canned Heat's subsequent career was marred by drug-related tragedies. First was the death of vocalist Alan Wilson in 1970, and in 1981 the demise of Bob "The Bear" Hite, whose falsetto blues style was part of the band's trademark sound.

Set List: I'm Her Man, Going Up the Country,

A Change Is Gonna Come / Leaving This Town,

(I Know My Baby?), Woodstock Boogie, On the Road Again

"We've always just fallen into something within a couple of days and then just gone out on the road and played. Sometimes it's shown it and sometimes it's been incredible. The Woodstock performance, which although there were a couple of tunes which weren't too good—'Going Up the Country' was one of them—there were some which were killers, stone killers. And that was with Harvey Mandel who had only been with us for one set before we'd done Woodstock and that was just a big jam. We all just like to play music." BOB HITE, CANNED HEAT

Right: Alan "Blind Owl" Wilson. Far right: Bob Hite encounters an over-zealous fan on stage.

canned heat

self-sufficiency

By the end of the first day, it had become clear the festival was in danger of turning into a catastrophe. The lack of preparation for nearly half a million fans (and an estimated million more in the vicinity, unable to reach the site) didn't just mean that the organizers couldn't cope with ticketing and such. The physical well-being of thousands of young people, exposed to the elements and often without sufficient food and drink, was at risk. Unable to respond quickly and efficiently on account of the traffic gridlock across Sullivan County, the authorities declared it a disaster area, even calling in units of the National Guard. But a real calamity was averted by the self-help ethos of the fans themselves, and the practical efforts of support groups within their ranks, primarily the Hog Farm and a growing number of volunteers.

Above, below, and opposite: With the overwhelming numbers involved, initial supplies of food and drink from regular concessions soon ran out.

"At one point I got on stage, this was on Friday, and said, 'If you're hungry, we're serving at the Hog Farm. We have serving booths, and you can get some food over there.' My husband Tom said to me, 'Oh, you shouldn't have said that.... They'll all get up and go over there at the same time.' And I said, 'No, no … they're not going to do that, there'll be a slow trickle over.' And I was right, they came over slowly. The lines sometimes were twenty-five people long, in ten lines, but that's not a lot.

And the concessions were done [exhausted] by the first day, so we ended up feeding everybody. Some people brought their own food. They'd have these little campfires and served themselves.

But all the people that didn't, we served.

The National Guard lowered down some food from their helicopters, but what they gave us was things like Melba toast, Hershey bars, Coca-Cola, things like that which would satisfy your hunger, but to me they weren't that healthy for people who were staying up for days on end.

So we felt that by going and buying vegetables from the neighbors, we could give them decent food.

When we started serving the food, the volunteers showed up. We were providing it, and the people were preparing and serving it. They just volunteered to help … you couldn't spend all the time in front of the stage, there were too many people. But the volunteers took their job very seriously, because the whole thing was like a big city, and a lot of people just decided to help out.

When it was time to get the vegetables, I would get a truck and drive to a nearby farm, and purchase loads and loads of food.... 'Give me that row of corn, give me that row of cabbage,' and we'd put it in the truck in big boxes and drive it back over." LISA LAW

"It's true there wasn't a lot of food that people had, but I remember from time to time there would be great big five or ten pound bags of oranges that were being passed around, maybe on the second day, or big bags of apples. And they would come to you and you were just like, 'Oh, okay, thanks,' and just take one and pass it on. And that would sort of sustain you for another half a day or something." DIANA THOMPSON, WOODSTOCK ATTENDEE

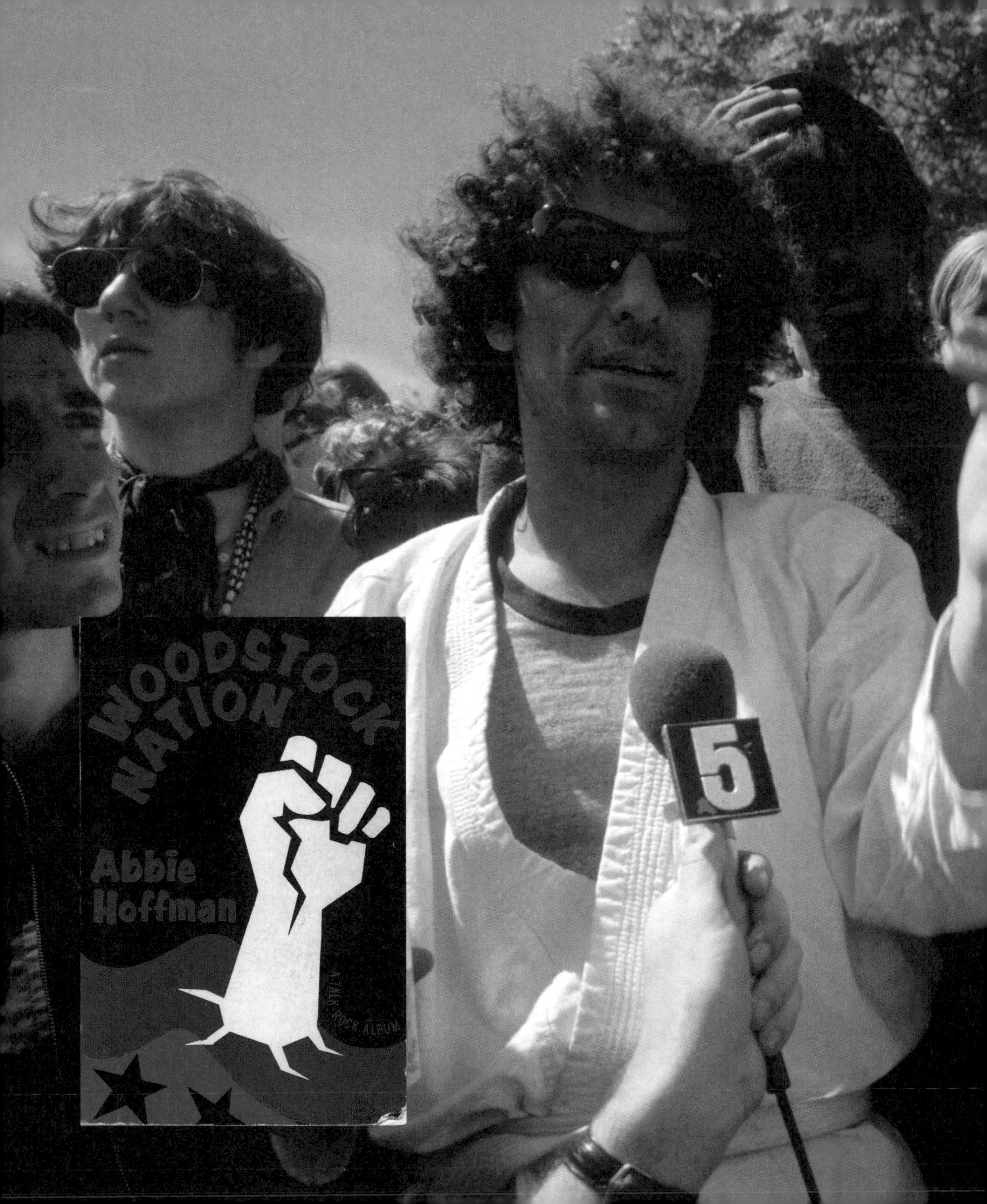
WOODSTOCK NATION
Abbie Hoffman
A TALK-ROCK ALBUM
5

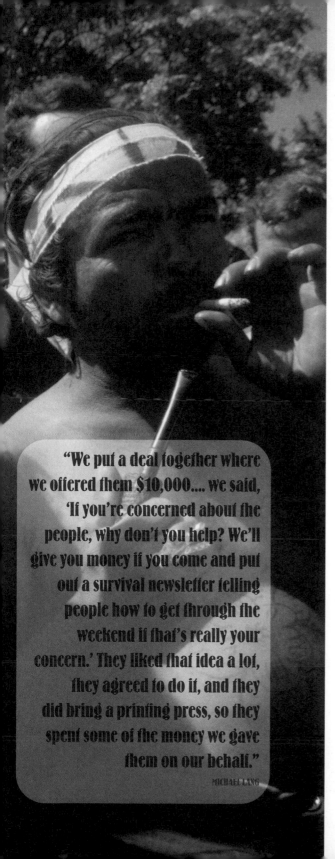

"I emerged exhausted, broke and bleeding from the Woodstock Nation. It was an awesome experience but one that made me have a clearer picture of myself as a cultural revolutionary." ABBIE HOFFMAN

Poised somewhere between the laidback nonconformity of the hippies and the right-on militancy of the radical members of the SDS (Students for a Democratic Society), the Yippies (Youth International Party) was an anarchistic political group that was more likely to use "guerrilla" street theater or public pranks than direct confrontation to draw attention to their cause. Founded by Abbie Hoffman, his wife Anita, Jerry Rubin, and others, the Yippies published absurdist manifestos calling for bizarre acts of civil disobedience, encouraged by Hoffman's fiery (but deliberately humorous) oratory and writings. Typical of the direct action they proposed was circling the Pentagon in order to make it levitate, and lacing a city's water supply with LSD.

When they did engage in more realistic action, as part of a coalition of various protest groups at the 1968 Democratic Convention in Chicago, they got police beatings—and in the case of Hoffman and Rubin, five-year jail sentences that were overturned on appeal.

After Abbie Hoffman threatened to disrupt the festival with some kind of Yippie mass demonstration, Woodstock Ventures agreed to let them have a booth in order to peddle their propaganda, as long as they also helped in a support capacity—which they did, at a price. With a financial handout of $10,000 they produced a newsletter giving information on medical help, and offering drug advice, though much of the money reportedly went towards Hoffman's upcoming trial, arising from the 1968 Chicago arrest.

The Yippie leader's own credibility at the festival was diminished, however, after he leapt on the stage during The Who's performance to deliver a diatribe against the arrest of fellow activist John Sinclair of the White Panther Party. He was booted into the press pit by a furious Pete Townshend—to a roar of approval from the crowd.

Abbie Hoffman recorded his own version of the Woodstock "spirit" in his book *Woodstock Nation* (1969), a stream-of-consciousness account of the festival and associated political issues, which he wrote immediately after the festival while awaiting trial.

"Abbie Hoffman was a brilliant deviant, a wonderfully imaginative creative guy—bust it up, break it down, make fun of it, ridicule it, destroy it, whatever—just for the heck of it. See what happens. I went to see Abbie on his request—an invitation that one doesn't refuse. I said, 'Look Abbie, I know you'd like to make a kind of big presentation at Woodstock, but it isn't that kind of a show, it's rock 'n' roll and it's really a weekend of peace and music,' and he said, 'I don't give a damn about that, you guys write a big check to my organization, and we're cool.' 'What are you talkin' about?' 'Here's what I'm talkin' about—$10,000.' "
JOEL ROSENMAN

Left: Abbie Hoffman (center) at the Democratic Convention demonstration in Chicago's Grant Park, August 1968. Inset: Hoffman's book *Woodstock Nation*.

"We put a deal together where we offered them $10,000.... we said, 'If you're concerned about the people, why don't you help? We'll give you money if you come and put out a survival newsletter telling people how to get through the weekend if that's really your concern.' They liked that idea a lot, they agreed to do it, and they did bring a printing press, so they spent some of the money we gave them on our behalf."

MICHAEL LANG

mountain

Saturday, August 16, approx. 9:00 p.m.

Leslie West: guitar, vocals

Felix Pappalardi: bass

Steve Knight: keyboards

Norman "N. D." Smart: drums

Felix Pappalardi, a graduate of Michigan Conservatory of Music, drifted around the Greenwich Village folk scene (briefly playing bass for Tim Hardin) before making a name for himself as a studio session player, arranger, and producer. He produced three albums for the British power trio Cream and, clearly influenced by the experience, put together Mountain in the mold of what was soon to be known as "heavy rock." He discovered guitarist Leslie West playing in a New York group he was producing, The Vagrants, and invited him to join. Next he found drummer Norman "N. D." Smart and, anxious for his new outfit not to seem a mere copycat of the UK supergroup, he also recruited keyboard player Steve Knight, a native of Woodstock.

Kicking off with what became their standard opener "Blood of the Sun," the set included the blues classic "Stormy Monday"—probably never played as heavily before—and "Theme for an Imaginary Western," written by Cream lyricist Pete Brown and bassist Jack Bruce.

Mountain had only played three previous dates when they appeared at the festival, but their blues-influenced, ultra-loud rock was perfectly in tune with the Woodstock vibe—and a harbinger of heavier things to come. Not many of the roadies at Woodstock would end up in the rock history books, but Corky Laing, who looked after Mountain at the time, took over as drummer later that year.

Set List: Blood of the Sun, Stormy Monday, Theme for an Imaginary Western, Long Red, For Yasgur's Farm (then untitled), Waiting to Take You Away, Dreams of Milk and Honey, Blind Man, Blue Suede Shoes, Southbound Train, Mississippi Queen

"Our routine—I mean we wouldn't have gone the night before—our routine was to get picked up in the limo in the morning and we would take the car all the way there. Then we started hearing that that's not possible, that the roads were impassable, that it was a big mess. So instead of our being picked up at ten o'clook in the morning, we were picked up a couple of hours later because we were going to go by helicopter, and the limo instead of taking us to the festival site took us to the [New York] East Side Heliport. Of course, approaching the site we got to look down to see the cars all laid up at ninety degrees to the roadway.... Anyway, I think the first time it really registered that there was something very extraordinary going on here was when we got on the stage to play, and I looked over the top of my [Hammond] B3 and there were little candles and little lighters, little points of light as far as you could see in the blackness.... It was enormous, and impossible to connect to, I mean you can't play to those people, you got to play to the guys you're playing with, where you are, and if you're lucky you've got a good crew who can deliver that out there. It was very well organized in terms of security. The helicopter got weaved in to a spot on the hilltop which was backstage, and there were these walkways—you couldn't get from here to there without going up on a catwalk. And there were people at each end of that, to make sure that the right people went and the wrong people didn't."

STEVE KNIGHT, MOUNTAIN

"The helicopter had to take us there in two trips because I was a lot heavier then. My manager brought five roast chickens. Janis Joplin had finished up all the bagels. We made a little campfire behind the stage and at two in the morning those chickens came in handy."

LESLIE WEST, MOUNTAIN

Opposite: Guitarist Leslie West. Inset: Mountain founder Felix Pappalardi.
Left: West, with drummer "N. D." Smart in the background.

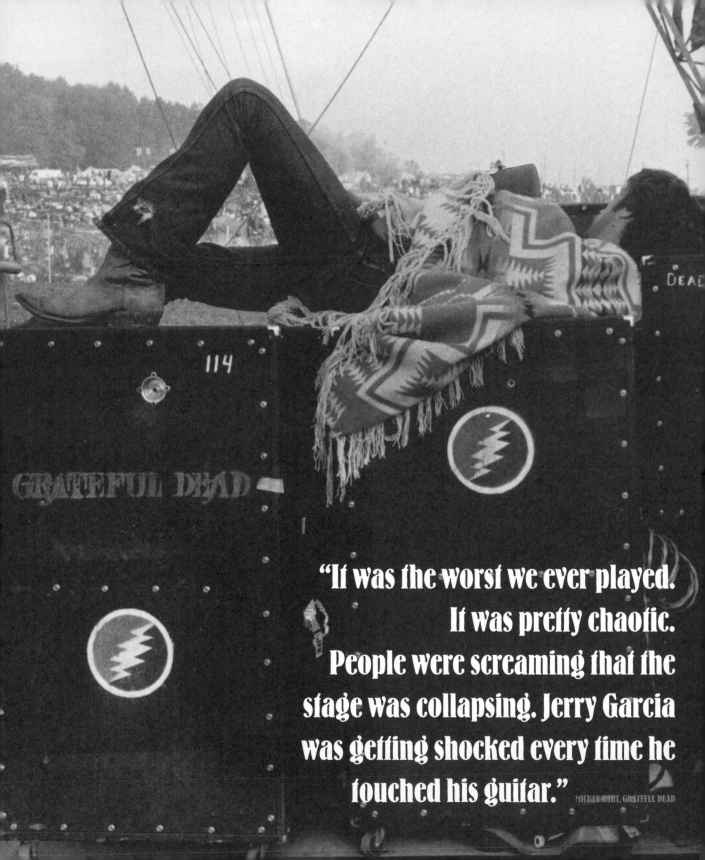

"It was the worst we ever played. It was pretty chaotic. People were screaming that the stage was collapsing. Jerry Garcia was getting shocked every time he touched his guitar."

MICKEY HART, GRATEFUL DEAD

grateful dead

Sunday, August 17, 12:00 midnight

Jerry Garcia: guitar, vocals

Bob Weir: guitar

Ron "Pig Pen" McKernan: keyboards, vocals

Tom Constanten: keyboards, vocals

Phil Lesh: bass

Bill Kreutzmann: drums

Mickey Hart: drums

They were never the most cohesive of groups (they first became known as the house band for Ken Kesey's notorious "acid test" LSD parties in 1966), but even by the Grateful Dead's anarchic standards their Woodstock performance was not one of their best. They were clearly stoned when they ambled on, already late because of a series of electrical problems, and their heavy equipment started to threaten the stability of the stage. Added to that was flooding from the rain, which put the band in real danger. Jerry Garcia and Bob Weir both received violent electric shocks, guitarist Weir being flung across the stage by the impact.

They struggled through some of their established hits, but the set was beset by sound problems, false starts, and long pauses. At one point about ten minutes elapsed between numbers, during which they babbled incoherently among themselves. Still waiting for the sound system to be fixed, they ended with "Turn on Your Lovelight," which turned out to be a forty-minute jam. Even many of the band's most ardent fans—the "Deadheads"—agreed that the Grateful Dead's Woodstock performance was a shambles. For others, though, the musical chaos was doubtless accepted as in keeping with the general mood of anarchy that characterized much of the Woodstock experience.

Set List: St. Stephen, Mama Tried, Dark Star/High Time, Turn on Your Lovelight

Left: Crew members taking it easy. At the time the Grateful Dead were famous for having more sound equipment than any other touring band. Below: Jerry Garcia.

"Every time I touched my instrument, I got a shock. The stage was wet, and the electricity was coming through me. I was conducting! Touching my guitar and the microphone was nearly fatal. There was a great big blue spark about the size of a baseball, and I got lifted off my feet and sent back about eight or ten feet to my amplifier." BOB WEIR, GRATEFUL DEAD

Above: Keyboard player and vocalist Ron "Pig Pen" McKernan and, opposite, with his girlfriend Veronica "Vee" Barnard. Below: (l to r) Jerry Garcia, Bill Kreutzmann, Bob Weir, and Mickey Hart.

"The people were just glad to be entertained, to get their minds off the rain and wind and mud, no matter what was happening. Had we played a good set, we probably would have transported them to another reality entirely. Some people made their careers at Woodstock, but we've spent about twenty years making up for it." BOB WEIR

creedence
clearwater
revival

Sunday, August 17, approx. 1:30 a.m.

John Fogerty: vocals, guitar, harmonica, piano
Tom Fogerty: rhythm guitar, vocals
Stu Cooke: bass
Doug "Cosmo" Clifford: drums

In terms of outright commercial success, Creedence Clearwater Revival were the biggest act to appear at the festival. They had already notched up two No. 2s in the *Billboard* singles chart during 1969—"Proud Mary" and "Bad Moon Rising"—and a third, "Green River," was heading for the same position when they appeared at Woodstock. They'd also had a Top 10 album, *Bayou Country*, early in the year, and the follow-up, *Green River*, was about to shoot to the top of the chart.

Over the previous two months Creedence had shared prominent billing with some of the biggest acts around, including The Mothers of Invention and Jimi Hendrix at the Denver Pop Festival in June, Hendrix, Jethro Tull, and The Byrds during the same month at the Newport '69 gathering in California, and Janis Joplin, Canned Heat, and Blood, Sweat & Tears at the Atlanta event in July. They were certainly no strangers to the festival circuit.

However, their eleven-song set of straightforward blues-tinged rock 'n' roll —although well received by the Woodstock audience—never actually appeared on the original Woodstock three-record compilation album, due to insurmountable contract problems between their label, Fantasy, and Atlantic Records, which produced the Woodstock collection.

Set List: Born on the Bayou, Green River, Nincty-Nine and a Half (Won't Do), Commotion, Bootleg, Bad Moon Rising, Proud Mary, I Put a Spell on You, Night Time Is the Right Time, Keep on Chooglin, Suzie Q

"Creedence had the privilege of following the Grateful Dead somewhere around 2:30 [sic] in the morning on the second day. Creedence was the hottest shot on earth at this moment, and we were really ready to rock out, and we waited and waited and waited, and finally it was our turn and my reaction was, 'Wow, we got to follow the band that put a half a million people to sleep.' I'm rocking and rocking and screaming, and about three songs into the set, I look out past the floodlights, and I see about five rows of bodies just intertwined— they're all asleep. Stoned and asleep. And I just looked out there, and I said, 'Well, we're up here having a great time. I hope some of you are, too.' What I meant was, I was searching to see if anybody was awake. Because there were a half million people asleep. These people were out; no matter what I did they were gone. It was sort of like a painting of a Dante scene, just bodies from hell, all intertwined and asleep, covered with mud. And this is the moment I will never forget as long as I live: a quarter mile away in the darkness, on the other edge of this bowl, there was some guy flicking his Bic [lighter], and in the night I hear, 'Don't worry about it, John. We're with you.' I played the rest of the show for that guy."

JOHN FOGERTY, CREEDENCE CLEARWATER REVIVAL

Left: John Fogerty. Right: (l to r) Tom Fogerty, Stu Cooke, Doug Clifford, John Fogerty.

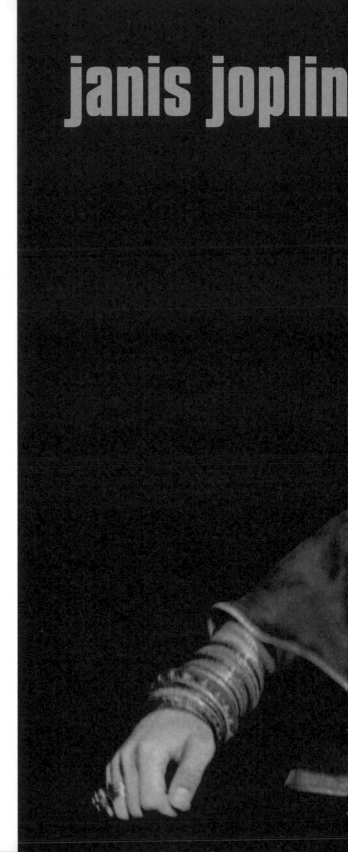

janis joplin

Sunday, August 17, approx. 2:30 a.m.

Janis Joplin: vocals

Terry Clements: tenor saxophone

Cornelius "Snooky" Flowers: baritone sax

Luis Gasca: trumpet

John Till: guitar

Richard Kermode: keyboards

Brad Campbell: bass

Maury Baker: drums

Janis Joplin's Woodstock appearance, supported by her new backing group, the Kozmic Blues Band, was distinctively stamped with her brash, searing style. The diminutive blues-shouting Texan had become a major figure on the San Francisco music scene between 1966 and 1968, with her original outfit, Big Brother & the Holding Company. Her performance at the Monterey Pop Festival, and the film record of the same, showed her at her sensational peak in 1967. As she lived up to her dual image of psychedelic queen and hard-drinking diva, alcohol and drugs were taking their toll. At Woodstock, following the long wait for her performance, the twenty-six-year-old appeared somewhat the worse for wear. In addition, she and the Kozmic Blues Band were still finding out how to perform compatibly together, having joined forces only in December 1968. As a result, she delivered a ten-song set that was well-received by the crowd, but which many Janis observers felt could have been even stronger.

Most of her set was taken from her first solo album, which was about to be released, *I Got Dem Ol' Kozmic Blues Again Mama!,* and included a cover of soul singer Eddie Floyd's "Raise Your Hand," a highly original interpretation of George Gershwin's "Summertime," and the Otis Redding classic "Can't Turn You Loose," which featured saxophone man "Snooky" Flowers on vocals with just a little help from Janis. The two encores, "Piece of My Heart" and "Ball and Chain," were both familiar to the audience from the repertoire of Big Brother & the Holding Company.

Just over a year after Woodstock, on October 4, 1970, Janis Joplin was found on the floor of a Los Angeles motel room, dead from a heroin overdose.

Set List: Raise Your Hand, As Good As You've Been to This World, To Love Somebody, Summertime, Try (Just a Little Bit Harder), Kozmic Blues, Can't Turn You Loose, Work Me Lord, Piece of My Heart, Ball and Chain

"I thought Janis was fabulous."
BILL HANLEY, SOUND ENGINEER

"We got in hours before she played. Even given that this was mid-August, still you're more than a month away from the equinox so it's not getting dark real early. But we got in there, and we just hung out in this tent backstage. I tend to wander around more, but Janis sat down with somebody she knew, talking and drinking.

I think probably part of the problem that night was that, even though they had had a day to catch up from the slow beginning and Richie Havens' legendary two-hour set or however long he played, they started with this lag, and this was a day and a half later, but everything was still running late. She was supposed to get on at nine or ten.

There's all these other folks to hang out with. There's musicians and it's the company of your peers. So it's social, it's not pacing up and down going 'Goddamn it, I want to go onstage!' Although there may have come a point later at night when she was thinking, 'I am getting tired, I want go out and play and then I want to go home and go to sleep.' But I think because it was social and because there were friends ... she sat around in the tent and socialized and talked, and what she did when she was doing those things was drink.

Nobody is disputing that probably she had had too much. I mean, she did try to pace herself before a show, and then she would reward herself after the show. What she always described was a level of a couple of drinks before the show, so you get that initial lift. And that's what she wanted when she went onstage. Not hours of sitting around drinking cocktails. But on the other hand, she wasn't gonna pace herself between, say, eight p.m. and eleven-thirty."

JOHN BYRNE COOKE, JANIS JOPLIN'S ROAD MANAGER

Left: Janis Joplin (right) backstage with her companion at Woodstock, long-time friend—and sometime lover—Peggy Caserta.
Overleaf: Janis with saxophone man "Snooky" Flowers contributing a vocal.

"Janis Joplin, the Texas singer, who became so popular as a member of the now disbanded San Francisco group Big Brother & the Holding Company, sang on Saturday night with her own band, as yet unnamed.

The special meaning of this concert for Miss Joplin is that her career was given its biggest push by the 1967 Monterey Pop Festival in California, the first of these large rock gatherings. Her appearance here was less spectacular. She sang hard and loud and was well received, but there were problems. Miss Joplin is a very emotional singer given to great outbursts of energy. Big Brother & the Holding Company was similarly inclined. Precision was dropped in favor of spontaneity and excitement, and it was a happy bargain. Her new band is ten times more precise and technically correct than Big Brother, but much less exciting. Miss Joplin sang some of her well-known songs, like 'Piece of My Heart' and the Bee Gees' 'To Love Somebody.' One of her best new songs, 'Work Me, Lord,' was written by Nick Gravenites, singer for another defunct band, The Electric Flag." MIKE JAHN, *NEW YORK TIMES*

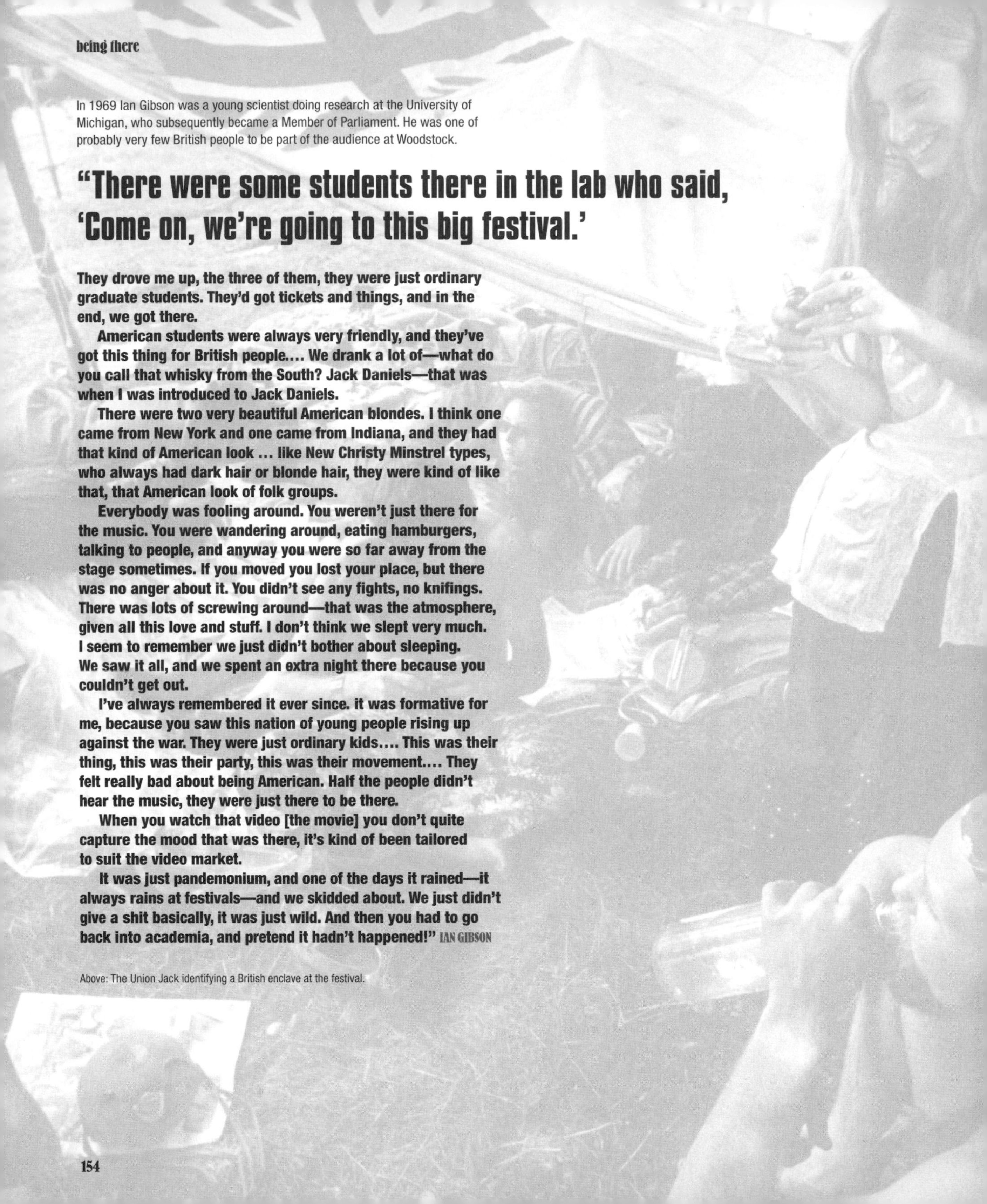

In 1969 Ian Gibson was a young scientist doing research at the University of Michigan, who subsequently became a Member of Parliament. He was one of probably very few British people to be part of the audience at Woodstock.

"There were some students there in the lab who said, 'Come on, we're going to this big festival.'

They drove me up, the three of them, they were just ordinary graduate students. They'd got tickets and things, and in the end, we got there.

American students were always very friendly, and they've got this thing for British people.... We drank a lot of—what do you call that whisky from the South? Jack Daniels—that was when I was introduced to Jack Daniels.

There were two very beautiful American blondes. I think one came from New York and one came from Indiana, and they had that kind of American look ... like New Christy Minstrel types, who always had dark hair or blonde hair, they were kind of like that, that American look of folk groups.

Everybody was fooling around. You weren't just there for the music. You were wandering around, eating hamburgers, talking to people, and anyway you were so far away from the stage sometimes. If you moved you lost your place, but there was no anger about it. You didn't see any fights, no knifings. There was lots of screwing around—that was the atmosphere, given all this love and stuff. I don't think we slept very much. I seem to remember we just didn't bother about sleeping. We saw it all, and we spent an extra night there because you couldn't get out.

I've always remembered it ever since. it was formative for me, because you saw this nation of young people rising up against the war. They were just ordinary kids.... This was their thing, this was their party, this was their movement.... They felt really bad about being American. Half the people didn't hear the music, they were just there to be there.

When you watch that video [the movie] you don't quite capture the mood that was there, it's kind of been tailored to suit the video market.

It was just pandemonium, and one of the days it rained—it always rains at festivals—and we skidded about. We just didn't give a shit basically, it was just wild. And then you had to go back into academia, and pretend it hadn't happened!" IAN GIBSON

Above: The Union Jack identifying a British enclave at the festival.

New York Times journalist Barnard Law Collier was the only reporter from a major newspaper to attend all three days of the festival—in fact the only one there for the first two days—and his dispatches often had the candid urgency of daily reports from a war zone. His bulletin dated August 16 included the stark warning of a possible major health disaster occurring on the site.

300,000 AT FOLK ROCK FAIR

BETHEL, N.Y., Aug. 16

Most of the hip-swinging youngsters heard the music on stage only as a distant rumble. It was almost impossible for them to tell who was performing, and probably only about half the crowd could hear a note. Yet they stayed by the thousands, often standing ankle-deep in mud, sometimes paying enterprising peddlers 25 cents for a glass of water.

Roadways leading from the site were tonight lined with thousands of weary-looking youths who had had enough, and were trying to reach places where they could get food and transportation.

During the first 24 hours of the fair, festival medical officers said that a thousand people had been treated at first-aid stations for various ailments, including exposure and a few accident cases. About 300 were ill because of adverse drug reactions.

NEW YORK TIMES, AUGUST 17, 1969

Above and below: Medical aid, drug advice, and general community support were an essential part of the "self-help" facilities that characterized Woodstock, especially when a genuine crisis seemed inevitable.

DOCTORS FLY TO SCENE

BETHEL, N.Y., Aug. 16

A dozen doctors, responding to a plea from the fair's sponsors, flew from New York to the scene, about 70 miles northwest of the city, near the Catskill Mountain resorts of Liberty and Monticello.

Michael Lang, the 24-year-old producer of the event, said that the medical help was summoned not because of any widespread illnesses, but because of the potential threat of a virus cold or pneumonia epidemic among such a large gathering.

NEW YORK TIMES, AUGUST 17, 1969

SUNDAY NEWS
NEW YORK'S PICTURE NEWSPAPER
FINAL ★★★ 20¢
Vol. 49, No. 16   New York, N.Y. 10017, Sunday, August 17, 1969*   WEATHER: Cloudy, warm and humid.

HIPPIES MIRED IN SEA OF MUD

They Don't Melt . . . Only slightly daunted by mud and other drawbacks, rockstars press on to the Woodstock folk-rock festival at White Lake, N.Y. Despite unplanned discomforts—and threat of medical emergency—more than 400,000 hold their ground on the Catskill farm in hope of catching some sounds. —Story p. 3; other pics, centerfold

Right: Nick and Bobbi Ercoline were unaware that the picture by Burk Uzzle, which became an iconic Woodstock image, was even being taken. They discovered it months later when it appeared on the cover of the Woodstock album release. "Five of us were sitting around and one of the guys had bought the album and we were listening to it, and we passed the cover around. And all of a sudden somebody said, 'Whoa! There's Herbie's butterfly. Whoa! There's Bobbi and Nick!'" The couple married two years later, and were still together when interviewed about the picture in 2005.

"By late on Saturday, even the least perceptive of the business managers for the bands began to realize that we might be in some kind of financial trouble. We got a call, I guess around midnight, and the two managers of the Grateful Dead and The Who called up and said, 'The rumor's going round that you guys are broke, and your check is no longer gonna do the job. We need cash.' So I said, 'Hey guys, I understand that you're concerned, but it's Saturday night around midnight, obviously there's no way I can get cash, so let's work this out tomorrow. Have your band play and we'll make good on it, don't worry.' And they said, 'We are worried … and your word, your check is not going to do it. We need cash or cashiers' checks.' I finally said, 'Well let's call [bank manager] Charlie Prince, it can't hurt…. Maybe he'll come up with a bright idea.'

And I said, 'Is there any chance you can get your hands on $50,000 for me,' and he [Prince] said, 'I don't think there is. We lock everything thing up in a time vault—the tellers' checks, the cashiers' checks, all the cash…. Wait a second, it was just going through my mind as I was saying it, there is one drawer of cashiers' checks that I may not have locked up on Friday night, it's a possibility…. Let me go take a look.'

I said, 'Charlie, this is so great, can you call me?' He said, 'Sure … but how do I get there? The last time I tried to get anywhere it was impossible.' I said, 'I'll take care of that, just wait out in your backyard and I'll send a helicopter.' And I hung up and got a helicopter up in the air and over to Charlie's in about twenty minutes. And he's waiting in his bathrobe, and it looked like a scene from *Close Encounters* as the chopper comes down and picks him up, and flies him over to the White Lake branch.

When he got into the bank the first thing he did was pick up the phone and call me, and tell me he was in the bank, and he was going to look around. He said, 'I'm gonna put the phone down, on the desk, and I'll come back to you as soon as I find these checks.'

Above: In the office, Michael Lang and Artie Kornfeld. Opposite top: Joel Rosenman and John Morris. Opposite bottom: Artie Kornfeld (left).

He put the phone down, and I could hear him rummaging around in the bank, and clattering, then I hear him—'Yeah, I found them!!' and in our White Lake office everyone went, 'Yeah!!' "

JOEL ROSENMAN

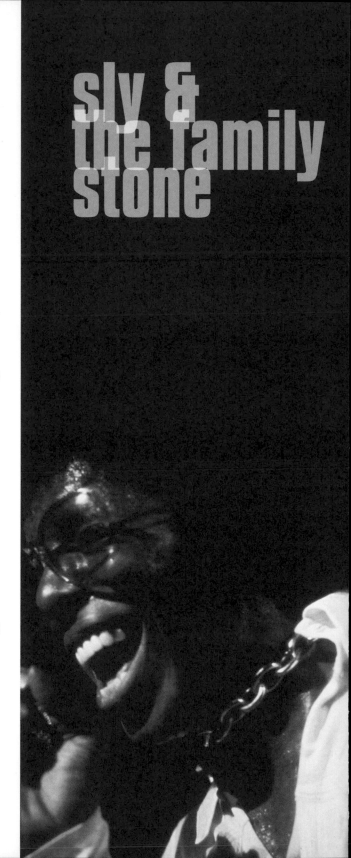

Sly & the family stone

Sunday, August 17, approx. 3:30 a.m.

Sly Stone: vocals, keyboard, harmonica

Freddie Stone: guitar, vocals

Jerry Martini: saxophone

Cynthia Robinson: trumpet

Rosie Stone: keyboard, vocals

Larry Graham: bass

Gregg Errico: drums

Formed in 1966 with a racially integrated, male-female lineup, Sylvester "Sly Stone" Stewart's soul outfit had already enjoyed several chart hits, including "Dance to the Music," "Everyday People" (a *Billboard* chart-topper), and "Hot Fun in the Summertime" when, late in the day, they were booked for Woodstock.

The organizers' initial doubts about booking the San Francisco band were a result of the group's reputation for being "difficult," typified in several instances of crowd hysteria—encouraged from the stage by the charismatic Sly—ending in near-riots. The most serious incident had occurred just a month earlier at the Newport Jazz Festival, when several hundred ticketless fans broke down fencing and swarmed through the 21,000-strong audience, driving paying customers from their seats as a rock-throwing running battle with security guards ensued.

But it was a forward-looking inclusion on the Woodstock roster: Sly's brand of psychedelic funk was pivotal in the development of soul music, impacting greatly on the disco movement of the early 1970s. And the political message of much of his material—calling for peace, love, and understanding but with a very deliberate black-consciousness edge to it—was equally in tune with the spirit of the times.

Set List: M'Lady, Sing a Simple Song, You Can Make It If You Try, Everyday People, (Medley): Dance to the Music./Music Lover./ I Want to Take You Higher, Love City, Stand

"Sly's effect on large audiences was amazing. At Woodstock, everybody was in their sleeping bags and he got everybody up out of their sleeping bags. Sly had this Napoleonic or Hitler-type control when he was on. He could make them riot. He could make them sit down. Make them do anything when he had the power." JERRY MARTINI, SLY & THE FAMILY STONE

"We thought that it was going to be a regular festival. We had no idea that it was going to be that big. We were staying in a little motel. We didn't play till the second night. We went over there and walked around in the mud. They didn't fly us in helicopters; they were being used for Medivac. They drove us in through the maze in a couple of limousines and treated us like royalty. We were supposed to start at ten o'clock. We sat around in tents and didn't go on until three-thirty in the morning. Everybody was asleep in their sleeping bags. We were a bit bummed, but people got up out of their sleeping bags. Everything was so late, we got onstage and just kicked ass."

JERRY MARTINI, SLY & THE FAMILY STONE

"We were scared. I've heard the other acts that were on it say the same thing; you look out there, butterflies. Before you even looked at the audience, you could feel the energy there and you knew it was intense. We were supposed to go on at eight o'clock. We were in the trailer, our adrenaline up, ready to go. Mike Lang kept coming in. Things were running behind, he said, hang in there. Two hours went by. We didn't go on 'till three-thirty. We were physically tired, just from all the adrenaline going through your body, peaking and coming down again, getting fired up to go on, for six or seven hours. We went on and you could feel the weight of it. It was heavy. This was the second day, the middle. People were sleeping, it was the middle of the night. It had just rained. Just the experience of getting there for the audience was a major no-one-had-planned thing. They had already been there for twenty-four, maybe thirty-six hours, hearing music, having to find food, standing in line to go to the bathroom. They were spent. It was night-time. You had been waiting to do your thing for hours now. They were in their sleeping bags, tired, burnt out, hungry, who knows what, asleep and you went on the stage to make these people get up and going. You could feel it. We started out and did the best we could. You could feel it drag and then, all of the sudden, the third song, I think, you started seeing heads bop up, people starting responding a little bit. Sly could feel it. He had it down by this time. He was great at working an audience in any situation, any diverse situation. He started talking to them. You could feel everybody start to listen to the music, wake up, get up, start dancing. Halfway through the show, the place was rocking. Really incredible experience." GREGG ERRICO, SLY & THE FAMILY STONE

Opposite: Sly and brother Freddie sharing vocals.

"I had no idea that is was going to be as big as it was. Getting to the concert, I realized that there were a lot of people, but still not how many until we played. Our songs would segue one into the other and many times there wasn't a place where you could get a big audience response. When we did stop playing, there was this tremendous roar unlike any thing we had ever heard. It was dark and you couldn't see all those people, but to hear that was like, wow."

LARRY GRAHAM, SLY & THE FAMILY STONE

"I got to witness the peak of the festival, which was Sly Stone. I don't think he ever played that good again—steam was literally coming out of his Afro." CARLOS SANTANA

the who

"It was chaos, wasn't it? What was going on off the stage was just beyond comprehension—stretchers and dead bodies and people throwing up and people having bad trips.... I thought the whole of America had gone mad." PETE TOWNSHEND, THE WHO

Sunday, August 17, approx. 5:00 a.m.

Roger Daltrey: vocals
Pete Townshend: guitar
John Entwistle: bass
Keith Moon: drums

Initially the archetypal UK Mod band, The Who created a teen anthem with "My Generation" (1965), which, like the band, endured through the years, and was as appropriate to the Woodstock audience as it had been to British youth in the mid-1960s. It was their explosive appearance at the 1967 Monterey Pop Festival that first established their reputation in the US, and by the end of 1968 seven singles on the charts, a Top 40 album, and heavy touring schedules across America had helped make them superstars. Their dynamic stage act was matched by Pete Townshend's musical vision, which in 1969 produced what many considered their masterwork, the concept album *Tommy*. It appeared on the *Billboard* chart in June, and quickly climbed to the No. 4 spot. Apart from the first two and final four numbers of their lengthy set at Woodstock, their whole performance consisted of songs from the so-called "rock opera," which told of the deaf, dumb, and blind kid Tommy who "sure played a mean pinball." According to eyewitnesses, the first rays of dawn illuminated the stage just as the band were playing Tommy's grand finale, "See Me – Feel Me." Their set was one of the best-received of the festival, but Pete Townshend was disparaging about the whole event—an attitude no doubt colored further by the infamous Abbie Hoffman incident, in which the agit-prop campaigner leapt up on the stage after the band had finished playing "Pinball Wizard," and harangued the crowd to protest at the unjust jailing of fellow activist John Sinclair. "I think this is a pile of shit, while John Sinclair rots in prison," yelled Hoffman. Townshend, incensed at the interruption, responded with "Fuck off! Fuck off my fucking stage!" and thumped the Yippie across the head with his guitar, before kicking him off the stage. Hoffman always claimed it was the stuff of legend, and that Townshend had merely bumped into him as he tuned up for the next number.

Set List: Heaven and Hell, I Can't Explain, It's a Boy, 1921, Amazing Journey, Sparks, Eyesight to the Blind, Christmas, Tommy Can You Hear Me?, Acid Queen, Pinball Wizard, Underture, Do You Think It's Alright?, Fiddle About, There's a Doctor, Go to the Mirror, Smash the Mirror, I'm Free, Tommy's Holiday Camp, We're Not Gonna Take It, See Me – Feel Me, Listening to You, Summertime Blues, Shakin' All Over, My Generation, Naked Eye

"Woodstock was probably the single best show in history. Townshend doesn't like it because he is an idiot...." ROGER DALTREY, THE WHO

All these hippies wandering about thinking the world was going to be different from that day on. As a cynical English arsehole, I walked through it all and felt like spitting on the lot of them, trying to make them realize that nothing had changed and nothing was going to change. Not only that, what they thought was an alternative society was basically a field full of six-foot-deep mud laced with LSD. If that was the world they wanted to live in, then fuck the lot of them." PETE TOWNSHEND

Left to right: John Entwistle, Roger Daltrey, Keith Moon, Pete Townshend.

"When you look back at the flower-power era, it all looks daft. I feel particularly cynical, because I thought it was daft at the time.... I didn't like Haight-Ashbury, I didn't like Abbie Hoffman, I didn't like Timothy Leary, and I didn't like Woodstock." PETE TOWNSHEND

"Abbie Hoffman interrupted The Who's set on Saturday night to berate the crowd for listening to music when John Sinclair, a Michigan activist, had just been sentenced to a long prison term for giving some marijuana to a cop. Peter Townshend hit Hoffman with his guitar, and that is more of a commentary on the relation of rock to politics than all of [underground rock magazine] Rat's fuzzy moralizing."

ELLEN WILLIS, *NEW YORKER*

"During the explosive set by The Who, Yippie founder Abbie Hoffman grabbed a microphone onstage and began to complain about a friend's arrest. Guitarist Peter Townshend coldly clubbed him in the neck with his guitar and kicked him offstage. No one in the audience protested Townshend's actions."

VARIETY

Sunday, August 17, approx. 7:00 a.m.

Marty Balin: vocals

Grace Slick: vocals

Paul Kantner: guitar, vocals

Jorma Kaukonen: guitar, vocals

Jack Casady: bass

Spencer Dryden: drums

Nicky Hopkins: piano

West Coast flower-power favorites from the Summer of Love in 1967, Jefferson Airplane were arguably past their peak by 1969, although some of the band enjoyed renewed success in the 1970s as Jefferson Starship. Booked to close the Saturday night at Woodstock, the Airplane had to wait for hours as a result of the incredible overrunning due to rain, technical problems, and changeover delays. They didn't actually take the stage until around 7:00 a.m. on Sunday. That morning they were joined by British session pianist Nicky Hopkins, a sometime guest on their recordings and then a fellow Bay Area resident. Despite a valiant effort from the band, even their most memorable numbers—including the two Top 40 hits from their seminal *Surrealistic Pillow* album of 1967, "White Rabbit" and "Somebody to Love"—failed to arouse the zonked-out audience. Jefferson Airplane did not appear in the original Woodstock film.

Set List: The Other Side of This Life, Somebody to Love, 3/5ths of a Mile in 10 Seconds, Won't You Try / Saturday Afternoon, Eskimo Blue Day, Plastic Fantastic Lover, Wooden Ships, Uncle Sam's Blues, Volunteers, The Ballad of You and Me and Pooneil, Come Back Baby, White Rabbit, The House at Pooneil Corners

"When we went on it was like, you know, dawn came up. I mean, most people were asleep anyway. I don't think we had a very good set because the sun was rising in our eyes and we had been up all night, naturally, partying. I've never seen the movie, but I remember it was kinda like, uh-uh, oh well." MARTY BALIN, JEFFERSON AIRPLANE

Opposite: Grace Slick. Overleaf: Top left: Drummer Spencer Dryden and Marty Balin. Bottom left: Paul Kantner, Jack Casady, Grace Slick, Spencer Dryden (in hat), and (standing) Country Joe McDonald with rock promoter Bill Graham.

"All right friends, you have seen the heavy groups, now you'll see morning maniac music, believe me, yeah ... it's a new dawn." GRACE SLICK, JEFFERSON AIRPLANE

"You saw musicians getting soaked by the rain. It brought everyone down to a common reality. That was the most precious thing about the festival. The egos all melted away."

JACK CASADY

"Woodstock everybody remembers with a little more fondness than I do. I have a bladder about the size of a dime and you couldn't get off the stage to go to the bathroom. It was not that well organized. But it was unique in that there were a half-million people not stabbing each other to death." GRACE SLICK

"I flew in on a helicopter, looking down at this enormous crowd and listening to the radio talking about it being one of the biggest cities in New York at the moment. I just thought it was the idealistic high point of the festivals that had been happening, Monterey and stuff like that, and then we got to Woodstock and that was like, 'Whoa!' And the idealism of what the musicians were all doing and the thrill of being a part of it, you know, kind of hit me when I looked down from the helicopter. I thought, 'Wow, maybe this actually is gonna be a positive vibe that's gonna be put out to the whole world.' So I was quite thrilled by it actually.

We had heard it on the radio. The broadcast people were saying, 'You can't get in. The roads are packed. There's so many people. You're gonna have to walk in.' And people were just walking in, and cars were parked every which way all along the highways and stuff. So it was pretty amazing.

And I had gone out a couple of times, because we were there like a couple days, and I think I got drunk and sober about three different times in the period of doing the whole show. So a couple of times I went down to the concert to see music and see different acts and just hung around. Milling around among the people, seeing the different things going on, and the diggers and different acts.

I remember one time I was standing in the rain, huddling under some digger's tents, you know where they're feeding people and some of these great people were there, Peter Coyote and Emmett Grogan, and all those guys. I remember Gravy talking about bad acid, making an announcement, and then everybody going, 'Uh-ohhh! Watch out!' Everybody was being very careful about what was going on. Of course by that time I was being very careful all the time." MARTY BALIN

day three

"It bombarded my senses, the sounds, the smells, and the visual stimulation. The smell, it was swampy. It was wood smoke. It was pot. It was body odor. It was cooking campfires. It just bombarded you. You could smell the rain that was about to come. It was humid. The sky was dark and gray. There was a hum, noise, voices, music in the background—not just from the concert; strumming of guitars, flutes, crying babies. And, the intercom—you could hear from the staging area calling for people, lost children, 'your wife is about to have a baby,' whatever. That bombarded you. The sounds and the smell, coupled with the movement—the activity, the commotion that was going on, whether it was people dancing to your left, people eating or sleeping or making love to your right, or people fighting—not physically fighting, but verbally fighting, which you didn't see much. Maybe a little argument now and again. And laughter, so much laughter. And, as the night went on and, as the sun went down, the sky had a red glow."

BOBBI ERCOLINE, WOODSTOCK ATTENDEE

Sunday, August 17, approx. 3:30 p.m.

Joe Cocker: vocals

Chris Stainton: keyboards

Henry McCullough: guitar

Alan Spencer: bass

Bruce Rowlands: drums

Although his debut LP *With a Little Help From My Friends* had just dented the *Billboard* Top 40 album chart, peaking at No. 35 in July, Joe Cocker had yet to make a real impact in America. He'd been a big name in his native UK since the previous October, when he topped the charts with a sensational version of The Beatles' "With a Little Help From My Friends," the hit coming after years on the road as a gigging rock 'n' roll singer. Cocker had begun his professional career in 1961, performing as Vance Arnold in the pubs of his northern hometown Sheffield.

Below: (l to r) Henry McCullough, Alan Spencer, Joe Cocker, Bruce Rowlands.

In fact, it was under that stage name that he got his first glimpse of the rock big time, when he and his group The Avengers supported The Rolling Stones at Sheffield City Hall in 1963.

Joe Cocker was the first act on the last officially booked day of the Woodstock festival, opening the events at around 3:30 p.m. His set was preceded by at least two unidentified "sound-check" instrumentals by The Grease Band, and after a slightly muted response to begin with, by the middle of the set—with his gritty voice and Ray Charles-inspired gyrations—Cocker had the crowd firmly on his side. For America it was a portent of things to come; within a year he had a No. 2 single, and his groundbreaking "Mad Dogs and Englishmen" tour, involving over thirty musicians, spawned both a bestselling live album and hit movie of the same name.

Set List: Dear Landlord, Something's Coming On, Do I Still Figure in Your Life, Feelin' Alright, Just Like a Woman, Let's Go Get Stoned, I Don't Need No Doctor, I Shall Be Released, Hitchcock Railway, Something to Say, With a Little Help from My Friends

joe cocker & the grease band

"In a year I'd gone with Chris Stainton (we both grew up in Sheffield), we'd gone from drinking beer every night to going through the whole gamut of smoking dope, and taking acid and everything, and our hair dropped from looking like greasers. I mean it all came on so quickly, that it was like a transformation of everything for us really.

There was like a breath of space, that was from about '67 to about '72, and then it kind of all just changed, and I think that's why a lot of us artists that were from that time period had a hard time suddenly moving over. Bands like Genesis were coming in, and whereas we used to be into jamming and being very loose, everything suddenly started tightening up. And like in the culture itself, suddenly—what happened, where did it all go? Because it was like another Renaissance period, that's the only way I can kind of think of it. It was a fantastic time, dressing up in outrageous clothes and that. I remember doing many shows when we'd be on the same bill as artists like The Byrds and Little Richard— the famous promoter, Bill Graham, he was great at doing that—putting together those mixed kind of bills, and that was a part of the times, too." JOE COCKER

"We played in Atlanta to about 50,000, and then we kept hearing that the word was out, that there was something really big coming up. We stayed in Connecticut, before the show, and we had to be helicoptered in, 'cause you just couldn't get there. Flying over the top of it, that was amazing. The band went ahead in one helicopter, and I went after them in one of those little bubble jobs.

I didn't get a chance to get nervous or anything, because when the helicopter landed, the band had already done a little sound check, and Michael Lang was there and said, 'Are you ready to go?' and I said, 'Sure,' and I just walked up the stairs, and we started straight into the set. So I didn't get a chance to get butterflies or anything....

If you remember on my [film] sequence, somebody says, 'Joe, look over your shoulder,' and there was a huge rain cloud, and that's when it all started, when it became a mudfest.... And I remember I just hung out with some hippies, like in a caravan, and waited for a few hours until we could get out.

I think we were lucky in some ways, we had a good day.... When you sing to that many people—I mean you can play to 50,000 people, and it's still a concert, but when you suddenly go over that line—I've done about three or four of them—it suddenly becomes something else. I remember by half the set I really didn't think we were getting through at all. Then we did 'Let's Get Stoned' [by Ray Charles], which fit the bill perfectly. Then of course everyone started coming alive.

We finished with 'With a Little Help From My Friends,' which has been a part of my history, I guess." JOE COCKER

"Two years before Woodstock, the most people I'd played to was 300 in a bar. It was hard getting the attention of such a crowd.

Even so, when I finally did 'With a Little Help From My Friends,' we got through to them.

And right as I finished, this huge black cloud came up and just poured on everything for hours." JOE COCKER

TIRED ROCK FANS BEGIN EXODUS

BETHEL, N.Y., Aug. 18

The storm, which struck at 4:30 p.m. after a sunny and breezy day, would have washed out any less-determined crowds. But at least 80,000 young people sat or stood in front of the stage and shouted obscenities at the darkened skies as trash rolled down the muddy hillside with the runoff of the rain. Others took shelter in dripping tents, lean-tos, cars, and trucks.

The festival promoters decided to continue the show but also to try to persuade as much of the audience as possible to leave the area for their cars or some sort of shelter.

The problem was, however, that most of those who remained unsheltered had parked their cars many miles from the festival grounds.

"It is really a problem because the kids are as wet as they can get already and they have miles to go before they can even hope to get dry," said Michael Lang, the executive producer of the festival.

The threat of bronchial disease and influenza was increased by the downpour, according to staff doctors here. Many boys and girls wandered through the mud nude, red mud clinging to their bodies.

When the storm struck, the performer on stage, Joe Cocker, stopped playing and the hundreds of people on the plywood and steel structure scurried off for fear of its being toppled by the winds, which were blowing in gusts estimated at up to forty miles an hour.

Amplifiers and other electronic devices were covered to avoid damage, and recorded music was played for the crowd.

As performers wandered onto the stage to look at the crowd and to decide whether to play, they were greeted by loud cheering. One naked man also came up on stage and danced.

At 6:15 p.m. the sun broke through and spirits rose again.

Artie Cornfeld [sic], a partner in the festival production company, said, "I guess this was meant to happen, and everybody is still with us. We're going to go on all night with the music."

NEW YORK TIMES, AUGUST 18, 1969

"We knew the rain was coming. Everybody could see it. I mean there was dark clouds coming. And at some point from the stage they were warning that we were going to get serious rain.

And we decided, you know, that we're not leaving. As long as they, they're going to play, we are not going to leave this hillside and go back to the tent or go find shelter. We had ponchos with us, and we had our food with us, and we just decided to stay. There was some sense of danger because of the lightning and the equipment, and people from the stage were telling people to get off the scaffolding because they would be electrocuted, but it wasn't really … we didn't feel that. We were farther up the hill, and we didn't feel that particular danger. And then it started to rain. And it rained a lot. And it rained more and it continued raining.

But you reach a point where you're so wet…. In the beginning you try to protect your shoes. You try to make sure that you're not walking in mud puddles, and you sort of step around, and sort of step from one newspaper to another, but at a certain point there is no reason. I mean, you are just soaked through, and it doesn't matter. At that point you transition to a whole different mindset about the rain. It's not a matter of going in and getting dry. Doesn't matter any more. It's almost like being in a swimming pool in the rain. What's the difference? You're wet anyway."

MARK KOSLOW, WOODSTOCK ATTENDEE

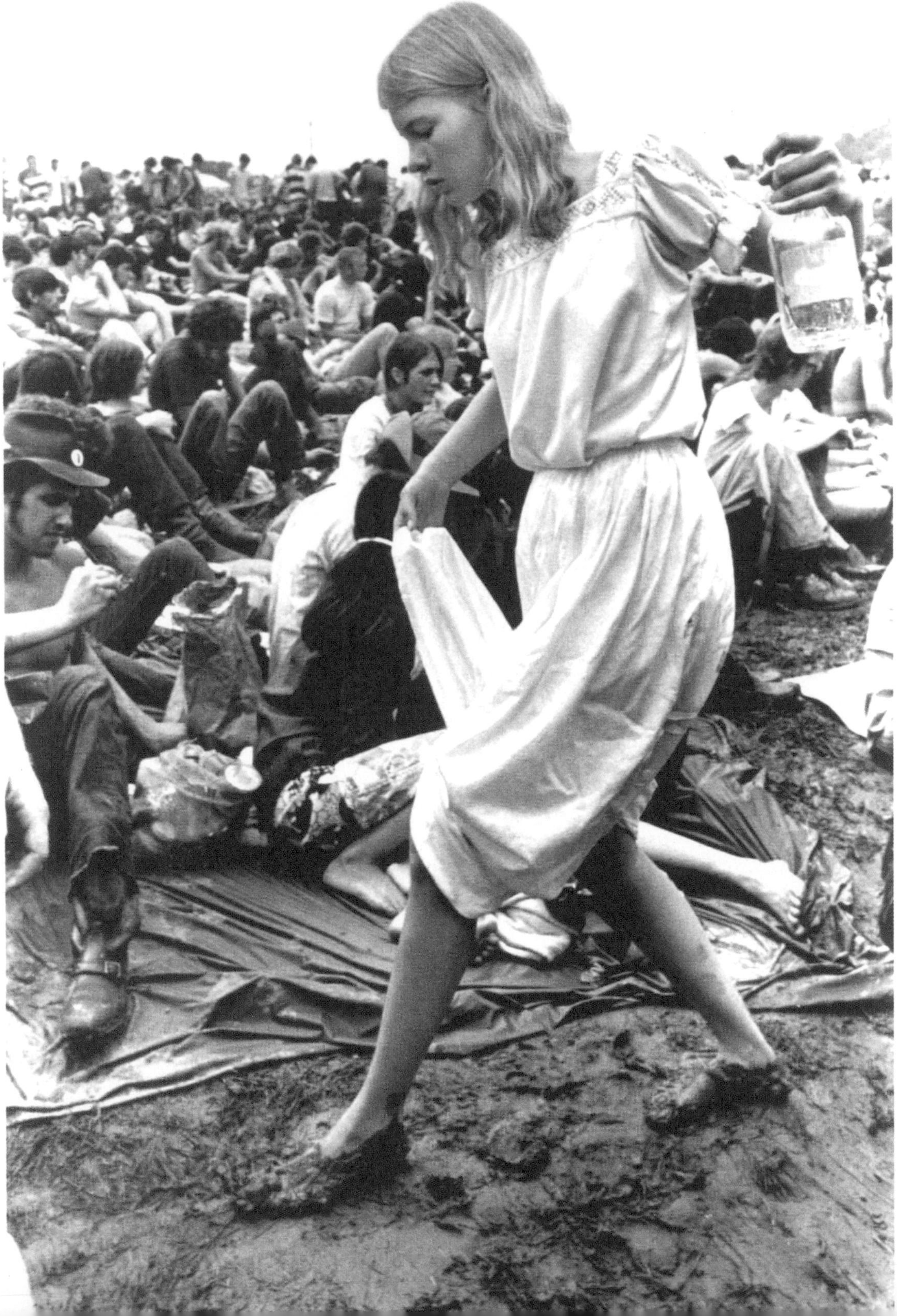

"Then everybody was just slobbing together. I mean Woodstock was just like a big pig sty, a big muddy mess. Everybody was bumping into each other, and slipping and sliding, and it was just like a playpen.

There was nothing you could do to avoid being soaking wet, muddy, and you just kind of had to let go of any preconceptions you had about how it was going to be, and you were just living in the moment. And that was a really great experience I think, breaking down all those expectations."

SUSAN COLE, WOODSTOCK ATTENDEE

Adjacent to Max Yasgur's farmland, a pond owned collectively by a group of farmers was leased to Woodstock Ventures as a water source for the festival. On behalf of the farmers' association, William Filippini signed over the rights to pump water out of the pond, for a fee of $5,000. But more famously, the pond became part of the media-driven folklore of Woodstock, when hundreds of mud-soaked and dirt-encrusted fans stripped off to go skinny-dipping in its waters.

"It was hot as hell, and all of these people were standing around the pond, the Filippini's pond, kind of standing there, round the edges. Everybody was waiting—you could sense, they wanted to go in, but they were kind of shy—what'd you do, with all these people here? And David [Myers] and I dropped our trousers and we just dove in. So we just didn't think anything of it, we just dropped our trousers and in we went, and right away—that was all it took—that gave everybody else permission to get naked, and jump in the water.

So some people can take credit for other things at Woodstock, but I take credit for being the one who broke the ice and got everybody nude swimming."

BARRY LEVINE, PHOTOGRAPHER

"Well *Playboy* didn't know what it was, and hardly anybody else did either. I wanted to go to Woodstock, and I wanted to go with an edge—you know, I didn't want to be just one of 300,000. I wanted get on the front row, to get up on stage. So I had worked for *Playboy*, done a cover for the magazine, in 1968 or whenever it was. So I called them up and said, 'There's gonna be a big concert, do you want me to cover it, I think we ought to cover this.'... And they didn't know what the hell it was I was talking about, and they said, 'Yes, you can use our name,' but not that they were interested in it. But it turned out to be such a big deal, they called me back after and said, 'Where's all the tits and ass?'... They saw my pictures, and said they weren't interested if there was no tits and ass.

I really just went to hear the music, not to shoot naked people. And when I was there, I didn't really feel like pointing my camera, you know, like—'I'm from Playboy, show us your tits'—it wasn't that kind of scene, at least it wasn't for me." ROWLAND SCHERMAN, PHOTOGRAPHER

Sunday, August 17, approx. 8:00 p.m.

Country Joe McDonald: guitar, vocals

Barry "The Fish" Melton: guitar

Mark Kapner: keyboards

Doug Metzner: bass

Greg "Duke" Dewey: drums

After the great rainstorm that closed Joe Cocker's set and lasted for several hours, Country Joe McDonald and his band The Fish took the stage in the early evening of what was officially the last day of the festival, drummer Greg Dewey entertaining the crowd with a spirited solo while Ten Years After were preparing to go on. They continued to play, preceding the British group with a full set. It wasn't the first appearance for Country Joe, who had stepped in on the second day to play an acoustic set without his band, to help fill time when the stage was waterlogged.

Of all the artists appearing at Woodstock, Country Joe and his group were arguably the most appropriate to the countercultural thrust of the event, having been central to the politico-protest movement on the West Coast since the mid-1960s.

Below: Country Joe McDonald. Opposite: Barry "The Fish" Melton.

Nevertheless, much of their repertoire consisted of non-protest songs, and Joe himself was wary of some of the extremes the "movement" could embrace. He canceled a booking to appear in Chicago during the protests surrounding the 1968 Democratic Convention, sensing there might be violence and not wanting to feel responsible for anyone getting hurt. On another occasion he was famously quoted as saying, "The most revolutionary thing you can do in this country is change your mind," a thinly veiled reference to erstwhile "comrades" who resented his shifting his position on the more militant aspects of the radical agenda.

Set List: Rock and Soul Music, Love, Sweet Lorraine, Sing Sing Sing, Summer Dresses, Friend Lover Woman Wife, Silver and Gold, Maria, The Love Machine, Ever Since You Told Me That You Love Me (I'm a Nut), Crystal Blues, Rock and Soul Music (reprise), The Fish Cheer, Fixin' to Die Rag

"When the performer comes on the stage, the rock 'n' roll musician, the hippies gave the rock 'n' roll musicians the chance to be the gurus of their generation, and they've in a sense blown it." COUNTRY JOE MCDONALD

country joe
& the fish

ten years
after

Sunday, August 17, approx 9:00 p.m.

Alvin Lee: guitar, vocals

Chick Churchill: keyboards

Leo Lyons: bass

Ric Lee: drums

Archetypal of the bands that characterized the second British blues boom (the first having been early in the decade, led by The Rolling Stones, The Yardbirds, The Animals, and others), Ten Years After were distinguished by lead man Alvin Lee, a genuine guitar virtuoso. Hailed in the press as the world's fastest player, Lee's technical prowess was matched by his artistry and the band's overall dynamic. They were scoring heavily in the US with their albums *Stonedhenge* and *SSSH* through 1969, supported by live performances that ensured their status as favorites on the touring circuit. It was a reputation borne out by their high-energy appearance at Woodstock: for the crowd their eleven-minute-plus "I'm Going Home" was one of the musical highlights of the festival. For Lee and the band, however, the legacy of the festival and the subsequent Woodstock movie had its downside, helping to create a "guitar-hero" image for the group that quickly became a rock 'n' roll stereotype in the early 1970s.

Set List: Spoonful, Good Morning, Little Schoolgirl, Hobbit, I Just Can't Keep from Crying Sometimes, Help Me, I'm Goin' Home

Above and opposite: Guitar ace Alvin Lee during the sensational set by Ten Years After.

"Ten Years After grew into something I didn't want—the heavy rock image thing, and we really tried to keep out of that. But it happened anyway through Woodstock, which was a complete accident, and it really changed a lot of people's attitudes to what we were doing. Before then it didn't seem so important, just go out there and have a good blow and get people off. Suddenly, it was really big gigs. Gotta play note for note. The fun seemed to disappear when the audience got to 12,000 … 15,000." ALVIN LEE, TEN YEARS AFTER

"I think [Woodstock] changed the whole business. Before the movie came out, it was pretty much an amateur business run by enthusiasts, with a few charlatans around, but then the media picked up on it and it became a huge business. Even promoters like Bill Graham—he was a great businessman and entrepreneur, but he was first and foremost a music fan. I think from Ten Years After's point of view, it became a bit too much for Alvin. Certainly after the movie there was a conscious shift. There were all sorts of rumors going around…. We had an American manager at the time, and according to one of the guys involved in making the film, Michael Wadleigh or someone, the American manager said, 'It's got to be eighty percent Alvin on the movie or we'll pull him out, and we'll pull Joe Cocker out as well.' So there was a conscious shift really, to make it Alvin Lee and Ten Years After at that time, and it's a matter of opinion whether it was a good idea or not. If I was a businessman looking at it, I'd have probably said, 'Well, that's a good idea'… but I think it did change things, it became too much, too much pressure." LEO LYONS, TEN YEARS AFTER

"We were a different band before Woodstock. We'd play the old Fillmore and be able to just play. We had respectful audiences then who would appreciate a jam or a swing. But after Woodstock the audience got very noisy and only wanted to hear things like 'I'm Going Home.'" ALVIN LEE

the band

"It was funny. You kind of felt you were going to a war.

I think we drove down to Stewart Airport, and they helicoptered us into the landing zone and then took us into motor homes to wait for the show. I remember walking around and checking out the thirty-foot stage, elevators in back, immense scaffolding, and an army of muddy people out on the hillside. They were set back about half an acre from the stage. It was the final day of the festival, and they'd run out of fresh food and water. There weren't any dressing rooms because they'd been turned into emergency clinics. There was lots of acid around—they were making announcements about it from the stage—and the audience was immensely under the influence of anything you could think of. This was Sunday, and some of them had been out there four nights already. The crowd was real tired and a little unhealthy. We just sat backstage and did our usual thing: go in, shake hands, eat, play the show, and split. We never hung around.

It rained pretty hard after we got there; a hard Catskill summer storm. So they stopped the show and then started it back up. I think we went on between Ten Years After and Johnny Winter: 'Ladies and gentlemen,' said Chip Monck, the voice of Woodstock, 'please welcome with us … The Band.'

Inhuman roar from the dark hillside. We looked at one another in disbelief. Garth was shaking his head. He started playing, and so did I. I played my cymbal, and he hit the bend pedal on the Lowrey organ, and we had a little duet until he slid into 'Chest Fever.' We were off. We played what was, for us, a real slow set: 'Chest Fever,' 'Tears of Rage,' 'We Can Talk,' 'Don't You Tell Henry,' 'Don't Do It,' 'Ain't No More Cane,' 'Long Black Veil,' 'This Wheel's on Fire,' 'I Shall Be Released,' and 'The Weight.' The encore was 'Loving You (Is Sweeter Than Ever),' which Rick sang for half a million soggy folks holding up lighters and matches.

Then we got the hell out of there, believe me. We took off from backstage in a rented station wagon, pulled through the mud by a bulldozer with a short chain. It took off with us, got us through a field, over a couple of ditches, and then finally onto some hard road. It took us a couple of hours to get the fifty miles back to Woodstock."

LEVON HELM, THE BAND

Sunday, August 17, approx. 10:30 p.m.

Robbie Robertson: guitar, vocals
Garth Hudson: organ, keyboard, saxophone
Richard Manuel: piano, drums, vocals
Rick Danko: bass, vocals
Levon Helm: drums, mandolin, vocals

Resident in the town of Woodstock, The Band were central to the whole genesis of the Music and Art Fair that eventually took place outside Bethel, forty-odd miles to the south. The group—formerly rock 'n' roller Ronnie Hawkins' backing band, The Hawks—had been working with Bob Dylan on an occasional basis since 1965. After the singer's motorcycle accident in 1966, by which time he was living in Woodstock, the band also moved to the town (specifically the nearby hamlet of West Saugerties), occupying a house they dubbed "Big Pink." It was there, during his furlough after the accident, that Dylan and The Band recorded most of what was later released as *The Basement Tapes,* as well as inspiring the title for The Band's acclaimed 1968 debut *Music From Big Pink.*

It was this, and subsequent musical activity in and around Woodstock, that gave Michael Lang and his associates the idea of building a state-of-the-art recording facility in the town, with the Music and Art Fair merely the means of raising some necessary capital. So The Band were an integral part of the Woodstock project right from the start—indeed, the event might never have been conceived without them.

Although not entirely happy with the sound system, from the first chords of the opener "Chest Fever" The Band seemed to personify the spirit of Woodstock, and the audience, enthralled, responded accordingly. The group closed its set with "The Weight," which had been featured in the counterculture biker movie *Easy Rider,* released earlier that summer, but the crowd wouldn't let them go until they had encored with "Loving You (Is Sweeter Than Ever)." Despite their tumultuous reception, however, The Band did not appear in the 1970 film or on the original soundtrack album because their manager, Albert Grossman, considered the fee offered for their services far too low.

Set List: Chest Fever, Tears of Rage, We Can Talk, Don't You Tell Henry, Don't Do It, Ain't No More Cane, Long Black Veil, This Wheel's on Fire, I Shall Be Released, The Weight, Loving You (Is Sweeter Than Ever)

> **"To me it [the set] was terrible. It was not our PA system, we were using other people's facilities, which means that we didn't have any control over it, and if you can't control it then I don't consider the people are getting their money's worth."** RICK DANKO, THE BAND

Opposite: Robbie Roberston (left) and Levon Helm. Above: Robbie Robertson. Left: Rick Danko (left). Overleaf: The Band leaving the site with manager Albert Grossman (left).

'After three days of people being hammered by the weather and music, it was hard to get a take on the mood. We played a slow, haunting set of mountain music. We lived up there, near Woodstock, and it seemed kind of appropriate from our point of view. We did songs like 'Long Black Veil' and 'The Weight,' and everything had a bit of reverence to it. Even the faster songs sounded almost religious. I thought, 'God, I don't know if this is the right place for this.' I remember looking out there, and it seemed as though the kids were looking at us kind of funny. We were playing the same way we played in our living room, and that might have given the impression that we weren't up for it. But it could've been that we just couldn't get that same intimate feeling with a few hundred thousand people.

I never thought it was an amazing musical experience. Just like in the movie, the music was only part of the entertainment. As for the event itself, you feel proud to have been a part of it, you feel it was amazing, you feel it was a first, you feel like it said something. In all of those ways it was huge. But as a musical experience for The Band, we were like orphans in the storm there."

ROBBIE ROBERTSON, THE BAND

johnny
winter

Monday, August 18, approx. 12:00 midnight
Johnny Winter: vocals, guitar
Edgar Winter: keyboards
Tommy Shannon: bass
"Uncle" John Turner: drums

Hailed as the latest guitar virtuoso by his record label Columbia, Johnny Winter, the albino rocker from Texas, was a name on every rock fan's lips when he appeared at Woodstock.

After years playing blues and rock on the tough club circuit, Winter's big breakthrough came in 1968, when *Rolling Stone* writers Larry Sepulvado and John Burks featured him in a piece on the Texas music scene, which prompted a bidding war among record companies that Columbia eventually won. His eponymous debut album for the label, featuring audacious covers of blues classics like Sonny Boy Williamson II's "Good Morning Little School Girl," and Robert Johnson's "When You Got a Good Friend," as well as a couple of originals, was plugged heavily on FM radio and peaked at No. 24 in the *Billboard* chart just a month or so before Woodstock.

His well-received blues-based set at the festival included such standards as "Johnny B. Goode" and "Tobacco Road," the latter the second of two numbers on which his brother Edgar (with whom Johnny had played intermittently since their teenage years) made a guest appearance on keyboards.

Set List: Talk to Your Daughter / Six Feet in the Ground, Leland Mississippi Blues, Mean Town Blues, You Done Lost Your Good Thing Now, I Can't Stand It [with Edgar Winter], Tobacco Road [with Edgar Winter], Tell the Truth [with Edgar Winter], Johnny B. Goode

"It was really muddy. Crowded too." JOHNNY WINTER

Monday, August 18, approx. 1:30 a.m.

David Clayton-Thomas: vocals, guitar

Steve Katz: guitar, harmonica, vocals

Dick Halligan: keyboards, trombone, flute

Jerry Hyman: trombone

Fred Lipsius: alto sax, piano

Lew Soloff: trumpet, flugelhorn

Chuck Winfield: trumpet, flugelhorn

Jim Fielder: bass

Bobby Colomby: drums

The original justification for the early 1970s jazz-rock combo Blood, Sweat & Tears' prominent place on the Woodstock bill was a reflection of their huge success in 1969, with two singles—"You've Made Me So Very Happy" and "Spinning Wheel"—making the No. 2 spot in the *Billboard* chart, and their eponymous debut album topping the list. By the time of the festival, founding member Al Kooper had left the horn-dominated band, but their flawlessly arranged mix of jazz, soul, and rock came as a refreshing contrast to the looser guitar-based sounds of most of the other acts—despite saxophone man Fred Lipsius claiming it was their worst gig ever.

Set List: More and More, Just One Smile, Something's Coming On, More Than You'll Ever Know, Spinning Wheel, Sometimes in Winter, Smiling Phases, God Bless the Child, And When I Die, You've Made Me So Very Happy

"Among the performers who would be at Woodstock approximately a month and a half after the Newport Jazz Festival was Blood, Sweat & Tears. This group was taking America by storm after replacing their founder and original lead singer, Al Kooper, with the dynamic David Clayton-Thomas. Blood, Sweat & Tears turned in a sensational, audience-pleasing performance at Newport, one of the main reasons that they were asked to play Woodstock."

JAMES PERONE, *AN ENCYCLOPEDIA OF THE MUSIC AND ART FAIR*

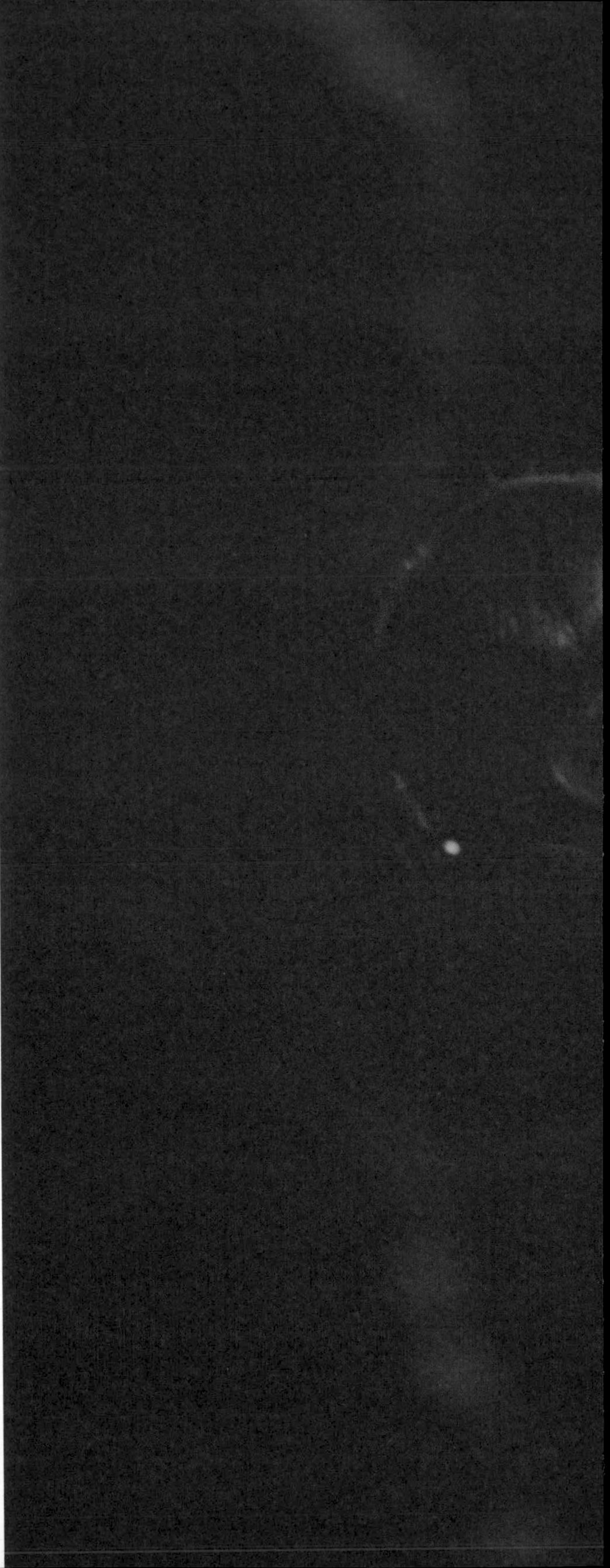

Right: Blood, Sweat & Tears vocalist David Clayton-Thomas.

Monday, August 18, 4:00 a.m.

David Crosby: guitar, vocals
Stephen Stills: guitar, vocals
Graham Nash: guitar, vocals
Neil Young: guitar, vocals
Greg Reeves: bass
Dallas Taylor: drums

One of the true "supergroups" of the era, the trio of Crosby, Stills & Nash had all made their mark on the rock scene before they got together—Crosby with The Byrds, Stills with Buffalo Springfield, and Nash with the British group The Hollies.

Crosby had left The Byrds in the fall of 1967, and in early 1968 Buffalo Springfield had fallen apart, leaving Stephen Stills also without a band. Graham Nash, who had first met Crosby when The Byrds were touring Britain in 1966, encountered him again when The Hollies were in California in 1968. An impromptu jamming session at a party early in 1969 convinced the three they had something worth developing, and soon after Nash (by this time not happy with The Hollies) joined the two Americans.

Although they had already debuted with their album *Crosby, Stills & Nash* in May, and entered the US singles chart with "Marrakesh Express" in July, they had been playing together just a brief time before Woodstock, and the date was only their second in public. Soon after their album release they had started rehearsing with an additional member, Neil Young—a graduate of the disbanded Buffalo Springfield along with Stephen Stills—who was to join them after their initial acoustic set.

Below: (l to r) Stephen Stills, David Crosby, Neil Young, and Graham Nash.

Following their somewhat fraught relationship in Buffalo Springfield, Stephen Stills had initially been dubious about adding Young to the Crosby, Stills, and Nash lineup. However, the Canadian singer was recruited, confirming further the band's "supergroup" status.

Young's Woodstock appearance began as just an acoustic duo with Stills, starting with the Buffalo Springfield song "Mr. Soul" (they were actually announced as "Buffalo Springfield"!). After three numbers Crosby and Nash reappeared, the quartet joined by a bass player and drummer for an electric set. Finally Crosby, Stills, Nash & Young rounded off a sensational performance with two acoustic encore numbers. The four would go on to mark the Woodstock spirit in song, when they covered Joni Mitchell's anthemic composition "Woodstock," a chart hit for them in April 1970.

Set List:
(acoustic, CS&N)
Suite: Judy Blue Eyes, Blackbird, Helplessly Hoping, Guinnevere, Marrakesh Express, 4 + 20
(acoustic, Stills & Young duo)
Mr. Soul, I'm Wonderin', You Don't Have to Cry
(electric, CSN&Y quartet plus bass and drums)
Pre-Road Downs, Long Time Gone, Bluebird, Sea of Madness, Wooden Ships
(acoustic, CSN&Y) Find the Cost of Freedom, 49 Bye-Byes

"This is the second time we've ever played in front of people, man, we're scared shitless." STEPHEN STILLS, TO THE WOODSTOCK CROWD

crosby
stills, nash
& young

"…We were scared, as Stephen said in the film. What wasn't said in the movie is why we were so nervous: everyone we respected in the whole goddamn music business was standing in a circle behind us when we went on. Everybody was curious about us. We were the new kid on the block, it was our second public gig, nobody had ever seen us, everybody had heard the record, everybody wondered, 'What in the hell are they about?' So when it was rumored that we were about to go on, everybody came. Every band that played there, including all the ones that aren't in the movie, were all standing in an arc behind us and that was intimidating, to say the least. I'm looking back at Hendrix and Robbie Robertson and Levon Helm and The Who and Janis and Sly and Grace and Paul, everybody that I knew and everybody I didn't know.

We were so happy that it went down well that we could barely handle it." DAVID CROSBY

Above: Stephen Stills. Right: David Crosby. Opposite: Neil Young.

"What effect did Woodstock have on music? That's when the market got big enough for the marketers to realize that they should go for it. They could isolate this whole group of people, target them as a consumer group—and they did. They used the music. That was the beginning of rock and roll being used in commercials. That's the long-term effect. Woodstock was a bullshit gig. A piece of shit. We played fuckin' awful. No one was into the music. I think Stephen was way overboard into this huge crowd. Everybody was on this Hollywood trip with the fuckin' cameras. They weren't playin' to the audience as much as to the cameras—these fuckin' cameramen were all over the stage. It was a distraction. I thought TV was a sellout. You get used to it after a while, and you even start getting into filming things to keep a record of it, but at first I never thought of being filmed while I was playin', and I could see everybody changing their performances for the fucking camera and I thought that was bullshit. All these assholes filming, everybody's carried away with how cool they are.... I wasn't moved. I wouldn't let them film me, that's why I'm not in the movie.

I said, 'One of you fuckin' guys comes near me and I'm gonna fuckin' hit you with my guitar. I'm playing music. Just leave me out.' Peace, love, and flowers. That's where I was at when we did Woodstock. So I was there ... but I wasn't. I left an imprint." NEIL YOUNG

205

Above and opposite: Medical problems among the crowd ranged from exposure, to minor cuts and injuries, to serious stretcher cases that had to be airlifted by helicopter to nearby hospitals.

"We were setting up teepees for the medical tent. We set up our teepee, and we set up the medical tent teepee because the doctors were coming in. We had to have medical tents for the doctors, then we put up little tents for the trip tents, and we put up another tent for the food-supply tent, next to the kitchen. So there were trip tents in the Hog Farm area, and over behind the stage, and when the doctors got someone who was tripping, they would send him over to the trip tent. If we found anybody needing medical attention, we'd send them over to the doctors. People got sick, and people cut themselves—and a lot of people didn't bring their pills for whatever they had, like asthma or something they had to have a pill for, so it was continuous note-giving to the stage, to announce someone needed this or that."** LISA LAW

"I was the dispatcher for the first-aid corps. I was able to go in with them and take the antibiotics on the first medical helicopter that went into Woodstock.... We never were paid for the antibiotics, which was no small donation, but it was something that we never considered—being paid. We felt that ... it's up to the people in the community to step up to the plate and try to get us through this weekend—because it was, it was a disaster area, really. A lot of people went to the festival and had a great time, and didn't have any bad feelings or anything. But I got to see the other side—the medical tents—that there were a lot of people that came that had unfortunate experiences.

The very first person I saw after I got into the pink tent came through the folds of the tent. He had split his head open, because he was tripping in Ben Leon's pond—and dove into the water, and didn't realize that the water was so shallow. He had a very bad laceration on his head.

I'm a registered nurse, but I had absolutely no experience in any type of drug or drug reaction. It was an enlightenment to get into a situation like that. And it was repeated over and over and over again." BARBARA HAHN, LOCAL RESIDENT

"It's like a city ... you got people cutting their fingers, you got people who forgot their medicine for their diabetes, you got people who are having babies, you got people who are overdosing on drugs.

You had a lot of LSD out there—people were taking LSD and not quite knowing what to do about it if they were a virgin LSD taker. So our job was to move these people into situations where they could finish their trip and be happy. Now at the beginning one of the doctors was giving Thorazine, and we immediately went over to the doctor and said, 'Look, if you give Thorazine, you stop a person's trip. It's not healthy for them, so just move those people you see towards us and we'll put them in our trip tents.

One guy was just freaking out on acid, he was just freaking out, and I took him back into the tent and I sat him down and I said, 'You're gonna be OK, we love you and all these people love you,' and he calmed down and I said, 'Why don't you take a nap right here?... And he calmed down, and he made it."

LISA LAW

"The most interesting thing for me was hanging around the Hog Farm's tent watching the counselors talk down the hippies who were dissociating on Brown Dot Acid. I thought they were heroes. They were very skilled. They helped a lot of people who were seriously flipping out. I think that may have been formative in my decision years later to become a drug counselor, which I am doing to this day."

ROBERT KIRKMAN, WOODSTOCK ATTENDEE

"And who was really beautiful was John Sebastian, Rick Danko, and Bobby Neuwirth, who was Dylan's sidekick. They came and they played for these people at the freak-out tent. They came over at night, and we let them go into the freak-out tent. In the Big Pink—that was the name of the [pink tent] hospital—and they did a couple of pickup concerts there, and it was fab-oo-lous. They just played acoustic guitars, they did it on the fly, no microphones or anything like that. It was really sweet." WAVY GRAVY (HUGH ROMNEY)

6:00 a.m.
Monday, August 18

Paul Butterfield: harmonica, vocals

Buzzy Feiten: guitar

Steve Madaio: trumpet

Keith Johnson: trumpet

Gene Dinwiddie: tenor saxophone

David Sanborn: alto saxophone

Trevor Lawrence: baritone saxophone

Teddy Harris: piano

Rod Hicks: bass

Phillip Wilson: drums

The Paul Butterfield Blues Band were favored in equal measure by fellow musicians and fans of Chicago-style electric rhythm & blues, and through the mid-1960s they established a huge following on the live club and concert circuit. Chicago-born Butterfield had apprenticed as a teenager, jamming with blues legends such as Muddy Waters, Little Walter, and Howlin' Wolf on the city's South Side, and when he formed his own band in 1963 it included ex-Howlin' Wolf bass player Jerome Arnold. He was duly credited with being one of the first white players to authentically capture the sound of the blues harmonica. His credibility with the burgeoning counterculture was guaranteed in 1965 when his band—minus Butterfield himself but including Mike Bloomfield on guitar and Al Kooper on organ—backed Bob Dylan on his mold-breaking electric set at the Newport Folk Festival in 1965. True to his roots, Butterfield's set list featured classic blues standards, including "Born Under a Bad Sign," written by Booker T. Jones and popularized by Albert King, and "Driftin' Blues," a 1945 hit for Texas blues man Charles Brown.

Set List: Born Under a Bad Sign, No Amount of Loving, Driftin' and Driftin', Morning Sunrise, All in a Day, Love March, Everything's Gonna Be Alright

Apart from some film outtakes, shown here, that were never used in the final Woodstock movie, there is no photographic record of the Butterfield band's set—but going on stage at six in the morning, perhaps it was not that surprising.

paul butterfield blues band

sha na na

Monday, August 18, approx. 7:30 a.m.

Donald "Donny" York

Rob Leonard

Alan Cooper

Frederick "Dennis" Greene

Dave Garrett

Richard "Richie" Joffe

Scott Powell: vocals

Reviving the glory days of 1950s rock 'n' roll (with outfits and stage choreography to match), Sha Na Na were undoubtedly an unexpected inclusion on the Woodstock bill. Formed by students at New York City's Columbia University, they specialized in doo-wop-driven vocals (hence their onomatopoeic name) and a repertoire of covers of hits by Elvis, The Coasters, Gene Chandler, and Danny & the Juniors. Their set at the festival was at first greeted with puzzlement on the part of many in the crowd—as can be seen in film footage of their performance—but they soon won over the majority when it became apparent it wasn't a joke. These guys, with their slicked-back hair, lamé suits, and sideburns, were deadly serious.

Set List: Get a Job, Come Go with Me, Silhouettes, Teen Angel, Her Latest Flame, Wipeout, Who Wrote the Book of Love, Little Darling, At the Hop, Duke of Earl, Get a Job (reprise)

"I was there—on stage! I was one of those Columbia University students who wound up at the right place at the right time—as original keyboard player for Sha Na Na! We played late Sunday night, or actually Monday morning. They kept bumping us; we were dressed in our rolled-up T-shirts, and it was COLD in them mountains at night! I remember huddling in the back of a big panel truck behind the stage trying to keep warm and listening to the groups that were supposed to have gone on AFTER us! We finally got on next-to-last—just before Jimi! Guess I ought to frame my Performer's Pass, huh?" JOE WITKIN, SHA NA NA

jimi
hendrix

Monday, August 18, 8:30 a.m.
(aka Gypsy Sons & Rainbows)
Jimi Hendrix: guitar, vocals
Larry Lee: rhythm guitar, vocals
Billy Cox: bass
Juma Sultan: percussion
Gerardo "Jerry" Velez: congas
Mitch Mitchell: drums

After his spectacular US debut at Monterey in 1967, Jimi Hendrix—already a big name in Britain—soon became a superstar in his own country, with three albums making the *Billboard* Top 10 (including the chart-topping *Electric Ladyland*) before his appearance at the Woodstock festival. He'd also become a regular visitor to Woodstock itself, and in July 1969 had moved to Shokan, a quiet village near the town, to spend the rest of the summer.

Officially billed as Gypsy Sons & Rainbows, a short-lived lineup that followed the disbandment of the Jimi Hendrix Experience a few weeks earlier, Hendrix's Woodstock performance could be seen as either a climax or anticlimax to the festival. It was an anticlimax only insofar as the Monday morning spot, almost half a day after the event was supposed to have finished, meant that only a tiny portion of the crowd—an estimated 30,000 to 60,000—was still there to hear him play. Most had begun the trek home, a mud-soaked exodus in the face of deteriorating conditions and potentially day-long traffic holdups. Somewhat ironically, Hendrix's manager had insisted that Jimi close the festival, seeing this as the "headline" spot.

But musically it marked a fitting climax to the three and a half days, with Hendrix in searing form as he blitzed his way through a two-hour set that featured such classics as "Foxy Lady," "Gypsy Woman," and "Hey Joe." The high point of his set, however, was the sensational, psychedelic rendition of the US national anthem, "The Star-Spangled Banner," which encapsulated both the musical and political spirit of Woodstock with blues-edged poignancy and other-worldly improvisation as the festival drew to an end. The Woodstock Music and Art Fair finally came to a close at 10:30 a.m., after Hendrix finished his set with "Hey Joe."

Set List: Message to Love, Hear My Train a-Comin'/Getting My Heart Back Together Again, Spanish Castle Magic, Red House, Master Mind (Larry Lee: vocals), Here He Comes (Lover Man), Foxey Lady, Beginnings/Jam Back at the House, Izabella, Gypsy Woman (Larry Lee: vocals), Fire, Voodoo Chile (Slight Return)/Stepping Stone, The Star-Spangled Banner/Purple Haze, Improvisation/Villanova Junction, Hey Joe

"I see that we meet again. Hmm. Yeah, well-well-well. Dig, dig, I'd like to get something straight. We, umm, got tired of the Experience, and every once in a while we're just blowing our minds too much, so we decided to change everything around, and I call it 'Gypsy Sons and Rainbows' for short. Cause we're nothing but a band of gypsies....

Give us about a minute and half to tune up, OK? Like we only had about two rehearsals, so we'll only do a primary rhythm thing.

**Voice in the crowd:
"Jimi, are you high?"
"I am high, thank you.
I am high, thank you, baby."**

JIMI HENDRIX

"Woodstock was the first gig I did with Jimi. That particular band was just for that season, because Jimi was trying to get himself together to go in another direction musically. Gypsy Sons and Rainbows was what Jimi called it. Jimi said that we had to get it together, so we rehearsed for it about three weeks. Up at a house he had in Shokan....

It was a *great* set. We were all together. Jimi was a perfectionist, and he wouldn't go on and let us play the music unless he felt we were ready for it. That's the type of musician he was. He didn't believe in half-assin' what he did. He believed in doing it all the way. He made sure that we had it all down before we performed it....

There was a lot of energy coming from the people, and Jimi said we'll take that energy and push it back to them. And that's how we did it. Some people may have left, but a lot of people just merged to the center to dig the music because everyone in the audience was into what we were all about. In fact, Jimi was the headliner. And everyone was anticipating his arrival. We stayed onstage for two hours, and they whisked us away right quick. I think we went somewhere down the road and got something to eat, and then we went back to the house at Shokan....

It was just a good gig. The great thing about it was it was peace and love and harmony, and some buzz, and everybody got along peacefully." BILLY COX, JIMI HENDRIX'S BASSIST

"Jimi Hendrix wanted to close the show because usually the headliner does close the show. His manager, Michael Jeffries [Jeffery], insisted; I said, 'Listen, it's not like that. They're all headliners. Why don't you go on around midnight?' Jeffries said no, Hendrix had to close the show; so I said, 'Okay, you got it,' even though I knew it was not really a good spot to have, waiting up all night and knowing many of the people would have left already. On Monday morning, Hendrix did play an incredible set, but by the time he got to the stage there were only about 40,000 people left."

MICHAEL LANG

 clearing up

"After the festival I got a job to clear up the field. The field was a mess, it was unbelievable if you look at how beautiful it is here today. It had the stench of a dump, like decay and rain, sleeping bags, mats, cartons of milk, so we were hired to clean it up. We had these long sticks with a nail on the end. We'd pick stuff up and make a pile of it, town trucks would pick it up, pump it in." DUKE DEVLIN, THE MUSEUM AT BETHEL WOODS SITE INTERPRETER

"After everybody left, there was so much mud that their sleeping bags were covered in mud, and they couldn't carry them. There were something like between 30,000 and 80,000 sleeping bags left, which we gathered up and put into a pile, and some people took them and others had to be trashed.

That's when one of the people died. He was in a sleeping bag over by the stage, and the honey wagon went up and ran over it ... actually Tom my husband held him in his arms as he passed away ... they thought that the sleeping bag was empty.

So afterward we cleaned up, the trash and the bags, with trucks and trailers, we were driving round picking up the trash and piling it in one area ... then they bussed us back to the airport.

At the very end we had a lot of helium left from blowing up balloons. We had these big long plastic bags which we filled with helium, joined them together and made into a peace symbol which we let float into the sky." LISA LAW

220

"My most vivid memory was leaving in a helicopter. John and Joel had left, I had to come and meet them at the bank. As we came up over the field we saw this huge peace symbol, and these kids were dragging garbage into this. So that was the image I sort of left, and the next thing I remember is landing on Wall Street! And it was a rude awakening! Y'know, coming from a dream." MICHAEL LANG

"A lot of kids—there was trash all over—started walking around with bags and picking up their own, trying to clean up the place on their own. That also affected me, the fact that not everybody was throwin' trash all over. Of course, there was a lot—tons of trash. That Sunday night they started picking up. A lotta people were leaving. The bands were still playing. But I knew it was a happening. I knew something—this was somethin', you know, beautiful.

I don't know how to describe it, but, after I got home and seen the amount of people here at the time, that even brought it more into focus for me."

JOE SCARDA, OFF-DUTY POLICEMAN HIRED AS SECURITY

223

As the bedraggled multitude left the Bethel site at the close of the festival, more than one eyewitness report compared the scene to a medieval army leaving a combat-scarred battlefield. In an article entitled "Grooving on the Sounds," however, in the British newspaper *The Guardian* of August 19, 1969, the veteran broadcaster and journalist Alistair Cooke made reference to a more recent, American, conflict:

"There was a vast relief today—in the Governor's mansion, the police departments throughout the State, the public health service, and probably also in the minds of thousands of parents around the country—when a camp-out involving twice the number of forces engaged in the Battle of Gettysburg broke out on the small country town of Bethel, New York, and went home."

The eminent observer went on to list the perils which, many feared, Max Yasgur was "inviting on himself"—"a rural version of the Chicago Democratic Convention riots that appalled the country just one year ago."

"There would be, he [Yasgur] was told, wholesale pot smoking at best, heroin at worst, an ocean of garbage, universal bad manners, an orgy of love-ins, and probably a wild and bloody encounter with the police."

Listing the various casualties that did befall the festival-goers—two deaths, four miscarriages, 400 treated for bad drug trips, over 3,000 minor injuries—Cooke nevertheless concluded that given the huge numbers attending (quoting a clear underestimate at 300,000), the festival had gone off surprisingly peacefully:

"But those casualties still left 296,000 or more in pretty good shape and incurable high spirits. The closest sizeable town is Monticello, and it had only twenty-five police, whose chief remarked at the end: 'Notwithstanding the personality, the dress, and their ideas they were and they are the most courteous, considerate, and well-behaved group of kids I have ever been in contact with in twenty-four years of police work.' "

Cooke then pointed out that the fact that a disaster was averted was in no small part due to the aid rendered by local residents, medical agencies, and voluntary groups:

"The 'facilities' of the countryside have never anticipated an invasion of 300,000 humans, either warlike or beautiful. The kids undoubtedly brought credit on their strange breed. They were abandoned to the elements until the local people, and the farmers and doctors and nuns and some Air Force helicopters, fed and tended and nursed them. It is difficult but it is not impossible to save 300,000 carefree hippies from hunger and disease when there is a supply and maintenance force gallantly on hand of sleepless doctors and radiologists, kindly farmers, and old ladies, the Stewart Air Force Base, volunteer ambulance drivers, the women of a Jewish community centre near by, and the sisters of the Convent of St. Thomas."

"The beautiful people who assumed that nature would provide were lucky in the availability at such desperate short notice of so much old-fashioned Christian, and Jewish, charity." ALISTAIR COOKE

Woodstock Facts and Figures

The price of a single-day ticket in advance was $7.00 • The price of a single-day ticket at the gate was $8.00 • The price of a two-day ticket in advance was $13.00 • The price of a three-day ticket in advance was $18.00 • The price of a three-day ticket at the gate was $24.00 • A total of 186,00 tickets were sold • Unable to get to the site, 4,062 ticket holders received a refund check • Over 6,000 patients were treated by 18 doctors and 36 nurses • An additional 50 doctors were flown in from New York City on August 16 • There were two births and four miscarriages during the festival • One death from a heroin overdose was reported, and one fan died after being run over by a tractor • It took an average eight hours to drive 98 miles from New York City to Bethel • Fans walked an average 15 miles to the site after abandoning their cars • At its peak there was a 17-mile bumper-to-bumper jam along Route 17B • The typical waiting time to make a phone call was two hours • The shortest waiting time between acts was 40 minutes • The longest waiting time between acts (excluding delays enforced by rain) was 120 minutes • There were 36 off-duty New York City policemen hired at $50 a day each, in addition to 150 volunteer police, 100 local sheriffs, and 100 State Troopers and deputies from 12 counties • The campers were joined by 450 unfenced cows for three days • Fans had access to 600 Port-O-San toilets • Emergency helicopters flew in 1,300 pounds of canned food, sandwiches, and fruit • The Women's Group of the Jewish Community Center of Monticello prepared 30,000 sandwiches, which were distributed by the Sisters of the Convent of St. Thomas

An estimated 250,000 people never made it to the site.

"Young people straggling into the Port of New York Authority bus terminal at 41st Street and Eighth Avenue last night were damp, disheveled, and given to such wild eccentricities of dress as the wearing of a battered top hat with a grimy jersey, blue jeans, and sandals. They were, according to the driver, Richard Biccum, 'good kids in disguise.' Mr Biccum, who is twenty-six years old, said: 'I'll haul kids any day rather than commuters,' because they were exceptionally polite and orderly. Reginald Dorsey, a Short Line Bus System dispatcher, agreed that the youths were 'beautiful people' who had caused no trouble."

NEW YORK TIMES, AUGUST 18, 1969

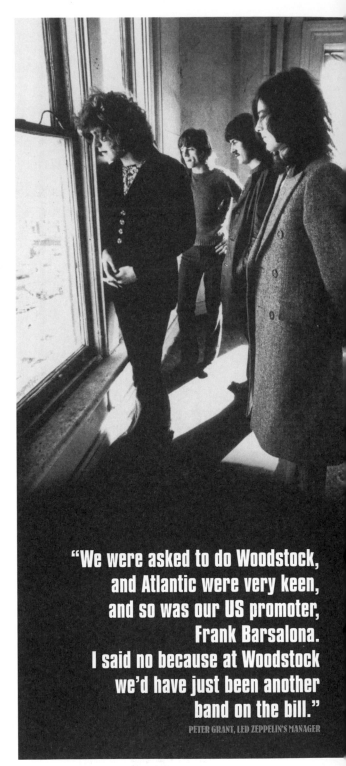

Refuseniks

A number of artists either pulled out of Woodstock at the last minute, or declined to perform when first invited, none having any idea that the festival would assume the significance that it did.

Joni Mitchell famously canceled just the day before she was due to travel to Bethel, reasoning that with the traffic snarl-ups she might not get back to New York City in time to appear on the prestigious *Dick Cavett Show*. As it turned out, Jefferson Airplane, Stephen Stills, and David Crosby all made it back from the festival by the Tuesday to join Joni on the TV chat show.

The Jeff Beck Group—which included Rod Stewart and future Rolling Stone guitarist Ronnie Wood in its ranks—were scheduled to appear at Woodstock, but disbanded just a week before the gig, while the heavy rock outfit Iron Butterfly were canceled by Woodstock Ventures after demanding a helicopter to fly them from New York, which Michael Lang refused.

Procol Harum declined the offer, as the festival was at the end of a long tour, and one of the band's members wanted to get back to England, where he was about to become a father. And The Doors were originally earmarked to play, but declined at the last moment, apparently because singer Jim Morrison hated playing large outdoor concerts and feared that if he performed at Woodstock he might be assassinated. Nevertheless, his bandmates Robby Krieger and John Densmore showed up, though they did not perform.

Other notable refusers included Jethro Tull (leader Ian Anderson was reported to have said he "didn't want to spend [his] weekend in a field of unwashed hippies"), Led Zeppelin, Tommy James & the Shondells, Paul Revere & the Raiders, Free, and Spirit. The Moody Blues, who played another event in Paris instead, had been booked (and appeared on posters) for the original Wallkill event.

Rumors abounded, before and during the Woodstock weekend, that The Beatles were going to make a surprise appearance. Although they hadn't played a concert since their US tour of 1966, the notion was fueled by the group's celebrated rooftop appearance on their London office building in January 1969. Michael Lang had made approaches to John Lennon via Chris O'Dell at The Beatles' Apple company, and Lennon was apparently keen on the idea. Any further negotiations were abandoned in the May, however, after Lennon was denied entrance into the US because of drug charges the previous year.

The most anticipated "surprise" performance that never materialized was an appearance on the Woodstock stage by Bob Dylan. Given his residence in nearby Woodstock itself—a factor in the original inspiration for the festival to be held there—and (albeit unwitting) his status as an icon of the counterculture, to some his eventual arrival at the Bethel site seemed inevitable. But it was never to be.

Dylan has gone on record many times saying that, by the end of the decade, the hippie fans who trekked to the town of Woodstock precisely because he lived there, were making his life and that of his family a misery. And he certainly didn't see himself as the "spokesman" of a generation with which, in many respects, he did not identify.

By the time Woodstock took place, Bob Dylan had signed to appear at the Isle of Wight Festival in England later in the month, and on August 15, the opening day at Bethel, he and his family were boarding the *Queen Elizabeth II* ocean liner to sail to Britain prior to the gig. Unfortunately, just before they set sail his three-year-old son Jesse hit his head on a doorknob, and they left the ship and returned to Woodstock, Dylan flying to the UK once he was assured his son was not seriously injured.

Right: Among the Woodstock "refuseniks," Led Zeppelin—(l to r) Robert Plant, John Paul Jones, John Bonham, Jimmy Page.

"We were asked to do Woodstock, and Atlantic were very keen, and so was our US promoter, Frank Barsalona. I said no because at Woodstock we'd have just been another band on the bill."

PETER GRANT, LED ZEPPELIN'S MANAGER

Above: Yoko Ono and John Lennon. Right: The Doors—
(l to r) Ray Manzarek, Robbie Krieger, Jim Morrison,
John Densmore.

Singer-songwriter Joni Mitchell was booked to play Woodstock, but when record executive David Geffen read the news reports he sent Crosby, Stills, Nash & Young on to the beleaguered site at Bethel, while he and Joni spent the evening in his New York apartment watching news reports of it on television. There she wrote her classic anthem to the three days of peace and music, "Woodstock," which CSN&Y made a worldwide hit the following spring.

"The deprivation of being stuck in a New York hotel room and not being able to go provided me with an intense angle on Woodstock. I was one of the fans. I was put in the position of being a kid who couldn't make it. So I was glued to the media. And at the time I was going through a kind of born-again Christian trip—not that I went to any church, I'd given up Christianity at a very early age in Sunday school. But suddenly, as performers, we were in the position of having so many people look to us for leadership, and for some unknown reason I took it seriously and decided I needed a guide and leaned on God. So I was a little 'God mad' at the time, for lack of a better term, and I had been saying to myself, 'Where are the modern miracles?' Woodstock, for some reason, impressed me as being a modern miracle, like a modern-day fishes-and-loaves story. For a herd of people that large to cooperate so well, it was pretty remarkable and there was tremendous optimism. So I wrote the song 'Woodstock' out of these feelings." JONI MITCHELL

"Then they [CSN&Y] heard the song, they recorded it, and it became the anthem for Woodstock. As for the movie, I would not allow them to use the footage of Crosby, Stills, Nash & Young in the movie unless they used Joni's song with Crosby, Still, Nash & Young singing it as the theme of the movie. That's how that happened." DAVID GEFFEN, ARTIST MANAGER AND RECORD EXECUTIVE

"Joni Mitchell and I were an item right around the time of Woodstock. We were in New York, and she was going to be doing *The Dick Cavett Show*. Rumors about Woodstock kept multiplying and multiplying. First, we hear 20,000 people will be there. Then, my God, we hear 100,000! Joni wanted to go, and I said, 'If you go, I can't guarantee that I can get you out of there and back to do the Cavett show,' which was an important show at the time. So Joni didn't go to Woodstock, and she was able to sing 'Woodstock' based on information given to her by us and Sebastian." GRAHAM NASH, CROSBY, STILLS, NASH & YOUNG

"I was bringing Crosby, Stills, Nash & Young ... and Joni Mitchell to Woodstock. And I arrived at La Guardia Airport. And I picked up the New York Times, and it says, '400,000 people sitting in mud.' And I thought, no way am I going to Woodstock. And so they went on to Woodstock. And Joni and I went back to my apartment on Central Park South, and we watched it on television. And she wrote the song 'Woodstock' in my apartment on 59th Street!"

DAVID GEFFEN
(SEE PAGE 288)

Opposite: Joni Mitchell at her home in Laurel Canyon, California, in 1969.

"That Woodstock festival ... was the sum total of all this bullshit. And it seemed to have something to do with me, this Woodstock Nation, and everything it represented. So we couldn't breathe. I couldn't get any space for myself and my family." BOB DYLAN

"**Woodstock—I didn't want to be part of that thing.**
I liked the town. I felt they exploited the shit out of that, goin' up there and getting
fifteen million people all in the same spot. That don't excite me. The flower generation—
is that what it was? I wasn't into that at all. I just thought it was a lot of kids out and around
wearing flowers in their hair, takin' a lot of acid. I mean, what can you think about that?" BOB DYLAN

Above: Bob Dylan on stage at the Woodstock 25th anniversary festival (known as Woodstock II)
at Saugerties, New York, in August 1994. Opposite: Dylan at a UK press conference, prior to his
appearance at the 1969 Isle of Wight Festival, just two weeks after Woodstock.

aftermath

" 'It was like balling for the first time,' said one campaigner, her voice shredded, her mind a tapioca of drugs. 'Once you've done it, you want to do it again and again, because it's so great.' And they will do it again, the threads of youthful dissidence in Paris and Prague and Fort Lauderdale and Berkeley and Chicago and London criss-crossing ever more closely until the map of the world we live in is viable for and visible to all of those that are part of it and all of those buried under it." *ROLLING STONE*, SEPTEMBER 20, 1969

POST-WOODSTOCK TIMELINE

1969 **August 29–31** Isle of Wight Festival of Music, England **August 30–September 1** Texas International Pop Festival **September 1** Category 5 Hurricane Camille hits the Gulf Coast, killing 248 people and causing over a billion dollars worth of damage **September 2** Ho Chi Minh, President of North Vietnam, dies aged 79 *(1)* **September 5** Lieutenant William Calley is charged with six counts of premeditated murder for his part in the My Lai massacre of 109 Vietnamese civilians *(2)* **September 24** "Chicago Eight" trial begins, arising from antiwar protests at the 1968 Democratic Convention *(3)* **October 15** National Moratorium across US protesting the Vietnam War **December 6** Altamont Speedway Free Festival ends in violence and death

1970 **April 22** First "Earth Day," launching the environmental movement **May 4** Four students killed by National Guard during antiwar demonstration at Kent State University, Ohio *(4)* **May 18** The Beatles release their final album, *Let It Be* **June 28** First Gay Pride march held in New York City *(5)* **September 18** Jimi Hendrix found dead of likely overdose in London **October 4** Janis Joplin found dead of heroin overdose in Los Angeles **December 30** Paul McCartney begins legal procedures to end The Beatles' partnership, signaling final breakup of the group

1971 **January 2** Ban on cigarette advertising on US radio and television **January 12** *All in the Family,* a long-running TV comedy challenging bigotry and ignorance, premieres on CBS **March 28** Final edition of TV's *The Ed Sullivan Show* **April 9** Charles Manson sentenced to death for Sharon Tate murder, later reduced to life imprisonment when California temporarily abolished the death penalty *(6)* **April 19** Soviet Union launches the first manned space station, *Salyut I* **June 27** Promoter Bill Graham closes his celebrated Fillmore East rock venue in New York City **July 3** The Doors singer Jim Morrison found dead in his apartment in Paris, France *(7)* **August 1** 40,000 attend George Harrison's fund-raising Concert for Bangladesh in New York City *(8)*

1972 **April 29** New York City mayor John Lindsay supports John Lennon's fight against deportation from the US *(9)* **June 17** Democratic party headquarters burglarized in the Watergate building in Washington **September 5–6** Terrorists kill 19 in siege at Munich Olympic Games

1973 **January 14** Elvis Presley's TV special, *Aloha From Hawaii,* is seen around the world by more than one billion viewers *(11)* **January 22** US Supreme Court decision (Roe *vs.* Wade) legalizes abortion nationwide **January 27** US role in Vietnam War ends with signing of Paris Peace Accords **March 29** The last US soldier leaves Vietnam **April 4** World Trade Center opens in New York City *(12)* **August 15** US ends bombing in Cambodia **December** Future mecca of punk rock, CBGB's club, opens in New York City *Also: Arab oil embargo causes fuel shortages and huge price rises (10)*

1974 **January 4** President Nixon refuses to hand over 500 tapes and documents, subpoenaed by the Senate Watergate Committee **February 4** Urban terrorist group the Symbionese Liberation Army kidnaps 19-year-old heiress Patty Hearst *(13)* **March 30** Punk band The Ramones play their first gig at the Performance Studio, NYC **April 15** Symbionese Liberation Army, joined by former captive Patty Hearst, robs San Francisco bank **August 9** Richard Nixon resigns as US President as a result of the Watergate scandal *(14)*

1975 **January 30** Weather Underground terror group bomb US State Department office in Washington, D.C. **March 10** *Rocky Horror Show* opens in New York City **April 30** Americans evacuated from Saigon as South Vietnam surrenders to the North, bringing the war to an end *(15)* **September 9** Hit TV comedy *Welcome Back, Kotter* premieres, featuring the poplar theme song (and 1976 No. 1 hit) by John Sebastian **October 11** NBC-TV's *Saturday Night Live* premieres, hosted by George Carlin **November 6** UK punk group The Sex Pistols play debut gig in London *(16)*

THE DICK CAVETT SHOW

The day after Woodstock ended—Tuesday, August 19—Jefferson Airplane, Joni Mitchell, Stephen Stills, and David Crosby all appeared as guests on ABC-TV's hour-long *Dick Cavett Show* in New York City. Aged thirty-two when this show aired, Cavett was considered the intellectual, hipper alternative to NBC-TV's much more popular late-night interviewer, Johnny Carson. Cavett, a graduate of Yale University and a former joke writer for Carson, encouraged more free-form discussion among guests than Carson, and was more comfortable with younger celebrities.

Most of the program served as a musical showcase for the assembled rock royalty. A twenty-five-year-old Joni Mitchell, looking very young and demure in a long, green velvet dress, performed "Chelsea Morning," "Willy," "For Free," and "The Fiddle and the Drum" solo on guitar and piano. Reportedly, her manager David Geffen had insisted that she couldn't appear at Woodstock because it might jeopardize her appearance on Cavett's show if she were trapped in the traffic jam. Stephen Stills performed an acoustic solo version of "4+20," and the Airplane opened and closed the show with rocking, tight versions of "We Can Be Together," "Volunteers," and (joined by Crosby and Stills) "Somebody to Love." The first number included the immortal phrase "Up against the wall, motherfuckers," which ABC censors noticeably failed to remove from the broadcast.

Jimi Hendrix had been booked for the appearance as well, but Cavett announced at the show's beginning that Hendrix had to cancel because of fatigue after finishing the festival so late. David Crosby confirmed that Hendrix had been playing until at least ten o'clock Monday morning.

During the brief "rap session" portion of the program, when all the performers gathered in-the-round in a circle of Naugahyde ottomans, Cavett asked a couple of general questions about the festival as well as about astrological signs and the perils of being long-hairs in 1969. But Cavett and his guests seemed rather ill at ease together, and straight answers were elusive. David Crosby proved the most relaxed and forthcoming in his comments about Woodstock.

"About two nights ago," volunteered Crosby, "that place up there was the second biggest city in New York. And it had no violence."

Less successful was Cavett's attempt to draw out Grace Slick of Jefferson Airplane about offstage goings-on. "What did you do, Grace, in your off-hours at the festival?" the host asked.

"Get it on," muttered Slick's boyfriend and bandmate, Paul Kantner, under his breath. Grace Slick looked mortified and covered her face in her hand, but quickly recovered by saying, "Listen, Jim, I wish I could tell you." To which Cavett replied in mock exasperation, "You've got to learn my name, Miss Joplin!"—thus steering the discussion safely away from the dreaded topic of free love.

Although the program did not contain any major revelations about the just-concluded festival, its broadcast signified that Woodstock was indeed a cultural milestone, and those who hadn't attended were eager to figure out just what had transpired in the fields of Bethel, New York.

Above: TV host Dick Cavett.
Right: David Crosby, Joni Mitchell, and Graham Nash.

"How was the festival in general?" Cavett asked the musicians. "Would you consider it a success?" "It was incredible," Crosby immediately replied. "It was probably the strangest thing that's ever happened in the world. Can I describe for you what it looked like flying in on a helicopter, man? It looked like an encampment of a Macedonian army on a Greek hill, crossed with the biggest batch of gypsies you've ever seen."

MAINSTREAM PRESS

Recognizing Woodstock as the social phenomenon that it was, over the days following the festival the mainstream press had time to reflect on the events in Bethel. The *New York Times,* in its stern, finger-wagging editorial the day after, scolded the organizers (and the counterculture generally) as if they were naughty children. *Newsweek* magazine, on the other hand, saw it in the context of the counterculture as a genuinely radical voice in American society, while *Life* took a characteristically objective stance in an eight-page photo feature.

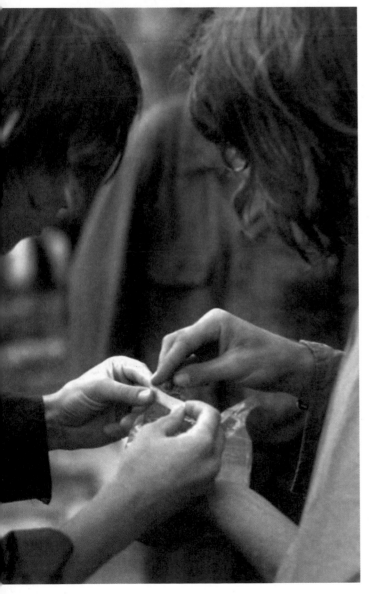

Nightmare in the Catskills

"The dreams of marijuana and rock music that drew 300,000 fans and hippies to the Catskills had little more sanity than the impulses that drive the lemmings to march to their deaths in the sea. They ended in a nightmare of mud and stagnation that paralyzed Sullivan County for a whole weekend.

What kind of culture is it that can produce so colossal a mess? One youth dead and at least three others in hospitals from overdoses of drugs; another dead from a mishap while sleeping in an open field. The highways for twenty miles around made completely impassable, not only for the maddened youths but for local residents and ordinary travelers.

Surely the parents, the teachers, and indeed all the adults who helped create the society against which these young people are so feverishly rebelling must bear a share of the responsibility for this outrageous episode. It is hardly credible that pot, acid, and other illegal drugs could be freely exchanged and used on the scale reported by reliable witnesses.

The sponsors of this event, who apparently had not the slightest concern for the turmoil it would cause, should be made to account for their mismanagement. To try to cram several hundred thousand people into a 600-acre farm with only a few hastily installed sanitary facilities shows a complete lack of responsibility.

The mix-up with the New York City Police Department, which left them without the services of several hundred off-duty policemen they had counted on for security purposes, greatly complicated matters. Apparently a high officer of the department encouraged them in the hope that they might be able to enlist some of the men.

When Police Commissioner Howard R. Leary learned of this he promptly and very properly forbade the men of his command from engaging in such activities. They are plainly a violation of the regulations against moonlighting, and the suggestion should never have been put forward by anyone familiar with the department's rules.

As always, there were redeeming features to the generally dismal situation. One was the genuine kindness shown by the residents of Monticello and other overrun communities, who boiled water and made thousands of sandwiches for the hungry, thirsty hordes of youngsters. Another was the help given by the doctors and nurses who flew to the scene.

Last, but by no means least, was the fact that the great bulk of the freakish-looking intruders behaved astonishingly well, considering the disappointments and discomforts they encountered. They showed that there is real good under their fantastic exteriors, if it can just be aroused to some better purpose than the pursuit of LSD."

NEW YORK TIMES EDITORIAL, AUGUST 18, 1969

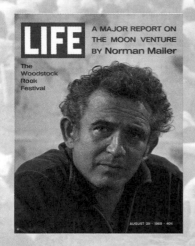

LIFE
The Woodstock Rock Festival

A MAJOR REPORT ON THE MOON VENTURE BY Norman Mailer

AUGUST 29 · 1969 · 40¢

"It was a real city, with life and death and babies—two were born during the gathering—and all the urban problems of water supply, food, sanitation, and health. Drugs too, certainly, because so many of its inhabitants belong to the drug culture. Counting on only 50,000 customers a day, the organizers had set up a fragile, unauthoritarian system to deal with them. Overrun, strained to its limits, the system somehow, amazingly, didn't break. For three days nearly half a million people lived elbow to elbow in the most exposed, crowded, rain-drenched, uncomfortable kind of community, and there wasn't so much as a fist fight. The promoters, however, discovered that city fathers always lose money—in this case, an estimated $2 million, which they hope to recoup on a film about the festival." *LIFE, AUGUST 29, 1969*

"Woodstock as an event in US social history was surely less cosmic than it looked to beat poet Allen Ginsberg (who called it 'a major planetary event') and less revolutionary than it seemed to the Yippies' Abbie Hoffman (who saw it as 'the birth of the Woodstock Nation and the death of the American dinosaur'). Yet adult America correctly saw something gently, amiably, and profoundly subversive in it all. Sociologists pondered it. Editorial writers puzzled over it. The New York Times one morning called it 'a nightmare of mud and stagnation,' slept on that judgment overnight, then decided next day that it had been something like 'the Tulipmania or the Children's Crusade ... essentially a phenomenon of innocence.' Pundit Max Lerner commended it to historians as an event in 'a cultural, not a political, revolution'—but a revolution nonetheless.... It would certainly be written large on maps of hip America. The festival was a disappointment to political activists, who remembered the confrontations on the steps of the Pentagon in 1967, in the streets of Chicago in 1968 and around People's Park in Berkeley this year. Woodstock belonged instead in another, parallel tradition born in San Francisco and the Monterey Pop Festival of 1967—the first of the great tribal feasts celebrating the culture of rock, drugs, and love as an end in itself. Woodstock marked a turning inward not unlike the impulse that produced the beat generation of the Eisenhower '50s—a retreat by the young from politics into the sanctuary of their youth and their senses." *NEWSWEEK, AUGUST 25, 1969*

WOODSTOCK MUSIC & ART FAIR
AN AQUARIAN EXPOSITION
1969
PRESS
Name Fred Stabl art
Affiliation

Opposite: Ordinary American kids (as opposed to fully commited members of the counterculture) experimenting with drugs was the main concern, as the mainstream press took stock after the events of August 15–18, 1969.

UNDERGROUND PRESS

The so-called "underground press" was a key element in the counterculture of the 1960s, with independently published and distributed newspapers and magazines that reflected the politics and lifestyle of the radical youth. Prominent among them was *The Village Voice*, the free New York weekly that had been running since 1955 (and still publishes), the *East Village Other*, launched in 1965—which the *New York Times* described as "so countercultural that it made *The Village Voice* look like a church circular" — and out on the West Coast, the San Francisco-based *Rolling Stone*, a powerful alternative voice before it evolved into the slick glossy that we know today. Significantly, in their post-Woodstock reports, all emphasized the sociopolitical implications of the festival over and above the impact of the actual music.

"Now if you can imagine a hip version of Jones Beach transported to a war zone in Vietnam during the monsoon maybe you'll catch a glimpse of what White Lake looked like a day after the long-haired troops occupied the area.... Perhaps most amazing was the physical stamina, tolerance, and good nature of a basically indoor, urban group of people caught in wretched outdoor conditions. It showed more dramatically than any planned demonstration could have that hip kids are fundamentally different from the beer-drinking, fist-fighting Fort Lauderdale crowds of yesteryear." *VILLAGE VOICE, AUGUST 21, 1969*

"... All I can say is that this has been the highest trip ever. We're too high and in such a different place. There are many, many stories still in all of us, but you'll just have to wait for them. Too hard to sort out and describe right now. We all want all our families and friends to be here and secretly hoped every head in the world would join us. The regular music thing is nice, but straight. The Hog Farm is just too much. We are home and at peace with each other and ourselves. I think you will find we have changed and grown. I don't want to leave, but I guess we must. The only thing is, how can I come back and do the old things? This is how we should live. Can we? ----- Peace – John." *EAST VILLAGE OTHER, AUGUST 20, 1969*

"No one in this century had ever seen a 'society' so free of repression. Everyone swam nude in the lake, balling was easier than getting breakfast, and the 'pigs' just smiled and passed out the oats. For people who had never glimpsed the intense communitarian closeness of a militant struggle—People's Park or Paris in the month of May or Cuba—Woodstock must always be their model of how good we will all feel after the revolution." *ROLLING STONE*, SEPTEMBER 20, 1969

THE WOODSTOCK
MOVIE

Independent filmmaker Michael Wadleigh, and his production partner Bob Maurice, had negotiated a deal with Woodstock Ventures in August 1969 to film the festival at their own expense and then try to get the movie placed with a distributor. Eventually Warner Bros. took up the film, paying Woodstock Ventures $100,000 advance against a royalty on the film and album, with Wadleigh-Maurice Productions receiving $90,000 for distribution rights. The film deal was agreed by Warner Bros. producer John Calley via Freddy Weintraub, a company vice-president (contrary to later claims by Ahmet Ertegun that it came along with the album rights he'd negotiated for

Atlantic Records, by then part of Warners). The movie *Woodstock: Three Days of Peace and Music* was a box-office blockbuster when released in 1970, making the Woodstock festival an international phenomenon. By 1999, the film had earned more than $100 million, and the soundtrack album a similar amount. It won an Academy Award for Best Documentary Feature.

"I originally bought that [album rights] because I thought a lot of our artists were gonna be on it. But, you know, I bought the rights for the whole thing. But I didn't have those artists. But after it happened, they all wanted to be on the record.

So we got permission from all the companies to use their artists. It was a great record. And do you know something? Paul Marshall [Woodstock Ventures' attorney] who did the deal, sold me the rights for $75,000. The right to record the concert. And I thought I was gonna get three or four—three live albums ... with different artists.

As it turned out, I think that Crosby, Stills & Nash were the only artists we had on the show."

AHMET ERTEGUN, ATLANTIC RECORDS CEO

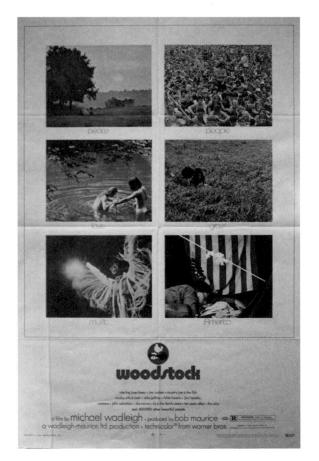

Right: Atlantic Records boss Ahmet Ertegun, who clinched the Woodstock record deal.

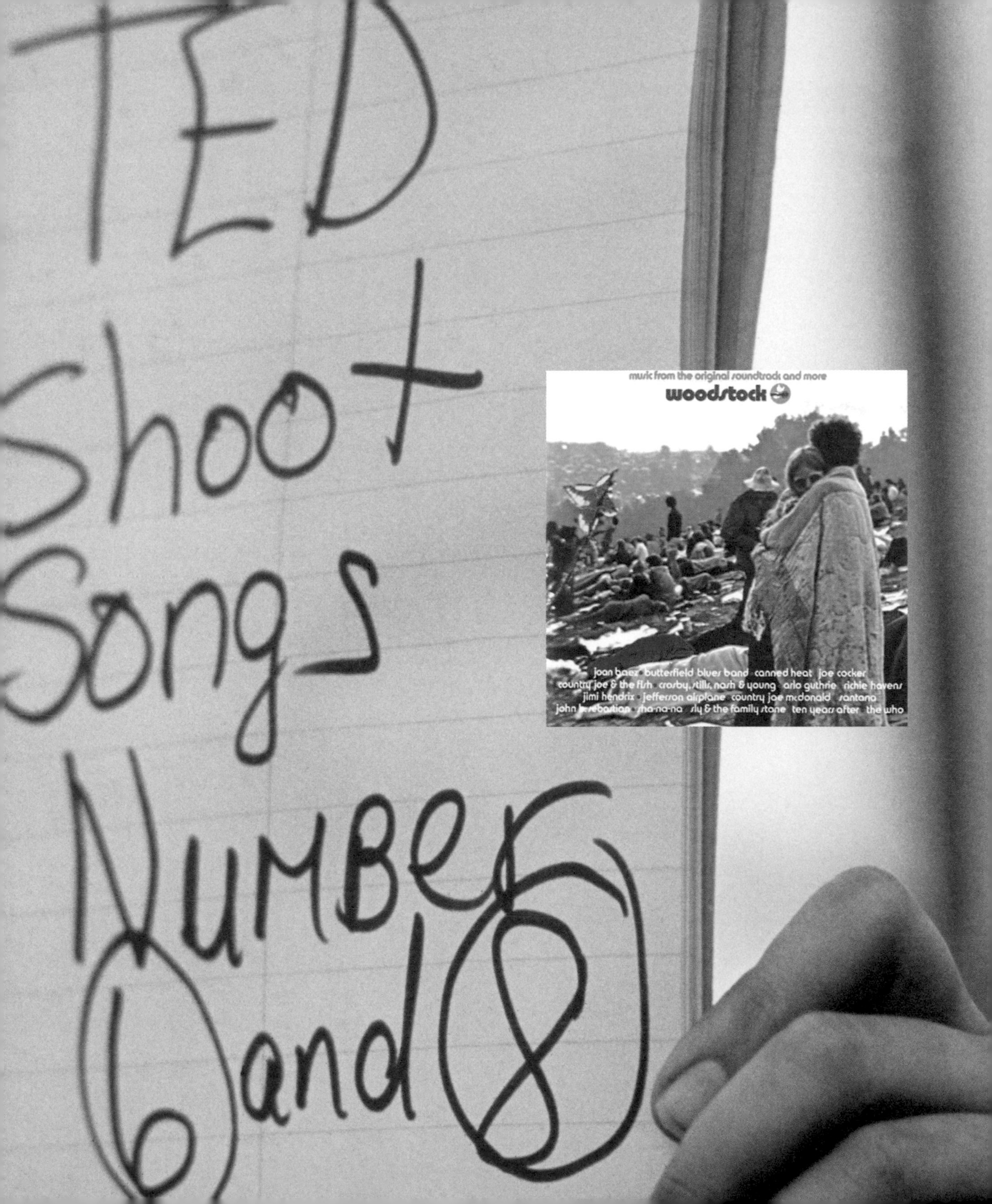

TED
Shoot
Songs
Number
6 and 8

music from the original soundtrack and more
woodstock

joan baez · butterfield blues band · canned heat · joe cocker
country joe & the fish · crosby, stills, nash & young · arlo guthrie · richie havens
jimi hendrix · jefferson airplane · country joe mcdonald · santana
john b sebastian · sha-na-na · sly & the family stone · ten years after · the who

"At that time, Freddie Weintraub was the guy. He was one of the vice presidents [of Warner Bros.] under Ted Ashley, and he decided that night. It was a Friday night. We were on the stage, and we didn't know. Wadleigh, myself, Thelma Schoonmaker, and all those wonderful cinematographers, we simply didn't know what was going to happen.

Michael Wadleigh and I had talked a year before about doing a rock 'n' roll revival show. At that time, people like Chuck Berry and Fats Domino and Little Richard were déclassé. Nobody wanted to do it. It was the time of Vanilla Fudge and the songs went on for twenty minutes, and also great stuff—The Doors, The Beatles, and, of course, The Stones. So, you know, the Fifties was something nobody dealt with. We said, 'Why don't we just get these guys, they're still around, and we'll do a show.'

And then he [Wadleigh] said, 'Listen, there's going to be this rock 'n' roll show apparently, up at a place called Woodstock, and I think maybe we should do it as a test.'

So he went up there with the cameramen. And after four days, we called him, and when he could get to a phone, he said, 'It's more than a test I'm afraid. This is going to be different.'

And by the time we got up there, we were stuck on the stage on that Friday night. We didn't know what was going to happen. I know we didn't know who was coming out. And when I say stuck on the stage, we were on the lip of the stage. And we were just photographing and working. We couldn't even get to the back of the [crowd], there were 500,000 people. We couldn't get food. There was no way you could move. You could maybe move down below the stage or come back up on the stage, that was it. You'd never make it.

And there were a number of people there at that time circling around, trying to buy the rights. And somehow, between Bob Maurice, who was the producer, and Mike Wadleigh, they worked out a deal with Freddie Weintraub, who used to run the Bitter End. He understood rock 'n' roll and the new music that was being played in the Village. And, he was the vice president.

And so next thing you know, I guess, he may have convinced them that this is the kind of picture that Warner Bros. should have. Warner Bros. in the Seventies was a very important studio. I mean … they were remarkable movies they made … and distributed. In any event, I stayed on as one of the editors, but I did not finish as one of the editors. It was finished by Thelma and Michael." MARTIN SCORSESE

"I was a freelance for Columbia Records in NYC, and had heard about this festival that was supposed to take place. When I came on to the site, it was just grass, fields, and I just happened to see somebody that I had worked with in advertising, Larry Johnson—L. A. Johnson.... And he said, 'We're trying to get a film together.'... It wasn't clear that they were going to be able to sign a deal ... and he said, 'What are you doin'?... We need a stills photographer for the film, but we can't pay any money up front, will you do it?' And I said the magic words, figuring they couldn't pay me up front, I said, 'Okay, but I own the photographs.'... As they weren't paying me, I said, 'I keep the negatives,' and he said, 'Okay.'

I went home and came back with all my equipment and joined the crew that was there. They had about seventeen primarily documentary filmmakers shooting—cameramen—and I joined the crew, and they took us to a bungalow colony nearby, and that was where we were supposed to sleep. And then drove us over to the site. We had a trailer there, and that was our base at the festival. As it turns out, none of us got back to the bungalow colony.... Everybody ended up just staying right there all the time. I slept about forty-five minutes for four or five days, and the forty-five minutes' sleep I had was on the stage, under the piano cover during Blood, Sweat & Tears.

There were teams of people that were set up by Mike Wadleigh, the director. He'd done a film on Aretha Franklin ... and he'd been in France in 1968 during the student uprising there ... but he didn't know too much about the contemporary acts that were supposed to appear. So as I worked in the record business, the music business, I sat with him and the crews and we went through every act. I described the act, how many people were in the act, what kind of music they played, whether they moved around a lot, who was the featured performer. So I briefed him on the acts, and the other cameramen as well. And he set up teams ... back in those days, the only way you could have synch sound was to be connected, literally connected with a wire, to the camera for the mic to be synched, and there was no in-camera sound, it was all external. So some of the cameramen had a sound person with them, who would carry a Nagra tape recorder and a mic, and they were synched into the camera. Some cameramen were, in Erich von Stroheim terms, without sound ... just shooting without any audio.

So I kind of, somehow, got attached to David Myers. He was like the old man on the crew, most of them were about my age, 25, 26, 27—David Myers was in his fifties I think, at the time. Most of the cameramen were from New York, he was from San Francisco. Wadleigh went to New York University, he knew Scorsese from NYU. Scorsese was a second director that Mike had brought up from New York with him, and Thelma Schoonmaker was Mike Wadleigh's editor.... That was the kind of overview of the crew.

I worked with him and the crew through the first rough cut, which was a five-hour rough cut.... They had a huge editing operation going on. Thelma Schoonmaker of course was the head of editing, but there were an awful lot of assistant editors.... Wadleigh came out of NYU, and Scorsese was an adjunct professor at NYU, so there were a lot of connections to the documentary filmmaking crowd in New York, and they drew a lot on interns from that pool of people." BARRY LEVINE, MOVIE STILLS PHOTOGRAPHER

Opposite: Movie director Michael Wadleigh flanked by the film's primary editors, Thelma Schoonmaker and Martin Scorsese. Right: Michael Wadleigh.

"I was a kid, and it was my first job in New York. I received a call from Warner Bros asking me if I wanted work. Well you could well imagine my shock. I was one of the kids who was hired for Woodstock! It was all shot in 16mm and lots and lots of cameras…. I was only there a day at Woodstock, then I came back to work on the film. It was such a mess there, I actually didn't stay.

They had about twenty cameras, and they had a master track, like an old-fashioned two-inch recording track. So that track was transferred to the film track. If you had a performance, say by Crosby, Stills, Nash & Young, you would have all the different cameras that were shooting, and you would have to synch them up to this master track. Now what was so awkward about it at the time—and how technologically backward things were—there was no way to do it except by the mouth movement, synching it literally to the mouth movement.

I, as an assistant editor, would have to synch it by eye, because it was so chaotic at Woodstock that they didn't have time to do things like a clapboard … and imagine there's twenty cameras all over the place, where do you put the clapboard?—there isn't any place to put the clapboard. It was all done in this kind of fashion, and it was quite a puzzle to put together. So I must have spent, I don't know how many weeks or days, just trying to synch up one performance.

And what was to be great fun, they would have three shifts. They had a daytime shift that I was fortunate enough to be on, then they had the night-time shift…. I would work from like nine till six, then they'd have a night shift that would come on and they'd be a bunch of other kids like myself. We were all in this big, big loft right on Broadway, right near the Lincoln Center—it was upstairs, I think it had been a dance studio. It was Broadway and 62nd Street or something like that, and they had all these editing machines piled into this loft. And we'd all be sitting there with these machines with earphones, and there were really many, many people there…. I can't remember if we were twenty on each shift, or thirty on each shift. And there was the graveyard shift, those people would come on at two in the morning to eight a.m.

But the fun part was that at the end of the day for the daytime shift, they would set up projectors so we could screen everything to see what it looked like. So if you can imagine there were twenty cameras that had been shooting, and they put 16mm projectors in the back of this big loft, and they would then begin projecting everything that had been synched up. So it was really virtually seeing a light show, because you'd have Camera One that would start with some sound, and then Camera Two would come in, and then there'd be Camera Three…. It was a big, big wall, and that was just an incredible fun part of it … it was basically a party, like a continuation of Woodstock, but much more fun because we were in there doing it.

And then of course Scorsese would come in, and Thelma [Schoonmaker] who happened to live next door to me in New York … she was the editor, and I was a bit in awe of her, but she was my neighbor."

SUSAN STEINBERG, ASSISTANT EDITOR ON THE MOVIE

"I couldn't believe what I was getting myself into. And then I found the truck, which was basically the back of a tractor trailer. We had one tiny little portion of it, in which was crammed a twelve-channel console, two Shure mixers, and two eight-track machines, one stacked up in an orange crate. It was very primitive to say the least....
Essentially we slept on the floor of the tractor trailer. And we did it in shifts. There were two of us doing it, and if I was sleeping the other guy would be running the board, but essentially we were up pretty much for three days....
As far as the wind thing was concerned, we just put tons of foam where we could on the microphones and hoped for the best. Rain, hey, it's gonna rain, there's nothing you can do, you just run for cover. That's what this covering was supposed to be on top of the stage. Of course the wind ripped it right off.
We just soldiered on, kept rolling tape. The main thing was to keep rolling the damn tape. If you didn't roll the tape, and even maybe there was a problem with the microphone, maybe there was a short, or distortion or whatever. You just deal with it. You just keep plowing on and roll that damn tape. And the fact of the matter is, that there are so many wonderful performances that have never seen the light of day. Who knows, one of these days that might actually occur."

EDDIE KRAMER, RECORDING ENGINEER

THE MONEY TRAIL

While Woodstock lived up to its billing as "3 Days of Peace & Music," it wasn't all love and harmony. Money was involved too—lots of it. In the aftermath of the festival, it wasn't always clear exactly how much everything had cost and how much Woodstock Ventures Inc. had made, but it soon became certain that the festival was a big money loser. Within days of the festival's end, the young promoters of Woodstock Ventures were acknowledging losses of well over $1 million.

Determined to make good on all debts, John Roberts took out more than $1 million in loans against his personal assets (he was heir to a fortune from the company that made Polident, a denture adhesive) and also used advance money from Warner Bros./Atlantic Records for the film and album rights. A year after the festival, partner Joel Rosenman told the *New York Times* Woodstock Ventures was still $1.2 million in debt. Rosenman and Roberts counted on royalties for the movie, albums, and licensing of the Woodstock trademark for merchandise to get them to the break-even point.

The royalty rates paid to Woodstock Ventures for the movie and albums were small—ten percent of net for the film and 0.5 percent of net for the albums, according to Roberts. The Warner Bros. 7 Arts corporation had secured rights to the albums through the wily Ahmet Ertegun, CEO of its Atlantic Records division, for an advance payment of $75,000 against royalties; Warner Bros. also acquired the film rights for a mere $25,000 against future royalties. Filmmakers Michael Wadleigh and Bob Maurice were paid a $90,000 advance for distribution rights by Warner Bros. Years later, Roberts admitted he had had first right of refusal on those film distribution rights (and a much larger share in future royalties) but turned them down because he was facing a rising tide of debt in the days before the festival. "In the context of so many bad decisions that summer," he later said, "this one looms large."

Nevertheless, thanks to the extraordinary popularity of the film and albums, Woodstock Ventures finally broke even in 1980. At that point, the film of Woodstock had grossed more than $50 million. In 1999, Roberts stated that the film had amassed gross receipts of more than $100 million and that the soundtrack album had sold more than six million units, grossing more than $100 million as well.

Culled from various news sources (*Variety*, the *New York Times*, *Rolling Stone*, *Billboard*), here are some of the key numbers in the Woodstock ledger.

Casual Contract Blank
AMERICAN FEDERATION OF MUSICIANS

INITIAL PROFIT AND LOSS ACCOUNTING (AS OF SEPTEMBER 1969)
Revenues (mostly advance ticket sales): $1.4 million ✪ Expenses: $2.7 million ✪ Initial losses: $1.3 million

ADVANCE TICKET PRICES
One day: $7 ✪ Two days: $13 ✪ Three days: $18

BREAKDOWN OF VARIOUS ANNOUNCED EXPENSES
Talent fees: $172,000 approx. (see breakdown below) ✪ Advertising: $200,000 ✪ Rent for Yasgur's Farm: $50,000
✪ Lease on additional Bethel acreage: $5,000 ✪ Insurance against damage to the Bethel area: $65,000
✪ Telephone lines for Wallkill site: $18,000 ✪ Telephone lines for Bethel site: $20,000
✪ Yippie headquarters: $10,000 ✪ Hog Farm's chartered airplane: $16,000
✪ Sound and stage lighting: $200,000 ✪ Garbage men for post-festival cleanup: $20,000
✪ 25% refunds to 4,062 ticket claimants: $25,000
✪ Emergency expenses: helicopter rentals, medical supplies, food: $600,000
✪ Miscellaneous production costs, including salaries for 750–1,000 workers: $1.3 million
✪ (The $1.3 million includes $500,000 in alleged duplicated costs due to the move from Wallkill)

AFTER THE CONCERT—BUYOUT OF WOODSTOCK VENTURES INC. SHARES
Michael Lang was paid $31,750 ✪ Artie Kornfeld was paid $31,750

TALENT FEES
Jimi Hendrix: $18,000 (+ $12,000 for film appearance) ✪ Blood, Sweat & Tears: $15,000 ✪ The Who: $11,200
✪ Joan Baez: $10,000 ✪ Creedence Clearwater Revival: $10,000 ✪ The Band: $7,500 ✪ Janis Joplin: $7,500
✪ Jefferson Airplane: $10,000 ✪ Paul Butterfield Blues Band + Bert Sommer: $7,500 ✪ Sly & the Family Stone:
$7,000 ✪ Canned Heat: $10,000 ✪ Richie Havens: $6,000 ✪ Arlo Guthrie: $5,000 ✪ CSN&Y: $5,000 ✪ Ravi Shankar:
$4,500 ✪ Johnny Winter: $3,750 ✪ Ten Years After: $3,250 ✪ Country Joe & the Fish: $2,500
✪ Grateful Dead: $2,250 ✪ Santana: $2,250 ✪ The Incredible String Band: $2,250 ✪ Mountain: $2,000
($5,000 acc. to Leslie West in 1989) ✪ Tim Hardin: $2,000 ✪ Joe Cocker: $1,375 ✪ Sweetwater: $1,250
✪ John Sebastian: $1,000 ✪ Melanie: $750 ✪ Sha Na Na: $700 ✪ Keef Hartley: $500 ✪ Quill: $375

WOODSTOCK MUSIC and ART FAIR
SATURDAY
AUGUST 16, 1969
10:00 A. M.
$7.00 Good For One Admission Only
B 03931
NO REFUNDS GLOBE TICKET COMPANY

NO REFUNDS FOR ANY REASON INCLUDING LOST OR STOLEN TICKETS.
The management reserves the right without notice to make changes or substitutions in the program. Commercial still photographs, motion picture film and sound recording rights with respect to Woodstock Music and Art Fair are expressly reserved. Any commercial use of photographs, film and/or sound recordings without the express written consent of the management is strictly prohibited. No alcoholic beverages or pets permitted on the premises. Positively no refunds weather permitting. SOLD AT DISCOUNT $6.50
The acceptance or use of this ticket shall release the management and all others, having any connection with the program or premises, from any liability for injury, damages or loss to person or property, including motor vehicles, and authorizes the management to reproduce or otherwise record and use the holder's name, likeness, voice and actions for all purposes.
THIS TICKET IS A REVOCABLE LICENSE AND ANY VIOLATION OF THE FOREGOING WILL BE A CAUSE FOR REFUSAL OF ADMISSION OR REMOVAL FROM THE PREMISES.

ISLE OF WIGHT

Frequently cited as "Britain's Woodstock," and held just two weeks later, at the end of August, the significance of the second Isle of Wight Festival (August 29–31, 1969) was largely due to the presence of one man—Bob Dylan. Having not played Woodstock itself, the much-publicized three-day event off the south coast of England was Dylan's first major appearance since his motorcycle accident three years earlier.

The 1968 Isle of Wight Festival, headlined by Jefferson Airplane, had been a much more low-key affair that drew a modest crowd of around 10,000, but it was successful enough for entrepreneurial brothers Ray, Ron, and Bill Foulk, and rock promoter Ricki Farr to plan something bigger for '69. An already ambitious lineup of acts that included The Who, Joe Cocker, and Richie Havens was eclipsed when the brothers signed Dylan for £35,000 ($50,000)—significantly more, it has been suggested, than he was offered for Woodstock.

After a Friday evening warm-up with just four acts, fans began to gather in their thousands on the Saturday, traveling from all corners of Britain to make the last leg of the journey by hovercraft from Portsmouth. Others chose more individual modes of water transport, from glitzy speedboats to simple canoes, and by midday the twenty-acre site outside the village of Wootton was already packed. And as at Bethel, the site was surrounded by a growing mass of tents—one of these spontaneous shanty towns even calling itself Desolation Row, after the Dylan song.

The Saturday lineup climaxed with the Moody Blues in the early hours of Sunday morning, and by the afternoon it was clear that this was the biggest gathering a UK rock concert had ever seen. Nearly a quarter of a million fans had arrived with seemingly one thought—to see Bob Dylan. The anticipation became palpable as celebrities arrived, from various Beatles and Stones to actors like Jane Fonda and Terence Stamp, they and their hangers-on fighting for position with reporters and photographers in the front-of-stage press and VIP enclosure.

At 10:20 p.m. The Band went onstage and played a dynamic forty-five-minute set, before Dylan, in a white suit that looked too big for him, finally took the stage. An hour later, after a two-song encore, it was all over. The man the British tabloid press hailed as some sort of messiah delivered a sensational set, and like all good showmen left the crowd howling for more. There was none of the rumored superstar jams, no words of wisdom to the faithful, just Bob doing his job. As the audience vainly chanted for their hero to return, MC Ricki Farr took the stage:

"He's gone ... he's gone. He came here to do what he had to do, he did it for you, and now he's gone. Really, there is no more."

Although the following year's Isle of Wight Festival was an even bigger (and certainly more fraught) affair, including Woodstock veterans Joan Baez, Ten Years After, Richie Havens, Sly & the Family Stone, John Sebastian, The Who, Melanie, and Jimi Hendrix, it was the 1969 "Dylan" Isle of Wight, that, like Woodstock itself, truly captured the spirit of the times as the 1960s drew to a close.

Opposite: Dylan on stage at the Isle of Wight Festival. Overleaf: Celebrities in the crowd included film director Roger Vadim and wife Jane Fonda (inset), actor Terence Stamp (inset), and Beatles George Harrison, John Lennon, and Ringo Starr (main picture).

"A sunset glorious enough to delight Turner. One of those long, endless skies streaked with lines of pink cloud, emerald light behind them, the on-coming darkness pouring through it, changing the upper greens to blue, to cobalt, to indigo, and the helicopters fluttering their red and amber guide lights overhead. It was as if Apollo had noticed us and, in passing, given the show a nod." CHRISTOPHER LOGUE, POET

ALTAMONT

Just as Woodstock was regarded as the high point of the rock-driven counterculture, so Altamont, less than four months later, was seen as its nadir. Organized and headlined by The Rolling Stones, the festival will forever be remembered for one incident, when a fan was fatally stabbed a few feet from the stage as Mick Jagger and the band were in the middle of their set.

The concert, originally planned to take place in San Francisco's Golden Gate Park, was moved north to the Sears Point Raceway, then at very short notice—only two days before the event—moved again to the then-disused Altamont Speedway, also in northern California. As a result the one-day festival suffered various problems, including a severe lack of toilet facilities, medical tents, and proper security.

The issue of security was central to the chaos that unfolded on the day of the festival—December 6, 1969. On the apparent recommendation of the Grateful Dead, The Stones seemingly hired members of the Hell's Angels motorcycle club to police the event, though the band later denied this, claiming they paid the bikers (in beer!) just to protect their equipment and keep fans off the four-foot high stage. Whatever the truth, the somewhat naïve idea that the Angels could keep order—an assumption based on their previous peaceful role at some Dead concerts, and the harmless presence of British bikers at The Stones' Hyde Park gig in London earlier in the year—was soon proved tragically wrong.

As the concert (also featuring Santana, Jefferson Airplane, The Flying Burrito Brothers, Crosby, Stills, Nash & Young, and the Grateful Dead) progressed, the mood among the audience of 300,000 got uglier, with the Hell's Angels, fueled by alcohol, becoming increasingly agitated and

violent. The Angels came armed with sawn-off pool cues to use as weapons to control the crowd, and in some instances aimed their bikes at troublemakers full-throttle, causing serious injuries. The violence even spilled on to the stage, with Jefferson Airplane's Marty Balin knocked unconscious mid-set after an argument with a drunken biker. Following the Balin incident, the Grateful Dead refused to play, and left the festival altogether.

But the full horror of Altamont culminated in the killing of an eighteen-year-old black teenager, Meredith Hunter, after an altercation with some of the Angels. The Rolling Stones were ending "Under My Thumb" when Hunter—clearly visible in the documentary film featuring the concert, *Gimme Shelter*—pulled out a long-barreled revolver and moved toward the stage. He was set upon by Hell's Angels, one of whom, Alan Passaro, pushed the gun away while stabbing the youth in the back. Hunter was stabbed five times in all and kicked to death, as The Stones, unaware that the fight had resulted in a fatality, decided to play on rather than provoke a possible riot. In 1972 a jury acquitted Passaro of murder, concluding he acted in self-defense as Hunter—allegedly under the influence of drugs—had drawn his handgun first. There were three other fatalities at Altamont, two caused by a car running over sleeping fans, and one by a drowning in an irrigation canal.

Coming at the very end of the 1960s, the catastrophe of Altamont was perceived as symbolic of the ending of an era, the era—for want of a better cliché—of "peace and love," which had found its most celebrated expression only a few months earlier at Woodstock.

> "Altamont became, whether fairly or not, a symbol for the end of the Woodstock Nation."
>
> MARK HAMILTON LYTLE, AUTHOR

Opposite: Hell's Angels attacking a man with sawn-off pool cues.
Left: Stones' tour manager Sam Cutler (left) and Michael Lang, appealing for calm at Altamont.

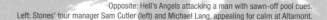

"The violence just in front of the stage was incredible. Looking back, I don't think it was a good idea to have Hell's Angels there. But we had them at the suggestion of the Grateful Dead. The trouble is it's a problem for us either way. If you don't have them to work for you as stewards, they come anyway and cause trouble."

KEITH RICHARDS, THE ROLLING STONES

Left: The Rolling Stones at Altamont (l to r) Keith Richards and (with their backs to the camera) Mick Taylor and Mick Jagger, at the moment Meredith Hunter was stabbed just feet from the stage.

259

SUMMERFEST TO GLASTONBURY

Over the forty years since Woodstock, big outdoor rock festivals have continued to be a central feature of youth culture in the US, Europe, and elsewhere. Not identified with a specific counterculture in most cases, they nevertheless, share the spirit of Woodstock in the coming together of large numbers of young people to listen to their own kind of music, in a common environment away from the home, college, or workplace.

The longest-running US event—which actually predates Woodstock, having started in 1968—is the Summerfest (also known as "The Big Gig"), in Milwaukee, Wisconsin. Held in Henry Maier Park, running for eleven days, and attracting up to a million people every year, it has been listed in *Guinness World Records* as the world's biggest music festival. Since the mid-1970s the event has always been staged from the end of June to the July 4 holiday, and the 2008 festival featured no fewer than sixty musical acts on twelve stages.

Doubling as a film and music festival, South By Southwest (SXSW), held in Austin, Texas, has become a music-industry showcase for new acts since its inception in 1987, with record-company talent spotters checking out over 500 hopefuls over four days every March. SXSW has inspired similar festivals, including North by Northeast (NXNE) in Toronto, Canada—a three-day live music festival and music conference held annually during the second weekend of June. On the East Coast, the largest event of recent years has been the HFStival. Run by radio station WHFS since 1990, and a July 4 holiday event, it moved from Washington, D.C. to Baltimore after the station relocated in 2005, where it has been held every May.

A springboard for the grunge-rock movement of the early 1990s, Lollapalooza began as a touring festival in 1991. It was founded by Perry Farrell, singer with Jane's Addiction, and, with its initial emphasis on alternative rock, punk, and hip-hop acts, it was instrumental in popularizing such bands as Nine Inch Nails, The Smashing Pumpkins, and Hole. Taking in a wider range of music styles each year, in 2005 it established itself as a non-touring, two-day event in Grant Park on the Chicago lakefront, with over seventy acts playing on five stages. It expanded to three days the following year, and now has a contract with the Chicago authorities that means it will be staged every August until at least 2011.

Outside tiny Manchester, Tennessee, on 700 acres in the countryside, the four-day Bonnaroo festival has been drawing festival crowds of around 80,000 annually since its debut in 2002. Held each June, the festival has featured a wide range of big-name rock acts (The Police, Pearl Jam, Neil Young, Radiohead), premier bluegrassers, and jam bands.

Another highly regarded outdoor event of recent years is the Coachella Valley Music and Arts Festival, held for three days in late April to early May in Indio, California. Catering largely for indie-oriented rock and dance music fans, it has grown in both size and reputation since it was first staged in 1999. It features six stages in its spectacular setting in the Colorado desert, where the temperature regularly rises to over a hundred degrees Fahrenheit then drops drastically after sunset.

Outside the US, rock festivals have an even longer history, with the UK's Reading Festival having its origins in the National Jazz Festival in 1961, and evolving into an all-rock event by the middle of the 1960s. It continues today as part of the two-pronged Carling Weekend, held in Reading (just west of London) and the northern city of Leeds. The festivals are held simultaneously over the national holiday weekend at the end of August and share basically the same bill of performers. Another double promotion of this kind, featuring a shared roster of artists, is the Oxegen/T in the Park festival. Running for three days over the second weekend in July, Oxegen is held in County Kildare, Ireland, and T in the Park in Kinross, Scotland.

The first UK festival to be held simultaneously on two sites in this way—and now one of the country's biggest—was the now annual V Festival, so called because it is organized by Richard Branson's Virgin commercial empire. Founded in 1996, it is now held in the London suburban town of Chelmsford, and South Staffordshire in the English Midlands, for two days over the third weekend of August. The overtly corporate nature of "V" sponsorship has given the festival a reputation for being more commercial than its UK rivals, although that has often meant better organization and avoidance of the crowd trouble that has frequently plagued other gatherings.

Elsewhere in Europe, one of the biggest events is the Roskilde Festival in Denmark, founded in 1971 by a group of high-school students. In 1972, it was taken over by the Roskilde Foundation, which has since run the festival as a nonprofit organization for "development and support of music, culture, and humanism." Opening on the last Sunday in June, the four-day extravaganza—180 bands were booked in 2007—attracts over 100,000 people each year. And the annual Rock Werchter in the Belgian village of Werchter, held over four days at the end of June, regularly has attendances of over 200,000 for a cutting-edge mix of alternative rock and pop.

Two events dominate the festival scene further east in Europe. The EXIT Festival—founded by college students in 2000, and held in the ancient Petrovaradin Fortress in Novi Sad, Serbia—draws over 100,000 to its four-day run every July. Meanwhile, the enormous Sziget Festival, staged for a week each August in Budapest, boasts more than 1,000 rock, pop, and alternative performances every year. The crowd numbers are of almost Woodstock proportions, with attendances peaking at 385,000 in recent years.

Further afield, the Big Day Out, which began in 1992, is an annual summer rock festival that tours Australia and New Zealand during the early weeks of each year. Now a major rock event in the Australasian music calendar, the 2009 lineup was headlined by Neil Young and the Arctic Monkeys.

But the non-US event that most directly evolved from the phenomenon of Woodstock is the Glastonbury Festival, held annually at the end of June since 1970, in England's rural West Country. Very much in the countercultural peace and love tradition of Woodstock, the first Glastonbury weekend (then called the Pilton Festival) attracted just 1,500 fans. Now 150–200,000 is the norm, for what has become the biggest rock festival in western Europe—and a far more corporate, commercially run enterprise than its idealistic original.

The Pilton event featured only UK acts, but the first "official" Glastonbury that carried that name, in 1971, included much bigger names (headlined by David Bowie) and two singers who had performed at Woodstock—Joan Baez and Melanie.

Over the subsequent years, a handful of artists who had played at Max Yasgur's farm in 1969 did "Glasto," including Melanie and Joan Baez in the early 1980s, Joe Cocker in 1985, and more recently The Who in 2007 and Joan Baez again in 2008. But it was the Glastonbury of the 1970s that, for most of the decade, carried on the Woodstock tradition of a music festival driven by a sense of community and countercultural values, rather than purely commercial considerations.

> **"After Woodstock, I became the festival queen—often called "the icon of Woodstock"—so wherever there was a festival, I got booked. And I think of all of them, Glastonbury was the closest, if inherited that spirit of Woodstock. That had a great feel, how people gathered to share a kindred spirit, and a support for humanity."** MELANIE

Below: Rapper Jay-Z at Glastonbury 2008. Opposite: Peace and love continued at the second Glastonbury Festival, 1971.

Since 1969, there have been numerous commemorations of Woodstock. At first they were informal affairs when fans gathered at the site near Bethel, but later they became large-scale commercial events that sought (unsuccessfully) to emulate the atmosphere and spirit of the original.

The first few years of the 1970s saw people making for the site on the three days of the anniversary, simply camping there in commemoration of the festival. Sadly Max Yasgur, whose heart trouble had grown worse since the events of 1969, passed away in 1973, the farm remaining in the hands of his widow, Miriam. Over the years increasing numbers of people would arrive August 15 through 17, but as she was increasingly unable to cope with the farm itself, Mimi (as Miriam was known) sold the property to Louis "Nicky" Nicadopolus and his girlfriend June Gelish in 1983.

Nicky and Gelish planned a concert on the site for the twentieth anniversary of Woodstock, but they could not get the necessary permits to stage the event, despite various arrangements having already been put in place. Then, just a day or so before the scheduled concerts, Nicky died. By this time 30,000 people had turned up for the event, and a spontaneous free festival took place over August 15, 16, and 17, even though it was midweek. A lineup of mainly lesser-known bands entertained the crowd over the three days, but at least two veterans of the original festival—Wavy Gravy and Melanie—made an appearance, as did Jimi Hendrix's father.

Above: Green Day at the 1994 Woodstock 25th anniversary festival. Below: Buildings on the Yasgur farm in 1999. Opposite: Flames and the aftermath, in the riot-hit 1999 Woodstock festival.

Before the 1989 gathering at the Woodstock site, there had been a tribute show at New York's Madison Square Garden in 1979 to mark the tenth anniversary. This featured a number of artists who had graced the stage at Bethel in '69, including Richie Havens, Country Joe & the Fish, Canned Heat, Paul Butterfield, and The Band's Rick Danko. Also that year, a commemorative "Woodstock in Europe" tour took place on the other side of the Atlantic, headlined by Joe Cocker.

The first official commemoration of the festival came in 1994, when Woodstock Ventures—which still comprised Lang, Roberts, and Rosenman—organized Woodstock '94 to mark the twenty-fifth anniversary. Billed as "2 more days of peace and music," and often referred to as Woodstock II, the poster for the event was a modified version of Arnold Skolnick's famous original, this time with two birds perched on the neck of the guitar. It was staged at one of the sites that had turned them down in 1969, the Winston farm in Saugerties, ten miles outside Woodstock itself. Having learned from past mistakes, the 1994 event was organized more professionally than the original at Bethel. Permits from the authorities were cleared months in advance, ticket sales were handled by an experienced agency, Ticketmaster, and food and other concessions involved corporate sponsorship from major companies.

Woodstock Ventures had acquired a new partner, John Scher of the PolyGram record company, and his influence was reflected in the choice of acts that celebrated the sounds of Woodstock '69, which included a cross-section of the music that had attracted young people over the quarter of a century since. The likes of Bob Dylan (whose performance was one of the highlights of the festival), Joe Cocker, Country Joe, and Santana appeared alongside more contemporary names, including Nine Inch Nails, Metallica, Sheryl Crow, Red Hot Chili Peppers, Salt-N-Pepa, and Cypress Hill. The concerts were set for August 13 and 14, but an extra day, Friday August 12, was later added. Echoing the original Woodstock, on the Saturday afternoon rainstorms reduced the site to a quagmire, and the press renamed the festival "Mudstock." Crowd estimates ranged from 250,000 to 350,000 by the Saturday evening.

Woodstock III, planned for the thirtieth anniversary, was sited on an ex-US Air Force base at Rome in upstate New York. Michael Lang was still involved, along with John Scher and Ossie Kilkenny, an Irish accountant who looked after the affairs of (among others) U2, Van Morrison, and UK rock band Oasis.

More than 200,000 people attended the festival, which—like the 1994 event—featured a variety of styles from across the spectrum of rock and pop music. Among the star names appearing over the three days of July 23–25, 1999, were soul legend James Brown, singer-songwriter Elvis Costello, rapper Ice Cube, rock band Counting Crows, rap-metal star Kid Rock, nu-metal favorites Limp Bizkit, the heavy metal Megadeth, Canadian vocalist Alanis Morissette, country pioneer Willie Nelson, and soul/funk specialists Parliament/Funkadelic.

With three stages accommodating all these styles and more, confusion often arose among fans of particular genres, who tried to move between areas to follow their favorites. And, as more than one commentator observed, a lot of punk and grunge-influenced music had made pop seem a lot uglier and potentially violent since the halcyon days of 1969.

Things came to a head on the Sunday night, when rioting broke out among a minority of the audience. With gangs of youths fighting, setting light to concession stands, and several rapes reported, it looked as if the crowds seen dancing around the blazing fires were a portent of dark times as the end of the millennium approached. Much of it was broadcast live on MTV, and it was a far cry from the peaceful optimism Woodstock had represented at the end of the 1960s.

"'99 was very edgy. I was convinced to let the booking reflect the times, and the times were very edgy. And so the audience consequently was more of an MTV audience than a Woodstock audience, and I think that's what lent that edge to the whole thing. Most people had a great time, but there were those incidents that were not great and which we obviously regret having happened…. As I look back on it I think that the booking strategy was wrong in '99. We should have stayed more with the jam bands and more true to what Woodstock had been. In '94 that was accomplished." MICHAEL LANG

In Bethel itself, the site of the original festival was the scene of various reunions, revivals, and commemorations through the 1990s, although they were all a lot lower key than the two Woodstock Ventures events of 1994 and 1999.

A twenty-fifth anniversary festival was planned on behalf of the National Multiple Sclerosis Society that was to be held at the same time as Woodstock II in 1994. It was to be a large-scale charity affair, with 40,000 tickets selling at between $150 and $5,000, but promoter Sid Bernstein (who had famously booked The Beatles at Shea Stadium in 1965) had to cut it back to less than 10,000 tickets due to a strict mass-gathering permit law that had been passed in Bethel in the wake of the 1969 festival. Eventually the event was canceled altogether, but 12,000 people turned up anyway for what proved to be (like the 1989 gathering) a far more spontaneous happening in the spirit of Woodstock '69. Melanie, a veteran of 1969 and sometimes dubbed "the icon of Woodstock," recalled the atmosphere: "They had a ceremony with Indian—that is, Native American—rituals going on, to bless the field, and it was beautiful."

By that time the Yasgur farm, though not including the festival site itself, had become the property of Jeryl Abramson and Roy Howard, who hosted semi-informal reunions on their land for several years following.

In 1996, cable television pioneer and Sullivan County native, Alan Gerry, bought the festival site and nearly 2,000 acres around it, to develop into what would become the Bethel Woods Center for the Arts (which opened in 2006). But before work started on the project, he staged two anniversary events in the Woodstock field, in 1998 and 1999.

Billed as "A Day in the Garden," named for Joni Mitchell's reference to "the garden" in her song "Woodstock," the two events were very different in both scale and emphasis. The earlier, three-day festival featured a Woodstock reunion of sorts, with '69 veterans Pete Townshend, Melanie, Richie Havens, and Ten Years After taking part, plus Joni Mitchell herself. But it was the newer names, The Goo Goo Dolls, Third Eye Blind, Joan Osbourne, and Marcy Playground, that proved the bigger attraction for many in the estimated 30,000-plus crowd.

For the thirtieth Woodstock anniversary in 1999, A Day in the Garden was a much smaller, one-day event, drawing about 13,000 visitors, but it was certainly a truer reunion, with Woodstock alumni outnumbering the few contemporary acts. They included Country Joe, Melanie, Rick Danko and Garth Hudson of The Band, Mountain's Leslie West, Richie Havens, Arlo Guthrie, David Crosby, and Johnny Winter.

"At the beginning we had like 10,000, and then it dwindled down.... We were only really capable of handling about 5,000, after that it was too big for us. The gate crew were mostly my girlfriends—we had all our kids in the Little League together—they loved it. The local high school band, we'd give them a spot. We had two stages running, it was terrific, and attracting infants to octogenarians.... We had some great people here." JERYL ABRAMSON, YASGUR FARM

Opposite top: The 1999 "A Day in the Garden" event at Bethel.
Above right: David Crosby. Right: Melanie. Below: Richie Havens.

WOODSTOCK TODAY

Back in 1969 the town of Woodstock became famous around the world by default, having turned down the proposal to hold the Music and Art Fair that bore its name. But today it's a different story, and the small Ulster County community has fully embraced the hippie heritage that actually manifested itself forty-seven miles to the southwest in Bethel.

Today hippie-themed stores—"head shops" as they would have been called in the late 1960s—abound, selling all manner of merchandise including posters, T-shirts, books, even pot-smoking paraphernalia, celebrating both the festival of 1969 and the music and culture it came to represent. The brightly colored psychedelic-style signage everywhere suggests that the peace-and-love era never went away—not here, at least. There's a lot more to Woodstock, however, than just a tourist industry based on the "Aquarian Exposition" of '69, which many visitors still imagine took place there.

The town's longer-established heritage as a center for the arts is very much in evidence, with numerous galleries and bookshops nestling somewhat incongruously beside the garish rock 'n' roll emporiums, on Tinker Street and its environs. The neoclassic town hall building on Tinker is the site of various performance events throughout the year, as well as the annual Woodstock Film Festival. Nearby, the Woodstock Artists Association and Museum houses a stunning permanent collection of the work of important American artists who lived and worked in the Woodstock area.

The tradition of America's oldest Arts and Crafts colony, established in the district of Byrdcliffe in 1903, is preserved by the Woodstock Guild in the Byrdcliffe Colony, sponsoring exhibitions, classes, concerts, and theater events. Likewise, the Maverick Concert Series, held in the picturesque "music chapel in the woods" since 1916, represents the oldest continuous chamber-music festival in America.

Woodstock's rock 'n' roll tradition, of course, goes back further than the heady days of the summer of '69. Indeed, the initial choice of the town as a festival venue was spurred by the rock-music community that was already settled and working there. Today, several alumni of the 1969 festival still live in the area, including Mountain's keyboard player Steve Knight (who served two terms on the town board from 1999 to 2007), John Sebastian, and veterans of The Band, Garth Hudson and Levon Helm. Helm's regular all-star "jam session" concerts, the Midnight Ramble, held in his home studio, are a highlight in the Woodstock musical calendar.

Compared to Woodstock's rich cultural history for a town of its size—fewer than 7,000 inhabitants were recorded there in the 2000 census—the festival site of Bethel has no such heritage to speak of, and until recently carried little acknowledgment of its one place in the history books. That changed, however, in June 2008, with the opening of The Museum at Bethel Woods, at the Bethel Woods Center for the Arts.

Above: A hippie-themed gift shop in present-day Woodstock.
Main picture: One of Levon Helm's Midnight Rambles in Woodstock, September 2008.

The Museum at Bethel Woods

When the cable television pioneer Alan Gerry finalized his purchase of the original Woodstock festival site in 1996, he set in motion his plan for an arts center that would also house a museum dedicated to the legendary festival. After $100 million was spent in development, the Bethel Woods Center for the Arts opened to the public in 2006. The centerpiece at the time was the outdoor performance amphitheater, which seats 17,000 and has since staged seasonal concerts by top names in the world of music, and given a much-needed boost to the economic prospects of the surrounding area. In June 2008, The Museum at Bethel Woods opened to the public and is the first exhibition space dedicated to telling the story of the Sixties, the Woodstock Music and Art Fair, and their legacies today.

In addition to a theater, classrooms for lectures, a museum shop, and other facilities, central to the Museum complex is the permanent exhibit gallery. It is an immersive environment incorporating traditional museum educational techniques as well as cutting-edge design, multi-media, and technology. Covering an area of nearly 9,000 square feet, the gallery exhibit includes five interactive installations, twenty films, a display of 164 artifacts and 330 photographs.

In the Sixties Gallery, the films include "The Sixties Timeline," which traces the images and sounds of the tumultuous decade, four short films covering popular culture in the 1960s (Fashion & Style, Radio, Television, and Suburbia), a ten-minute documentary produced by History© outlining the traumatic social and political events of 1968, and "A Musical Revolution," describing the evolution of rock 'n' roll through the 1960s.

In the Festival Gallery there are four short films covering all aspects of the planning and birth of Woodstock, a rear-projection on the windshield of a psychedelically painted ex-school bus (like the vehicle that brought the Merry Pranksters to Bethel) depicting the many cross-country journeys to the site, and four shorts addressing various aspects of the Woodstock experience— "The Hog Farm Commune," "The Security Plan," "Stories in the Field," and "Local Observers." And an impressive twenty-one-minute documentary entitled "Woodstock: The Music," projected in high-definition in its own dedicated theater onto a twenty-two by thirteen foot screen, captures some of the outstanding performances at the festival, many rarely or never seen before. The commentary, contributed by performers who were there as well as contemporary rock players, gives a unique musician's insight to the images and sounds.

But undoubtedly the visual high point of the exhibit is "The Festival Experience"—an eleven-minute surround-sound film projected by nine video projectors on to four screens measuring sixty-two feet wide by fifty feet high. Creating a seamless 270-degree visual landscape, including a "sky" that changes as night follows daylight and gathering storm clouds herald a downpour, it places the visitor in the festival audience, immersed in the sights and sounds of Woodstock as the three days unfold.

Interactive elements at the exhibit include excerpts from the great songs of each year from 1960 through 1968, with narration placing each in the context of its time, and a "Music of 1969" feature that is selected by the visitor and accompanied by a narration saying why that artist did or did not play at the festival. An interactive map of the Woodstock Music and Art Fair allows visitors to locate and learn more about places on the site, including the Hog Farm, the woods, the stage area, and even the portable bathrooms!

In the Impact Gallery, visitors can leave their own impressions of Woodstock, the 1960s, or their experience at the Museum itself in the "Personal Stories" booths, sample "The Music After Woodstock" that reflects its heritage, and watch a film called "Woodstock & the Sixties: What Do They Mean Today?"

And Museum patrons can visit the adjacent Woodstock site, the field where the performances actually took place, which is now marked by a commemorative plaque, and usually hosted by longtime "Site Interpreter," festival veteran Duke Devlin.

Alongside the photographs and articles of memorabilia, collected over several years by the Museum staff, one of the Museum's greatest resources is the visual testimonies and oral histories, excerpts from which are used throughout the exhibit in both the films and on text panels. An ongoing project, and totaling over seventy contributions at the end of 2008, they include in-depth interviews with a huge range of people associated with the festival, including musicians, organizers, security people, technical staff, Hog Farmers, local residents, and, of course, fans who were there. Stored permanently in the Museum's archives, the interviews have proved an invaluable asset in putting together this book.

Below: Exterior view of The Museum at Bethel Woods. Opposite, clockwise from top left: One of the interactive features at the Museum; a 1969 "peace flag" artifact in the Sixties Gallery; the Museum's "psychedelic" bus. Overleaf: Scenes from the permanent exhibition.

"Let the word go forth from this time and place, to friend and foe alike, that the torch has been passed to a new generation of Americans."

PRESIDENT KENNEDY

THE 1968 THEATER

LABOR ASSEM FOR PEACE

WORLD PEACE

OUT OF VIETNAM NOW!

COMING APART
"There's battle lines being drawn"
BUFFALO SPRINGFIELD, FOR WHAT IT'S WORTH

The events of 1968 challenged many Americans' faith in the power of idealism and the promise of peaceful change. When civil rights leader Martin Luther King was assassinated on April 4th, riots broke out in more than 100 cities across the country. In June, Americans lost another emblematic leader when Robert F. Kennedy was shot and killed while campaigning for president. In response to the escalating war in Vietnam, student activists seized campus buildings and clashed with police at increasingly violent demonstrations.

Where Are They Now?

Joan Baez (b. 1941)
With over thirty albums to her credit, Joan Baez records and tours regularly after a performance career spanning fifty years. Highlights have included her 1975 gold-selling album *Diamonds & Rust,* the 1985 Live Aid concert in Philadelphia, and receiving the Grammy Lifetime Achievement Award in 2007.

The Band
The group (who first got together in the early 1960s backing rockabilly singer Ronnie Hawkins as The Hawks), were active as The Band from 1967 to 1976, reforming from 1983 to 1999 without Robbie Robertson (b. 1943). Richard Manuel (1943–86) and Rick Danko (1942–99) are deceased, while Garth Hudson (b. 1937) and Levon Helm (b. 1940) both still reside in the Woodstock area.

Blood, Sweat & Tears
Formed in 1967, the ever-changing lineup of BS&T—which included three separate periods with lead singer David Clayton Thomas (b. 1941)—currently features founder members Bobby Colomby (b. 1944) on drums, and guitarist Steve Katz (b. 1945), the latter after an absence of thirty-five years.

Opposite: Joe Cocker on stage in Sydney, Australia, 2006.
Below: Joan Baez on a European tour in July 2008.

Paul Butterfield (1942–87)
The highly influential Paul Butterfield Blues Band was on the road from 1963 until 1970, before Butterfield reformed it working with an entirely new lineup through the mid-1970s. During the late 1970s and 1980s he pursued a solo career, until his death from a heart attack in 1987 at the age of forty-four.

Canned Heat
Debuting at the Monterey Pop Festival in 1967, the classic lineup of Canned Heat came to an end with the death of Alan "Blind Owl" Wilson (1943–70), which was followed by that of Bob "The Bear" Hite (1943–81). In a currently active version of the band, only drummer Adolpho "Fito" de la Parra (b. 1946) remains from the group that played at Woodstock.

Joe Cocker (b. 1944)
In the years since Woodstock, Joe Cocker's many successes have included a *Billboard* No. 1 duet with Jennifer Warnes on "Up Where We Belong" in 1982, and his 1986 album *Cocker,* which earned a platinum disc in Europe. He continues to tour on an occasional basis, and currently lives on the Mad Dog Ranch in Colorado, from which he and his wife run the Cocker Kids Foundation for disadvantaged children. In 2007 he was awarded an OBE (Order of the British Empire) in the Queen's Birthday Honours list, for services to music.

Country Joe & the Fish

After the band broke up in 1971, Country Joe McDonald (b. 1942) reformed them sporadically with fellow founder Barry "The Fish" Melton (b. 1947). Elsewhere his energies have been devoted to a solo career and political activism. In 2004 he toured with a group as the Country Joe Band, playing the US western seaboard, New York state, and a ten-date visit to the UK.

Creedence Clearwater Revival

Hot on the heels of their Woodstock appearance, CCR had another huge hit in January 1970 with "Travellin' Band," followed by what many considered their finest album, *Cosmo's Factory,* in the following July. Although the chart-topping band broke up in 1972, founder John Fogerty (b. 1945) is still recording, and undertaking extensive world tours on a regular basis.

Crosby, Stills, Nash & Young

David Crosby (b. 1941), Stephen Stills (b. 1945), and Graham Nash (b. 1942) have all pursued illustrious solo careers while reuniting from time to time, along with Neil Young (b. 1945) whose reputation as a singer-songwriter has earned him almost legendary status. Their frequent reunions as a quartet have included the Philadelphia Live Aid concert in 1985, 1988's *American Dream* album and *Looking Forward* in 2000, and full-blown tours in 2000, 2002, and 2006—plus a Crosby, Stills & Nash trek in 2008.

Rona Elliot (b. 1948)

Since the days of Woodstock Rona Elliot has become a well-known music journalist and media interviewer. Currently she writes a column for *USA Today,* is a coach on the *American Idol* TV show, teaches a music business class at UCLA, and is on the Grammy advisory committee.

Stanley Goldstein (b. 1939)

Woodstock Ventures' "headhunter," Stan Goldstein has worked in the music and film industries as a consultant, mixer, production and project manager, line producer, and producer of shows, festivals, and events. He also continues to work on the production side of documentary films.

Grateful Dead

Following the death of founder and main man Jerry Garcia (1942–95), the remaining members formally disbanded, but over the years have come together for reunions and one-off appearances. In 1998 Bob Weir (b. 1947), Phil Lesh (b. 1940), and Mickey Hart (b. 1943) reformed as The Other Ones, along with Grateful Dead collaborator Bruce Hornsby; Lesh left in 2000, while another Woodstock veteran of the band Bill Kreutzman (b. 1946) joined. After various lineup changes, in 2003 The Other Ones changed their name to The Dead.

Arlo Guthrie (b. 1947)

Guthrie has released over thirty albums since his debut in 1967, and is an established figure on the US folk-music circuit. His first big hit after his Woodstock appearance was with the song "City of New Orleans" in 1972, written by singer-songwriter Steve Goodman. Through the late 1970s and 1980s he toured and recorded with his band Shenandoah, and in 1991 established the Guthrie Center in Massachusetts, an interfaith meeting center serving people of all religions.

Bill Hanley (b. 1937)

Following Woodstock Bill Hanley confirmed his position as a world leader in sound engineering with numerous large-scale projects. In 2006 he was awarded the prestigious Parnelli Lifetime Achievement Award for service to the sound industry.

Tim Hardin (1941–80)

Despite some critically acclaimed albums during the decade after Woodstock—including *Suite for Susan Moore and Damion, Bird on a Wire,* and *Painted Head,* all on the Columbia label—Hardin's troubled lifestyle ensured he never had the commercial success he enjoyed in the 1960s, the singer succumbing to a fatal heroin and morphine overdose in 1980.

Keef Hartley (b. 1944)

Hartley was making records up till the end of the 1990s. In 2007 his autobiography, *Halfbreed (A rock and roll journey that happened against*

all the odds), was released, covering his career as a drummer through to the years immediately following his band's appearance at Woodstock. Now retired but making occasional live appearances, he lives in his native town of Preston, England.

Richie Havens (b. 1941)
Havens followed his success via the *Woodstock* film with the 1971 album *Alarm Clock,* which became his first Top 30 chart hit. Since then he has become one of the hardest-working veterans of Woodstock, continuing to tour—particularly North America and Europe—and release new studio albums. In 2007 he appeared in the Todd Haynes film *I'm Not There,* singing Bob Dylan's "Tombstone Blues."

Jimi Hendrix (1942–70)
Soon after his Woodstock gig Hendrix formed his Band of Gypsies with the same bass player, Billy Cox (b. 1941), and drummer Buddy Miles (1947–2008), releasing a live album in April 1970. Just five months later Jimi Hendrix was found dead in a London hotel room. Drummer Mitch Mitchell (1947–2008), who'd played with both Hendrix's Experience and the guitarist's band at Woodstock, died in a Portland, Oregon hotel during a 2008 "Experience Hendrix" tour.

The Incredible String Band
Two months after Woodstock the ISB released *Changing Horses* in November 1969, followed by *I Looked Up* in April 1970, but neither album achieved the acclaim or success of their previous work. After disbanding in 1974, the front line "Incredibles" of Mike Heron (b. 1942) and Robin Williamson (b. 1943) got together with a new lineup for two concerts in 1997. A permanent reunion ran from 1999 to 2003, after which Heron continued to fly the ISB banner until 2006.

Jefferson Airplane
Released in November 1969, *Volunteers* would be the final album by the classic Airplane lineup, making the *Billboard* No. 13 spot early in 1970. After their appearance at the Altamont concert, in which Marty Balin (b. 1942) was knocked unconscious, drummer Spencer Dryden (1938–2005) quit the band in February 1970, precipitating the gradual disintegration of the group. Following their eventual breakup in 1973, Balin, Grace Slick (b. 1939), Paul Kantner (b. 1941), Jack Casady (b. 1944), and Jorma Kaukonen (b. 1940) have been involved in a number of Airplane spinoffs and reunions over the years, including Jefferson Starship, the KBC Band, and Hot Tuna. Spencer Dryden died of colon cancer in 2005.

Janis Joplin (1943–70)
Her Kozmic Blues Band having broken up at the end of 1969, Janis was working with the Full Tilt Boogie Band when she died of a heroin overdose in October 1970. Prior to her death she had been working on a new album with the band, the posthumously released *Pearl,* which became the biggest-selling LP of her career (a *Billboard* chart-topper), and included her bestselling single (also No. 1), a cover of Kris Kristofferson's "Me and Bobby McGee."

Artie Kornfeld (b. 1942)
Following Woodstock, Kornfeld continued in the recording business, earning over 100 Gold and Platinum discs during a highly successful career.

Eddie Kramer (b. 1941)
For the last forty years, since producing the Woodstock soundtrack, Kramer has worked with numerous top artists including Kiss, Anthrax, Buddy Guy, Sting, Brian May, and in 2006, the Red Hot Chili Peppers.

Michael Lang (b. 1944)
Since the early 1970s Lang has worked in artist management—with clients including Joe Cocker and Rickie Lee Jones—film production, his own record company (signing Billy Joel among others), and event production. Projects in 2009 include an event to mark the 50th anniversary of the Lincoln Center in New York City.

Chris Langhart (b. 1940)
Theater designer and Woodstock's technical director, Langhart went on to establish the Rainbow venue in London alongside John Morris, with whom he also coordinated various festivals and rock tours in Europe. He now teaches lighting and stagecraft at Solebury School in Pennsylvania, and is technical director of the School's theater.

Mel Lawrence (b. 1935)
Since Woodstock, site director Mel Lawrence has been producing and directing film documentaries. He also helped create the Jamboree in the Hills country music festival, now running for over thirty years, and currently produces action/reality shows for television.

Melanie (b. 1947)
Melanie's Woodstock-inspired "Lay Down (Candles in the Rain)" made the *Billboard* Top 10 in the summer of 1970, followed by other hits including a cover of The Rolling Stones' "Ruby Tuesday" the same year, and 1971's chart-topping "Brand New Key," which sold over three million copies worldwide. Melanie continues to record, and perform live on an international basis. An appearance at the Meltdown Festival at London's Royal Albert Hall was released on DVD as *Melanie: For One Night Only,* in October 2007.

Chip Monck (b. 1939)
After Woodstock, Monck did the lighting for many prestigious events including the Concert for Bangladesh, the Broadway production of *The Rocky Horror Show,* and the Los Angeles Olympics. Since 1988 he has lived in Melbourne, Australia.

John Morris (b. 1940)
In the early 1970s Morris repeated his success running New York's Fillmore East at London's famous Rainbow venue. Since the 1990s he has been in antiquities show production, owning and organizing the traveling Antiquities Show sales presentations across the US.

Mountain
The group's debut album was released after their Woodstock appearance, in 1970. Entitled *Climbing!,* it reached the Top 20 album chart, with the spinoff single "Mississippi Queen" making the Top 40. The 1971 follow-up *Nantucket Sleighride* also made the Top 20 albums. Disbanding Mountain in 1972, then reuniting briefly in 1974, after the death of Felix Pappalardi (1939–83) guitarist Leslie West (b. 1945) reformed the band for a second time in 1985. They continue to tour and record, even featuring on an edition of the *Guitar Hero 3: Legends of Rock* video game.

Opposite: Florida, August 2006 (l to r) Graham Nash, Stephen Stills, Neil Young, and David Crosby.

Wes Pomeroy (1920–98)

After heading security at Woodstock, Pomeroy worked for a number of US rock tours, including a Led Zeppelin trek, before going back to law enforcement and various governmental posts. Retiring in 1995, he died in 1998 following a series of heart problems.

Quill

Following their Woodstock appearance, Quill released a self-produced album, the eponymously titled *Quill,* on Atlantic Records' Cotillion label (to which they had been signed in the summer of 1969), which achieved little success. Subsequently cofounder Jon Cole left a few months later, and the remaining four members disbanded in the spring of 1970.

John Roberts (1945–2001)

Although he was involved with Michael Lang and Joel Rosenman in the Woodstock 25th anniversary festival in 1994, in the main Roberts distanced himself from the music business in the years that followed the Bethel event. He died of cancer in 2001, aged fifty-six.

Joel Rosenman (b. 1942)

Still in the investment business, in an interview in 2001 Joel Rosenman said he examines a handful of business projects every week—"I am still doing the same thing as in 1968." With John Roberts he co-authored *Young Men with Unlimited Capital,* a nonfictional account of their exploits as producers of Woodstock.

Santana

Released just after their sensational Woodstock appearance, the band's debut album *Santana* reached No. 4 in the US charts. This was followed a year later by the chart-topping *Abraxas,* and a year after that *Santana III,* another No. 1. Over the next ten years the band had eleven Top 30 album

hits, and since then Grammy Award winner Carlos Santana (b. 1947) has fluctuated between a solo career and leading a band bearing his name. In 2003 *Rolling Stone* listed him at No. 15 in its 100 Greatest Guitarists of All Time.

Swami Satchidananda (1914–2002)

Over the years following his Woodstock appearance, the Swami wrote numerous books and lectured extensively on yoga and enlightenment, founding the Light of Truth Universal Shrine (LOTUS) at Yogaville in Buckingham, Virginia in 1986. He died in his native India in 2002.

John Sebastian (b. 1944)

A long solo career has included a chart-topping single, "Welcome Back," in 1976, and more recently jug-band gigs billed as John Sebastian and the J-Band. He has hosted several TV programs on the music of the 1960s, including *The Golden Age of Rock and Roll,* and a PBS Lovin' Spoonful retrospective in 2007. Since 2008 Sebastian has been regularly touring and recording with the celebrated bluegrass musician David Grisman.

Sha Na Na

Post-Woodstock success was immediate for the revivalist rock 'n' roll outfit, including their own syndicated TV show, which ran from 1977 to 1982, and a Top 40 album—*The Golden Age of Rock 'n' Roll*—in 1973. Still gigging on an occasional basis, in the current line-up only vocalist Donny York and drummer Jocko Marcellino remain of the original band that played Woodstock.

Ravi Shankar (b. 1920)

Now in his late eighties, Shankar has been the recipient of many prestigious awards over the years, including India's highest civilian accolade, the Bharat Ratna, in 1977. In 2002 he composed a sitar piece for the George Harrison memorial concert, performed by his daughter Anoushka (b. 1971). He is also the father of the jazz singer-pianist Norah Jones (b. 1981).

Arnold Skolnick (b. 1937)

The designer of the Woodstock poster worked in graphics for a number of years before moving into book publishing. He now heads up his own publishing house based in Chesterfield, Massachusetts.

Sly & the Family Stone

Coinciding with Woodstock, the band had a hit single with "Hot Fun in the Summertime" which made the No. 2 spot, followed by the chart-topping "Thank You (Falettinme Be Mice Elf Agin)")" in January 1970. But despite further chart successes (including the single "Family Affair" and album "There's A Riot Goin' On, " both No. 1 in 1971), the original band broke up in 1975, and Sly Stone (b.1943) went solo—though still collaborating with Family Stone members from time to time. In 2003, members of the original band, except Sly and bassist Larry Graham (b.1946), reunited to record an album, and Sly himself rejoined for a 2007 European tour.

Bert Sommer (1949–90)

Sommer released his second album, *Inside Bert Sommer,* early in 1970, followed by *Bert Sommer* later that year. After completing his fourth solo album—also simply titled *Bert Sommer*—in 1977, Sommer joined his friend Johnny Rabb in The Fabulous Newports, based in Albany, NY. He died in 1990 after a long battle with respiratory illness.

Left: Guitar veteran Johnny Winter in July 2008.
Opposite: Roger Daltrey (left) and Pete Townshend fronting The Who, October 2008.

Sweetwater

The group eventually disbanded following the near-fatal motor accident involving lead singer Nancy Nevins (b. 1949) in December 1969, though initially they carried on awaiting her recovery, releasing two albums—*Just For You* in 1971, and *Melon* the following year. Of the original line-up, Albert Moore, Alan Malarowitz, and August Burns are all deceased, but Sweetwater have reformed from time to time, with Nevins back on vocals.

Ten Years After

TYA's popularity burgeoned after Woodstock and the subsequent movie, reflected in four chart albums—*Cricklewood Green* and *Watt*, both in 1970, *A Space In Time* (1971) and *Recorded Live* in 1973. But the pressure of Alvin Lee's increasing "guitar-hero" image took its toll. Splitting up in 1974, the band reunited in 1988, played a few concerts and released the 1989 album *About Time,* then disbanded again. Front man Alvin Lee (b. 1944) now plays under his own name, while Leo Lyons (b. 1943), Chick Churchill (b. 1946), and Ric Lee (b. 1945) still operate as Ten Years After.

Elliot Tiber (b. 1935)

Author and screenwriter Tiber has written a number of books about his part in the Woodstock festival, one of which—*Taking Woodstock*—has been made into a 2009 feature film by director Ang Lee.

Michael Wadleigh (b. 1939)

Woodstock director Wadleigh made two spinoffs, a 1974 documentary about Janis Joplin, and 1999's *Jimi Hendrix: Live at Woodstock*, and also the 1981 horror movie *Wolfen*. More recently he has worked with a human-rights organization in the Darfur region of Sudan, also producing a documentary on the Turkana people of Kenya and southern Sudan.

Wavy Gravy (b. 1936)

It was two weeks after Woodstock that Hog Farm founder Hugh Romney was dubbed Wavy Gravy by bluesman B.B. King, during the Texas International Pop Festival. For many years he and his wife Johanara have run a circus and performing arts camp (Camp Winnarainbow) for children in California.

The Who

Through the 1970s The Who had a plethora of hit albums, including the much-acclaimed *Live At Leeds* (1970), *Who's Next* (a US No. 4 that featured groundbreaking synthesizer effects), the teen-angst "rock opera" *Quadrophenia* in 1973 (spawning a cult film in 1979), and 1978's *Who Are You,* which was overshadowed by the death of Keith Moon (1946–78). Since Moon's death, and the subsequent loss of John Entwistle (1944–2002), Pete Townshend (b. 1945) and Roger Daltrey (b. 1944) have continued recording and occasionally touring with various lineups as The Who.

Johnny Winter (b. 1944)

In the early 1970s Winter struggled with a heroin problem but kicked the habit in 1973, at which point he released the appropriately titled *Still Alive And Well*, making the *Billboard* Top 40 for the fourth time in his career. He went on to fulfill a lifelong ambition, producing three albums with his guitarist hero Muddy Waters, and since then has never stopped astonishing audiences with his interpretations of classic blues.

Max Yasgur (1919–73)

Less than two years after Woodstock, in 1971 Yasgur sold his dairy business, though not the farm itself. And just nineteen months later, he died of a heart attack at the age of fifty-three. It was the only time a humble farmer was given a full-page obituary in *Rolling Stone* magazine.

Discography

A selection of albums by the artists who performed at Woodstock, released before, or in the years immediately following, the festival. Where the editors feel appropriate, a later compilation album has also been included.

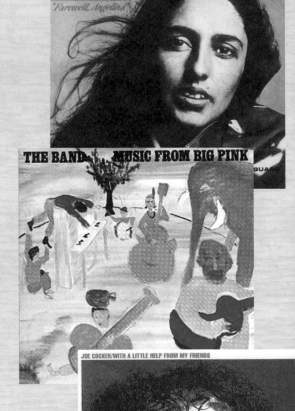

Joan Baez
Joan Baez Vol. 2 (1961)
Farewell, Angelina (1965)
The First Ten Years (compilation/1970)
Diamonds & Rust (1975)

The Band
Music from Big Pink (1968)
The Band (1969)
Stage Fright (1970)

Blood, Sweat & Tears
Blood Sweat & Tears (1969)
Greatest Hits (compilation/1972)

Paul Butterfield
The Paul Butterfield Blues Band (1965)
East-West (1966)
The Resurrection of Pigboy Crabshaw (1968)

Canned Heat
Canned Heat (1967)
Living the Blues (1969)
Let's Work Together: The Best of Canned Heat
   (compilation/1989)

Joe Cocker
With a Little Help from My Friends (1969)
Joe Cocker! (1969)
Mad Dogs & Englishmen (live/1970)

Country Joe & the Fish
Electric Music for the Mind and Body (1967)
I-Feel-Like-I'm-Fixin'-to-Die (1967)

Creedence Clearwater Revival
Creedence Clearwater Revival (1967)
Bayou County (1969)
Green River (1969)
Willy & the Poor Boys (1969)

Crosby, Stills, Nash & Young
Crosby Stills & Nash (1969)
Déjà Vu (1970)

Grateful Dead
Live Dead (1969)
Workingman's Dead (1970)
American Beauty (1970)

Arlo Guthrie
Alice's Restaurant (1967)
Running Down the Road (1969)
Hobo's Lullaby (1972)

Tim Hardin
Tim Hardin 1 (1966)
Tim Hardin 2 (1967)
This Is Tim Hardin (1967)

Keef Hartley
Halfbreed (1969)

Richie Havens
Mixed Bag (1967)
Richard P. Havens, 1983 (1969)
Stonehenge (1970)
Alarm Clock (1971)

Jimi Hendrix
Are You Experienced? (1967)
Axis: Bold As Love (1967)
Electric Ladyland (1968)

Incredible String Band
The 5000 Spirits or the Layers of the Onion
   (1967)
The Hangman's Beautiful Daughter (1968)

Janis Joplin
Big Brother & the Holding Company (1967)
Cheap Thrills (1968)
Got Dem Ol' Kozmic Blues Again Mama! (1969)
Pearl (1971)

Jefferson Airplane
Surrealistic Pillow (1967)
Crown of Creation (1968)
Bless Its Pointed Little Head (live/1969)
The Worst of Jefferson Airplane (compilation/
   1970)

Melanie
Melanie (aka Affectionately Melanie) (1969)
Candles in the Rain (1970)

Mountain
Climbing! (1970)
Nantucket Sleighride (1971)

Quill
Quill (1970)

Santana
Santana (1969)
Abraxas (1970)
Amigos (1976)

John Sebastian
The Best of the Lovin' Spoonful (compilation/
   1969)
John B. Sebastian (1970)

Sha Na Na
Rock and Roll Is Here to Stay (1969)

Ravi Shankar
The Sounds of India (1968)
The Essential Ravi Shankar (compilation/2005)

Sly & the Family Stone
Dance to the Music (1968)
Stand! (1969)
There's a Riot Goin' On (1971)

Bert Sommer
The Road to Travel (1969)

Sweetwater
Sweetwater (1968)

Ten Years After
Stonedhenge (1968)
Ssssh (1969)

The Who
My Generation (1965)
The Who Sell Out (1967)
Tommy (1969)
Live at Leeds (1970)
Who's Next (1971)

Johnny Winter
The Progressive Blues Experiment (1969)
Johnny Winter (1969)
Second Winter (1969)
Johnny Winter And (1970)

Various Artists
Woodstock: Music from the Original Soundtrack
   and More (1970, re-released 1994, 2009)
Woodstock 2 (2 LPs/1971)

Bibliography

Baez, Joan, *And a Voice to Sing With: A Memoir,* Signet, 1990

Bell, Dale (ed.), *Woodstock: An Inside Look at the Movie that Shook up the World and Defined a Generation,* Michael Wiese Productions, 1999

Bennett, Andy (ed.), *Remembering Woodstock*, Ashgate Publishing, 2004

Bonds, Ray (ed.), *The Vietnam War: The Illustrated History of the Conflict in Southeast Asia,* Crown Publishers, 1979

Bowman, John S. (ed.), *The Vietnam War: An Almanac,* World Almanac Publications, 1985

Boyd, Joe, *White Bicycles,* Serpent's Tail, 2006

Clarke, Donald (ed.), *The Penguin Encyclopedia of Popular Music,* Viking, 1989

Crosby, David and Carl Gottlieb, *Long Time Gone: The Autobiography of David Crosby,* Doubleday, 1988

Echols, Alice, *Scars of Sweet Paradise: The Life and Times of Janis Joplin,* Henry Holt, 1999

Evers, Alf, *Woodstock: History of an American Town,* The Overlook Press, 1987

Farber, David, *et al., The Sixties Chronicle,* Publications International, Ltd., 2004

Hajdu, David, *Positively 4th Street,* Bloomsbury, 2001

Havens, Richie and Steve Davidowitz, *They Can't Hide Us Anymore,* Spike, 1999

Helm, Levon and Stephen Davis, *This Wheel's on Fire: Levon Helm and the Story of The Band,* William Morrow & Company, 1993

Henderson, David, *'Scuse Me While I Kiss the Sky: Jimi Hendrix,* Doubleday, 1978

Hoffman, Abbie, *Woodstock Nation,* Vintage/Random House, 1969

Hoskyns, Barney, *Across the Great Divide: The Band and America,* Hyperion, 1993

Landy, Elliott, *Woodstock 1969, The First Festival,* Square Books, 1994

Lang, Michael, with Holly George-Warren, *The Road to Woodstock,* Ecco/HarperCollins, 2009

Lang, Michael and Jean Young, *Woodstock Festival Remembered,* Ballantine Books, 1979

Lewis, Dave, *Led Zeppelin: The Concert File,* Omnibus, 1997

Lytle, Mark Hamilton, *America's Uncivil Wars: The Sixties Era from Elvis to the Fall of Richard Nixon,* Oxford University Press, 2006

Makower, Joel, *Woodstock: The Oral History,* Doubleday, 1989

Marsh, Dave, *Before I Get Old: The Story of The Who,* Plexus, 1983

McDonough, Jimmy, *Shakey: Neil Young's Biography,* Random House, 2002

McNally, Dennis, *A Long Strange Trip: The Inside History of the Grateful Dead,* Broadway Books, 2002

Miles, Barry, *Hippie,* Cassell, 2003

The Nuclear Age: TimeFrame AD 1950–1990, Time-Life, 1990

Perone, James E., *Woodstock: An Encyclopedia of the Music and Art Fair,* Greenwood Press, 2005

Rosenman, Joel, John Roberts, and Robert Pilpel, *Young Men with Unlimited Capital: The Behind-the-Scenes Story of Woodstock* (rev. ed.), Bantam Books, 1989

Rotolo, Suze, *A Freewheelin' Time: A Memoir of Greenwich Village in the 60s,* Broadway, 2008

Selvin, Joel, *On the Record: Sly & the Family Stone,* Simon & Schuster, 1997

Shaar-Murray, Charles, *Crosstown Traffic: Jimi Hendrix and Post-war Pop,* Faber & Faber, 1989

Shankar, Ravi, *Raga Mala,* Welcome Rain, 1999

Shapiro, Harry and Caesar Glebbeek, *Jimi Hendrix: Electric Gypsy,* St. Martin's Press, 1990

Shapiro, Marc, *Carlos Santana: Back on Top,* St Martin's Press, 2000

Smith, Joe, *Off the Record: An Oral History of Popular Music,* Warner Books, 1988

Sounes, Howard, *Down the Highway: The Life of Bob Dylan,* Grove Press, 2001

Tamarkin, Jeff, *Got a Revolution! The Turbulent Flight of Jefferson Airplane,* Atria Books, 2003

Tiber, Elliot, *Woodstock Derilium,* Knock on Woodstock, Derilium Press, 2001

Tiber, Elliot and Tom Monte, *Taking Woodstock,* Square One Publishers, 2007

Ward, Ed, Geoffrey Stokes, and Ken Tucker, *Rock of Ages: The Rolling Stone History of Rock & Roll,* Rolling Stone Press/Summit Books, 1986

Whitburn, Joel, *Top Pop Singles, 1955–2002,* Record Research, 2003

Zinn, Howard, *A People's History of the United States, 1492–Present,* HarperCollins, 1999

Numerous articles were consulted from the following publications: *Billboard, Business Week, Life, The New York Times, The New Yorker, Newsweek, Rolling Stone, Time* and *Variety*.

Sources

14 Suze Rotolo, *A Freewheelin' Time: A Memoir of Greenwich Village in the 60s*, Broadway, 2008; 16 Dick Gregory, stand-up comedian, at the Playboy Club Chicago, 1961, from the unfinished documentary film *Color of Funny*; 20 Isabel Stein, talking to Mike Evans; 21 Mike Heron, talking to Mike Evans; 25 From the Port Huron Statement of the Students for a Democratic Society, 1962, Courtesy Office of Sen. Tom Hayden; 27 Paul Kantner, in *Hippie* by Barry Miles, Sterling, 2003; 28 Bill MacAllister, *Jazz on a Summer's Day* DVD liner notes, Charly Licensing APS, 2001; 29 George Wein, in *Positively 4th Street* by David Hajdu, Bloomsbury, 2001; 30 Lou Adler, from *Off the Record: An Oral History of Popular Music* by Joe Smith, Warner Books, 1988; 32 Michael Lang, in *Woodstock Festival Remembered*, Ballantine, 1979; 34 George Quinn, Woodstock resident, from expectingrain.com/dok/atlas; 36 John Roberts, *The Woodstock Diaries*, 1994, prod. Alan Douglas, Warner Bros./Time Warner Entertainment; 37 Michael Lang, talking to Paul Kingsbury; 40 John Roberts, *The Woodstock Diaries*, 1994, prod. Alan Douglas, Warner Bros./Time Warner Entertainment; 41 left "Peaceful Rock Fete Planned Upstate" by Louis Calta, *New York Times*, June 27, 1969; 41 right Howard Mills, Jr., Wallkill site owner, video testimony, The Museum at Bethel Woods; 43 Michael Lang, talking to Paul Kingsbury; 44 "Pop Rock Festival Finds New Home" by Richard F. Shepard, *New York Times*, July 23, 1969; 45 Richard Gross, video testimony, The Museum at Bethel Woods; 46 Sam Yasgur, video testimony, The Museum at Bethel Woods; 50 Rona Elliot, talking to Paul Kingsbury; 51 Michael Lang, talking to Paul Kingsbury; 52-53 Arnold Skolnick, talking to Mike Evans and Colin Webb; 57 Bill Hanley, talking to Paul Kingsbury; 59 Michael Lang, talking to Paul Kingsbury; 60-61 Eddie Kramer, video testimony, The Museum at Bethel Woods; 62 "346 Policemen Quit Music Festival," *New York Times*, August 15, 1969; 64 Cecelia, quoted on www.woodstock69.com; 65 "200,000 Thronging to Rock Festival" by Barnard L. Collier, *New York Times*, August 16, 1969; 67 "300,000 at Folk Rock Fair" by Barnard L. Collier, *New York Times*, August 17, 1969; 69 Richie Havens, quoted on www.classicrockpage.com; 72 Richie Havens, video testimony, The Museum at Bethel Woods; 75 Diana Thompson, video testimony, The Museum at Bethel Woods; 78 Fred Herrera, talking to Paul Kingsbury; 79 Alex Del Zoppo, talking to Paul Kingsbury; 81 top Rona Elliot, talking to Paul Kingsbury; 81 bottom Michael Lang, in *Woodstock Festival Remembered*, Ballantine, 1979; 82 Bert Sommer, quoted on www.inkui.com; 83 Ira Stone, quoted on www.bertsommer.com; 85 Michael Lang, in *Woodstock Festival Remembered*, Ballantine, 1979; 89 Ravi Shankar, from his autobiography *Raga Mala*, Welcome Rain, 1999; 90-91 Melanie, talking to Mike Evans; 93 Arlo Guthrie, interviewed by Steve Lane in BrooWaha online newspaper, March 31, 2008. Copyright © 2009 BrooWaha LLC; 95-97 Joan Baez, from her autobiography *And a Voice to Sing With: A Memoir*, Signet, 1990; 99 top "How You Gonna Keep Em Down In The Town," *Variety*, August 20, 1969; 99 bottom Isabel Stein, talking to Mike Evans; 102 Lisa Law, *The Woodstock Diaries*, 1994, prod. Alan Douglas, Warner Bros./Time Warner Entertainment; 104 bottom Joel Rosenman, *The Woodstock Diaries*, 1994, prod. Alan Douglas, Warner Bros./Time Warner Entertainment; 108 Lisa Law, talking to Mike Evans; 110 Lisa Law, *The Woodstock Diaries*, 1994, prod. Alan Douglas, Warner Bros./Time Warner Entertainment; 111 Jean Young, in *Woodstock Festival Remembered*, Ballantine, 1979; 112 Eric Stange, video testimony, The Museum at Bethel Woods; 115 Michael J. Fairchild, liner notes for the album *The Woodstock Diary*, Atlantic Records, 1994; 118 Country Joe McDonald, video testimony, The Museum at Bethel Woods; 120 Jerry Gilbert, *Zig Zag* magazine, December 1974; 121 John Sebastian, video testimony, The Museum at Bethel Woods; 124 left "Farmer With Soul," *New York Times*, August 18, 1969; 124 right Max Yasgur, addressing the Woodstock crowd, August 16, 1969; 125 Sam Yasgur, video testimony, The Museum at Bethel Woods; 126 Carlos Santana, in *Carlos Santana: Back on Top* by Marc Shapiro, St Martin's Press, 2000; 128 Carlos Santana, talking to David Sinclair, *Q* magazine, October 1990; 131 Joe Boyd, in *White Bicycles*, Serpent's Tail, 2006; 132 Mike Heron, talking to Mike Evans; 134 Bob Hite, talking to Steven Rosen, *Sounds* magazine (UK), March 2, 1974; 137 top Lisa Law, talking to Mike Evans; 137 bottom Diana Thompson, video testimony, The Museum at Bethel Woods; 139 left Michael Lang, *The Woodstock Diaries*, 1994, prod. Alan Douglas, Warner Bros./Time Warner Entertainment; 139 top Abbie Hoffman, *Woodstock Nation*, Vintage/Random House, 1969; 139 bottom Joel Rosenman, *The Woodstock Diaries*, 1994, prod. Alan Douglas, Warner Bros./Time Warner Entertainment; 141 top Steve Knight, talking to Mike Evans and Paul Kingsbury; 141 bottom Leslie West, quoted on www.classicrockpage.com; 142 Mickey Hart, quoted on www.classicrockpage.com; 144-145 Bob Weir, in "Woodstock Remembered" by David Fricke, *Rolling Stone*, August 24, 1989; 147 John Fogerty, in "Twentieth Anniversary: John Fogerty" by James Henke, *Rolling Stone*, December 10, 1987; 150 Bill Hanley, talking to Paul Kingsbury; 151 John Byrne Cooke, talking to Paul Kingsbury; 153 Mike Jahn, *New York Times*, August 18, 1969; 154 Ian Gibson, talking to Mike Evans; 155 "300,000 at Folk Rock Fair" by Barnard L. Collier, *New York Times*, August 17,

1969; 158 Joel Rosenman, *The Woodstock Diaries*, 1994, prod. Alan Douglas, Warner Bros./Time Warner Entertainment; 160-162 *On the Record: Sly & the Family Stone* by Joel Selvin, Simon & Schuster, 1997; 163 Carlos Santana, in "Woodstock Remembered" by David Fricke, *Rolling Stone*, August 24, 1989; 165 top Pete Townshend, quoted on www.alternativereel.com; 165 bottom Roger Daltrey, quoted on www.wikiquote.org; 167 Pete Townshend, in *Amazing Journey; The Life of Pete Townshend* by Mark Wilkerson, lulu.com, 2006; 168 left Pete Townshend, *San Francisco Examiner*, July 24, 2002; 168 right Ellen Willis, *New Yorker*, September 6, 1969; 169 "How You Gonna Keep Em Down In The Town," *Variety*, August 20, 1969; 170 Marty Balin, talking to Paul Kingsbury; 172 Jack Casady, quoted on www.classicrockpage.com; 173 top Grace Slick, in *Got a Revolution! The Turbulent Flight of Jefferson Airplane* by Jeff Tamarkin, Atria Books, 2003; 173 bottom Marty Balin, talking to Paul Kingsbury; 177 Bobbi Ercoline, video testimony, The Museum at Bethel Woods; 179-180 Joe Cocker, talking to Mike Evans; 181 Joe Cocker, quoted on www.classicrockpage.com; 182 "Tired Rock Fans Begin Exodus," *New York Times*, August 18, 1969; 183 Mark Koslow, video testimony, The Museum at Bethel Woods; 185 Susan Cole, video testimony, The Museum at Bethel Woods; 186 Barry Levine, talking to Mike Evans; 188 Rowland Scherman, talking to Mike Evans; 190 Country Joe McDonald, talking to Greg Shaw, *Mojo Navigator*, November 22, 1966; 193 top Alvin Lee, talking to John Ingham, *Sounds*, October 11, 1975; 193 middle Leo Lyons, talking to Mike Evans; 193 bottom Alvin Lee, in "Alvin Lee's Long Road to Freedom" by Barbara Charone, *Rolling Stone*, February 13, 1975; 194 From *This Wheel's on Fire: Levon Helm and the Story of The Band*, by Levon Helm and Stephen Davis, 1993. Reprinted by permission of HarperCollins Publishers; 195 Rick Danko, talking to Richard Williams, *Melody Maker*, May 29, 1971; 196 Robbie Robertson, in "Woodstock Remembered" by David Fricke, *Rolling Stone*, August 24, 1989; 199 Johnny Winter, talking to Sean McDevitt, *Guitar World*, March 2007; 200 James Perone, *An Encyclopedia of the Music and Art Fair*, Greenwood Press, 2005; 204 From *Long Time Gone: The Autobiography of David Crosby* by David Crosby and Carl Gottlieb, Doubleday, 1988; 205 Neil Young, in *Shakey: Neil Young's Biography* by Jimmy McDonough, Random House, 2002; 206 top Lisa Law, talking to Mike Evans; 206 bottom Barbara Hahn, video testimony, The Museum at Bethel Woods; 207 top Lisa Law, *The Woodstock Diaries*, 1994, prod. Alan Douglas, Warner Bros./Time Warner Entertainment; 207 middle Robert Kirkman, personal story for The Museum at Bethel Woods; 207 bottom Wavy Gravy (Hugh Romney), talking to Paul Kingsbury; 213 Joe Witkin, quoted on www.woodstock69.com; 217 Billy Cox, talking to Paul Kingsbury; 219 Michael Lang, in *Woodstock Festival Remembered*, Ballantine, 1979; 220 top Duke Devlin, talking to Mike Evans; 220 bottom Lisa Law, talking to Mike Evans; 222 Michael Lang, *The Woodstock Diaries*, 1994, prod. Alan Douglas, Warner Bros./Time Warner Entertainment; 223 Joe Scarda, video testimony, The Museum at Bethel Woods; 224-225 "Grooving on the Sounds" by Alistair Cooke, *The Guardian*, August 19, 1969; 227 "Tired Rock Fans Begin Exodus," *New York Times*, August 18, 1969; 228 Peter Grant, in *Led Zeppelin: The Concert File* by Dave Lewis, Omnibus Books, 1997; 230 top left Joni Mitchell, from the Crosby, Stills & Nash boxed-set booklet by Chet Flippo, Atlantic Records, 1991; 230 top right David Geffen, in *Long Time Gone: Autobiography of David Crosby* by David Crosby and Carl Gottlieb, Doubleday, 1988; 230 middle right Graham Nash, in *Off the Record: An Oral History of Popular Music* by Joe Smith, Warner Books, 1988; 230 bottom David Geffen, in *Atlantic Records: The House that Ahmet Built*, directed by Susan Steinberg, Rhino/WEA, 2007; 232 Bob Dylan, in "Bob Dylan: The Rolling Stone Interview" by Kurt Loder, *Rolling Stone*, June 21, 1984; 233 Bob Dylan, with Jim Jerome, November 10, 1975, in *Shakey: Neil Young's Biography* by Jimmy McDonough, Random House, 2002; 235 "It Was Like Balling For the First Time" by Jan Hodenfield, *Rolling Stone*, September 20, 1969; 240 "Nightmare in the Catskills," *New York Times* editorial, August 18, 1969; 241 top "The Big Woodstock Rock Trip," *Life*, August 29, 1969; 241 bottom "Age of Aquarius," *Newsweek*, August 25, 1969; 242 left "The 10th Largest City in the United States" by Steve Lerner, *Village Voice*, August 21, 1969; 242 right John "The Swede" Hilgerdt, *East Village Other*, August 20, 1969; 243 "I Looked at My Watch…" by Andrew Kopkind, *Rolling Stone*, September 20, 1969; 244 Ahmet Ertegun, in *Atlantic Records: The House that Ahmet Built*, directed by Susan Steinberg, Rhino/WEA, 2007; 246 Martin Scorsese, interviewed by Richard Schickel; 247 Barry Z. Levine, talking to Mike Evans; 248 Susan Steinberg, talking to Mike Evans; 249 Eddie Kramer, video testimony, The Museum at Bethel Woods; 255 Christopher Logue, *The Times*, September 13, 1969; 257 Mark Hamilton Lytle, *America's Uncivil Wars: The 60s Era from Elvis to the Fall of Richard Nixon*, Oxford University Press, 2006; 259 Keith Richards, John Burks, *London Evening Standard*, February 7, 1970; 260 Melanie, talking to Mike Evans; 263 Michael Lang, talking to Paul Kingsbury; 265 Jeryl Abramson, talking to Mike Evans and Paul Kingsbury; 288 WOODSTOCK, Words and Music by JONI MITCHELL, © 1968 (Renewed) CRAZY CROW MUSIC.

Index

Bold references indicate a section devoted to a performer or subject. *Italic* references indicate illustrations.

Acknowledgments

This book is dedicated to Michael Lang, the founder and true spirit of Woodstock

The editors would like to thank the following individuals and organizations for their considerable help and support of this publication:

Jeryl Abramson; Marty Balin; Gary Burr; John Byrne Cooke; Joe Cocker; Billy Cox; Alex Del Zoppo; Duke Devlin; Alan Douglas; Rona Elliot; Peter Golding; Michael Gray; Fred Herrera; Mike Heron; Bill Hanley; Roy Howard; Steve Knight; Michael Lang; Lisa Law; Barry Levine; Bill Lloyd; Leo Lyons; Jeff Manzelli; Marc Margolis; Rick McNamara; Anthony Pomes; Hugh Romney; Melanie Safka; Daryl Sanders; Rowland Scherman; Richard Schickel; Martin Scorsese; Arnold Skolnick; Isabel Stein; Susan Steinberg; Elliot Tiber; Jeff Weinstein.

Belmont University Library; Country Music Hall of Fame & Museum; The Golden Notebook bookstore, Woodstock; Nashville Public Library; Vanderbilt University Library; and Michael Egan; Wade Lawrence; Robin Green; Rosie Vergilio; Elaine Muscara; Paul Hein; Alan Gerry at The Museum at Bethel Woods Center for the Arts.

Picture Credits

Every effort has been made to trace the copyright holders. The picture editor apologizes in advance for any unintentional omissions and would be pleased, if any such case should arise, to add an appropriate acknowledgment to any future edition of the book.

Robert Altman/altmanphoto: 256-257, 257. **John Byrne Cooke:** 29t. **Corbis:** 11, 12-13, 14, 15t, 15br, 16, 17 t&b, 18t&b, 19, 20, 23b, 23t, 24t, 26b, 66tl, 232, 236, 237 all except br, 238, 252, 254tl, 262t, 263t&b, 272, 274, 276, 277. **Daily News Pix:** 37t, 156l. **Jeff Dexter:** 254-255. **Henry Diltz/Corbis:** 31t&b, 32, 33 all, 36, 58bl, 59m, 84, 224, 229b, 239. **Henry Diltz/morrisonhotelgallery.com:** 38, 39t&b, 45, 47, 48-49, 56, 57, 58tl,tr,br, 59t&b, 61, 70-71, 74-75, 93, 94, 99, 103t&b, 105, 106-107, 108, 109b, 116background, 121, 130t, 132, 146, 147, 151, 152, 158b, 159t, 160, 166-167, 170-171, 173, 176tl, 185b, 194, 198, 199t&b, 203t, 204l&r, 205, 214, 218-219, 220-221. **Rona Elliot Collection:** 42-43, 50, 51 all. **Mike Evans Collection:** 138, 266b. **Eyevine/Librado Romero/The New York Times:** 62, 63 all. **Michael FredericksTopfoto/ The Image Works:** 8, 102, 136tl, 137 background, 184, 185t, 241b, 242. **Getty Images:** 15bm, 21, 26t, 28t&b (Bob Parent/ Time Life), 37b (Bill Eppridge/Time Life), 66t&background, 80-81 (Bill Eppridge/Time Life), 114-115 (Bill Eppridge/Time Life), 129 (Tucker Ransom), 138-139 (Santi Visalli), 155b (John Dominis/Time Life), 158t (Bill Eppridge/Time Life), 183 (John Dominis/Time Life), 191 (Bill Eppridge/ Time Life), 241t, 254tr, 260, 273. **Eddie Kramer/kramerarchives.com:** 216. **Jason Laure/Frank White Photo Agency:** 3, 69t, 110br, 111b, 119, 122t&b, 123, 126bl&br,

127, 130b, 131, 140l, 141, 153, 162t, 165, 168b, 169l, 188, 189t&b, 211. **Lisa Law:** 98b, 109t, 117, 196-197. **Barry Z Levine/woodstockwitness.com (all rights reserved):** 60, 76, 78, 79l&r, 86l, 86-87, 91b, 92, 96-97, 100-101, 124, 125, 134-135, 140br, 161, 164 (and back endpaper), 168t, 169r, 176br, 179, 181, 192, 195t&b, 202, 212l&r, 213, 217, 245, 287. **Jim Marshall/ marshallphoto.com:** 5, 15bl, 22, 30, 54-55, 58m, 68all, 72-73, 77, 82-83, 84-85, 87r, 88-89, 90-91, 95, 104t & background, 110 background, 111t, 116bl, 118, 120, 126t, 128, 135t,m&b, 142, 143, 145, 148-149 (and front endpaper), 150, 155t, 159b, 162-163, 172t&b, 174-175, 190, 258-259. **Tom Miner/Topfoto/The Image Works:** 2, 9, 98t, 136b, 154, 176bl, 177tr, 182, 206, 215, 223t, 240. **Thomas Monaster/ monasterphoto.com:** 29b. **The Museum at Bethel Woods:** 1 (Rich Law); 5t (Rich Law), 21t (Rich Law), 23b (Rich Law), 23t 40, 40-41, 42bl 234-235, 241m, 244l, 251bl&br, 268, 269 all, 270 all, 271 all. **Bill Owens:** 256. **Ron Pownall:** 25. **Paul La Raia:** 266-267. **Redferns:** 26m, 34-35 (Douglas R. Gilbert), 228 (Herb Greene), 229t (Tommy Hanley), 237br (Chris Morphet), 244r, 252-253 (David Redfern). **Ken Regan/Camerafive:** 67, 136tr, 144t&b, 176tr, 178, 208-209, 226-227, 233, 247. **Retna:** 24b. **Rex Features:** 27 (David Magnus). **Rowland Scherman:** 112, 200-201, 203b. **Joe Sia/Wolfgangsvault.com:** 193 **Topfoto/The Image Works:** 46 (Dan McCoy), 177tl (John Dominis), 180 (Ron Arenalla), 225 (Charles Gatewood). **Burk Uzzle:** 156-157. **Warner Bros.:** 7, 210, 246, 248, 249. **Wenner Media/Rolling Stone:** 243. **Edd Westmacott:** 261. **Frank White/Frank White Photo Agency:** 262b, 264 all, 265 all. **Baron Wolman/ fotobaron.com:** 11 (pic 9), 53b, 64-65, 69b, 113, 133, 137bl, 176ml, 177b, 186, 187, 207t&b, 222, 223b, 227t, 231, 250, 288. **Woodstock69.com:** 250-251. **Woodstock Ventures:** 52, 53t, Nick Zungoli: 234-235.

WOODSTOCK

I came upon a child of God
He was walking along the road
And I asked him where are you going
And this he told me
I'm going on down to Yasgur's farm
I'm going to join in a rock 'n' roll band
I'm going to camp out on the land
I'm going to try an' get my soul free

We are stardust, we are golden
And we've got to get ourselves
Back to the garden

Then can I walk beside you
I have come here to lose the smog
And I feel to be a cog in something turning
Well maybe it is just the time of year
Or maybe it's the time of man
I don't know who I am
But you know life is for learning

We are stardust, we are golden
And we've got to get ourselves
Back to the garden

By the time we got to Woodstock
We were half a million strong
And everywhere there was song and celebration
And I dreamed I saw the bombers
Riding shotgun in the sky
And they were turning into butterflies
Above our nation

We are stardust
Billion year old carbon
We are golden
Caught in the devil's bargain
And we've got to get ourselves
Back to the garden

JONI MITCHELL